THIS BUSINESS OF
CONCERT PROMOTION AND TOURING

A Practical Guide to Creating, Selling, Organizing, and Staging Concerts

RAY D. WADDELL

RICH BARNET

JAKE BERRY

BILLBOARD BOOKS

AN IMPRINT OF WATSON-GUPTILL PUBLICATIONS / NEW YORK

Executive Editor: Bob Nirkind
Project Editor: Ross Plotkin
Production Manager: Salvatore Destro
Interior Design by Lisa Hamilton
The principal typefaces used in the composition of this book were Janson Text and
Frutiger Condensed

First published in 2007 by Billboard Books,
an imprint of Watson-Guptill Publications,
Nielsen Business Media, a division of The Nielsen Company.
770 Broadway, New York, NY 10003
www.watsonguptill.com

Library of Congress Control Number: 2007921236

ISBN-13: 978-0-8230-7687-1
ISBN-10: 0-8230-7687-3

Printed in the United States

First printing, 2007

2 3 4 5 6 7 8 9 / 14 13 12 11 10 09 08

ACKNOWLEDGMENTS

RAY D. WADDELL'S ACKNOWLEDGMENTS

Portions of text and certain quotes in this book were taken from articles previously written by Ray Waddell for *Billboard* magazine. The authors would like to thank *Billboard* for the use of this material and those who helped create it. Waddell would also like to thank the following for their input, expertise, and support: Michael Arfin, Charles Attal, Terry Barnes, Jeffery Bischoff, Bart Butler, Ashley Capps, Jamie Cheek, Jay Coleman, Andy Donkin, Arthur Fogel, Dell Furano, Nick Gold, David Goldberg, Steve Hauser, Trent Hemphill, Dave Holmes, Patterson Hood, John Huie, Seth Hurwitz, Greg Janese, Terry Jenkins, Billy Joel, Allen Johnson, Brock Jones, Marty Kern, Joe LaGuardia, Peter Luukko, Kevin Lyman, Fred Maglione, Pam Matthews, Eric Mayers, Kathleen O'Brien, Randy Phillips, Bob O'Neal, Bob Ringe, Doug Rountree, Bob Roux, John Scher, Mitch Schneider, Seth Sheck, Mark Shulman, Scott Siman, Kirk Sommer, Ed Stack, Livingston Taylor, Rick Whetsel, Buck Williams, Rick Zeiler, and Danny Zelisko.

RICH BARNET'S ACKNOWLEDGMENTS

The authors thank Middle Tennessee State University for graciously providing Rich Barnet a noninstructional assignment in order to complete this book. Barnet would like to thank the following professionals for helping make this book possible: Doug Adams, Paul Allen, Jerry Bailey, Phil Casey, Marci Allen Cardwell, David Chadwell, James Chippendale, Charles Dorris, *E!*, Paul Fischer, Melanie Hansel, Chris Haseleu, Ian Jeffery, Marie Kun, Darin Lashinsky, Steve Lassiter, Bernie Leadon, Bill Lee, Greg McCarn, Chuck Melton, David Moser, Dave Natale, Scott Nichols, Norm Parenteau, Jason Pitzer, Steve Powell, Pat Price, Chris Rabold, Rocko Reedy, Chris Salamone, Heather Story, Crystal Taliefero, Butch Taylor, Peter Tempkins, Flory Turner, Ethan Weber, Bob Williams, Patrick Woodroffe, and Jeremiah "Ice" Younossi.

JACK BERRY'S ACKNOWLEDGMENTS

I would like to thank all the bands and managements I have worked for, all the crews that have worked for me, and all the vendors who have supplied equipment to my tour over the years, AC/DC for giving me a start, Gerry Barad, Bono, Charlie, Adam Clayton, Michael Cohl, Dale, Danny O, Duane, the Edge, Arthur Fogel, John Giddings, Glen, Steve Howard, Ian, Mick Jagger, Lisa, Maria, Martin, Megan, Melissa, my girls Jessica, Rachel, and Rebecca, my mother, my brother, Paul McGuinness, Larry Mullen Jr., Wendy Overs, Richard, Keith Richards, Robert, Simone, Lori Tierney, Toby, Charlie Watts, and Ronnie Wood.

This book is dedicated
to our friends and loved ones,
and all the bands in vans.
Support live music!

CONTENTS

The arena is packed and the anticipation is palpable. An electric buzz crackles amid the 18,000 in attendance as the final minutes tick down toward a show that has been on everyone's calendar for weeks. The merchandise tables and concessions stands are swamped. Seats are rapidly filling. Suddenly, the house lights dim and a roar erupts from the throng. Only the outline of the drum riser and the red lights from production gear are visible on stage. The fans voice their approval as shadowy figures take the stage and pick up instruments. As the opening chords are struck, this thing is on!

Welcome to the explosive world of the concert business. In this digitized era, when entertainment beams from sixty-foot video walls and flickers from two-inch handheld screens, when the world can be delivered to your desktop, there is still absolutely no substitute for the live concert experience. The live mojo cannot be bootlegged, ripped, stripped, downloaded, or delivered in any way, shape, or form that beats the firsthand experience. Simply put, you have to be there.

This basic fact makes touring the single most important facet of an artist's career, and the one career segment where artists can control their own destiny. If an act has the live chops, is booked into a venue people enjoy attending at a price they feel is fair, you've got critical mass. As artists see revenue streams from record sales and publishing royalties diminish, the potential for touring revenue has never been greater. Popular acts today can command ticket prices they could only dream about a decade ago and, for those that attract eyes and ears, lucrative opportunities in merchandising and sponsorships are available that did not exist only a few years ago. If an act can make it on the road, they can make it, period.

Star-making television shows aside, an artist's career usually and should begin with live performances. If he or she is lucky and good, income from concerts will increase over time. For classic artists, touring revenue can sustain a career long after the hits are gone and platinum sales have diminished. For baby acts, the stage is where the buzz begins. For many artists, particularly heritage acts and those in such niche genres as jam band, bluegrass, heavy metal, or blues, concerts and ancillary revenues from touring, like merchandise sales and sponsorships often bring in the lion's share of all revenue, as much as 70 percent or more of an act's annual income.

But perhaps more importantly, live performance is where the artist connects with the fans, which is rewarding to artists on a level well beyond the money earned. Most artists prefer the concert stage to any other aspect of their careers. It's something they do not take lightly. "I'd have to say that live performance is as real as this unreal life gets," James Taylor told *Billboard* in 2005. "It's a reality check for us to play music in real time to an audience who's responding or not responding. It's compelling, because you agree to show up at a certain place at a certain time, you sell tickets and it's like you have responsibility for a lot of people's time. There is a lot of gravity to it."

One could say the same for the touring industry at large. The business of concert promotion becomes more competitive each year, and is a constantly evolving industry. Therefore, it is paramount that one continues to reeducate oneself and one's staff regarding this dynamic business. What holds true one day may be irrelevant the next, so professionals must always look forward.

According to figures reported to *Billboard* Boxscore, gross North American concert dollars topped out at more than $2.8 billion in 2005, with attendance of more than 52 million music fans. When nonreporting shows, festivals, fairs, casinos, private dates, performing arts centers, clubs, and other events are taken into consideration, the North American concert business likely tops $4 billion in gross and is probably close to 100 million in attendance. People love live music, and they don't mind paying for it.

The live business has changed dramatically in the past decade, however. Once dominated by local and regional entrepreneurial promoters who controlled their market fiefdoms like feudal lords, today's concert business is a mixture of large corporate promoters and small, often regional, independent promoters who deal with a complex network of agencies, managers, producers, and venues that intertwine and interact through a daily dance that routes tours across the country and around the globe.

There have never been more opportunities in the concert business. But this business also has never been more volatile and rife with potential booby traps. On the surface, the concert business is and should be simple. As professions go, the touring industry is relatively young, with the roots of the modern concert model dating back to the late 1960s and pioneering promoters like Bill Graham and agents like Frank Barsalona. In basic terms, the concert business is about buyers (promoters) buying a commodity (live performers) from sellers (agents) and reselling this commodity in a marketplace (the venue) where the end-user (concertgoers) will consume it (rock out). The traditional promoter/agent/venue triumvirate, though, has morphed into a model where the lines are blurred, roles shift, margins are razor thin, and the pie is sliced and resliced in ever slimmer pieces. At the same time, a cottage industry of ancillaries has exploded far beyond the simple concert T-shirt into instant live concert CDs, digital delivery, and VIP packages.

Although there is no shortage of books about the music business in general and legal issues in particular, there is little practical information about the concert business available. Furthermore, because few, if any, colleges have ever offered comprehensive educational programs to train individuals for careers in the concert industry, anyone working in this business has had to either learn their craft through on-the-job training or via fairly well-structured mentoring systems at booking agencies, venues, and concert promotion companies. As industries go, the touring industry is small in terms of numbers, and the concert business society has always been somewhat closed by its own nature. While such trade publications as *Billboard* and *Pollstar* cover industry trends and news, highly competitive promoters have never been quick to reveal trade secrets or tricks of the trade, and to fully learn this business by observation could take many years. The industry is full of stories about promoters whose careers lasted exactly one failed show. A mistake can cost you your house.

Our goal with *This Business of Concert Promotion & Touring* is to provide readers with information that will help accelerate this learning process and help them to avoid pitfalls that can be costly and damaging. We endeavor, as well, to help readers discover new career paths by offering an overview of who does what in a complex industry. Finally, we present an introduction to terminology of the concert and touring industry that will help ease the reader's entry into this specialized field within the music business.

Much of what follows is geared toward the artist's perspective, but the information is pertinent for those involved at any level in live performance. When we write about festivals, for example, we will not only explain the pros and cons of playing these unique bookings for artists, but also the issues involved in booking acts into festivals for agents, the huge risks for promoters, the challenges for production and security professionals, the legal components for attorneys, and the impact on an act's career for managers. Readers should benefit from each of these perspectives.

This book will also benefit developing artists looking to make their time and efforts in live performance pay off in terms of revenue and career development. If you are an aspiring artist who hopes to make the transition from low-paying local gigs to more profitable tours, this book will be especially important. More and more artists are taking a DIY approach, and they need to understand what types of employees to hire for tours; how to create a tour budget, negotiate contracts, capitalize on merchandising opportunities; and many other things that go well beyond putting gas in the van and packing extra guitar strings. To launch a concert tour you need a team who can provide the technical and logistical help to produce a show and present it with consistent quality at each city on the route. Not understanding the basics of tour production and budgeting may cause you to hire too many employees for your road crew, a mistake that can quickly eat into tour profits. Equally disastrous, you may hire someone, like a friend or relative, who lacks the necessary expertise to keep the tour running smoothly.

Anyone who works in the concert industry, or hopes to enter this field, should benefit from this book. It will be especially valuable to you if you want to land a job in the concert business, because you will get a clear understanding of what types of positions are available in this unique industry. For example, you will learn what personal managers, booking agents, tour managers, venue managers, production managers, tour technicians, and concert promoters do and how they earn a living in a world where profit margins are small and risks are great. And, if you work for a venue, advertising agency, radio station, production company, or any other organization that works in or around the concert business, you will see how the pieces all fit into the concert promotion puzzle.

The same holds true if you are a record label employee who works in publicity, promotion, or tour support, as you will learn ways to help and advise your artists when they tour.

The information in this book provides a blueprint. For instance, because artist fees are typically the single biggest expense for a concert promoter and negotiating fees is critical, we present numerous fee structures for paying artists that should be considered. We also explain many performance agreement clauses, and how to create a concert or festival budget and work within the constraints of shrinking profit margins.

A common refrain in the touring industry is that there are no bad shows, only bad deals. A show is not successful unless all parties—band, promoter, venue, fans—are happy. In the following pages, we will demonstrate how to make it rock without breaking the bank. No bad shows, no bad deals.

PART I

CREATING THE SHOW: THE ARTIST'S TEAM

CHAPTER I Key Representatives for Touring Artists

For many of us, there is a moment in our lives that feels like a reward for all of our hard work and sacrifices. The milestone in an artist's career can be when they hear their song on the radio for the first time, or, perhaps, when he or she steps onto the stage to perform the opening show of his or her first major tour. At that instant, drenched in the gazes of thousands of fans and bathed in the unique roar that only an adoring crowd can create, the years of practicing music, playing in smoke-filled bars, and struggling to learn about the business finally come to fruition. This is the fun part.

Unfortunately, only a fraction of those who aspire to be a successful touring artist are fortunate enough to reach that career milestone. Although the media often present us with glamorous images and enviable accounts of individuals who have become successful, respected touring artists, they rarely reveal that the overwhelming number of aspiring acts have disappointing careers and "can't quit their day job." True "overnight" successes are extremely rare and generally only happen after years of hard work. Executives at record labels, music publishing companies, and booking agencies responsible for signing new talent report that they reject hundreds of talented acts for each one they sign. For each platinum artist, there are thousands who dream of someday reaching that level of success but who will never come close to achieving it.

Why do artists develop successful careers while most others do not? Successful artists' careers unfold in stages, but the majority of musicians are unaware of what it takes to move from one level to another. If you aspire to a career in music (or, for that matter, to work for a successful artist), you must possess the necessary talent; understand the business of music; and assemble a team of experts to help you reach your goals. Most veterans of the industry agree that finding a team of music business professionals is the most important variable in the equation. This explains why an extremely talented musician might find little success, while a less talented artist with an excellent team of representatives may enjoy a lucrative career. The music industry is definitely a "team sport" when it comes to developing an artist's potential.

An artist's team of professionals will handle most business-related functions so he or she can spend more time on songwriting, recording, rehearsing, and performing. Creative individuals are usually happy to give up a percentage of their income to experts who can provide advice, counsel, and business services. Therefore, the focus should be on what can be gained from these representatives rather than how much of your income you are "giving away." A more logical way to look at the money you pay artist representatives is, "I can keep 100 percent of a little or a smaller percentage of a lot." History has shown that managers, agents, attorneys, and other artist representatives are able to secure much more lucrative deals for developing artists than the acts are able to attain by themselves, so the smaller percentage can clearly be the larger total sum for an artist.

It is important to understand clearly the role of each member of your team and your options for paying them. These choices usually include paying each representative a percentage of your gross or net income, a salary, or hourly wages. You will likely enter into a contractual agreement with each of your representatives to define both your rights and obligations. Before you bind yourself to anyone who may represent you, you should explain what you expect them to do for you in exchange for their compensation. Place yourself in the role of a CEO who is hiring executives to advise and help run the "company." Like any other CEO, you need to gather opinions and information about each professional before you invite them to join your team. Like it or not, you must become a business entity as well as a creator of music.

Before you begin to plan and launch a tour, your core team of representatives—attorney, manager, booking agent, business manager, tour manager, and production manager—will provide critical advice about hiring and supervising tour employees, negotiating performance agreements, and developing payment structures. It is important to remember, though, that you hire these representatives to give *advice*, not to take *total control* of the decision-making process. Some artists are more hands-on than others, but ideally you should make your own career decisions after listening to the appropriate team members. The music industry is rife with examples of artists who relegated too much authority to their handlers and realized too late that their career would have been more successful had they paid more attention to the business decisions being made on their behalf. It is, therefore, critical for you and your representatives to understand how the business of concert promotion and touring works in the marketplace.

ENTERTAINMENT ATTORNEY

Some veterans of the music industry recommend that an artist hire an entertainment attorney before hiring any other representatives. There is sound logic to this notion. The primary reason you need an entertainment attorney is to read, draft, and evaluate all contractual agreements between you and your manager, booking agency, record label, music publisher, and concert promoters. Because most of these agreements bind you for a significant period of time, advice from an entertainment attorney is important before you sign anything. Lawyers are regulated by a code of ethics and risk being disbarred if they violate these codes. Although there is no guarantee, your attorney has the highest probability of representing you with honesty, integrity, and confidentiality because he or she is regulated in the same way that physicians and accountants are regulated. Your other representatives, including your manager, business manager, and agent, have no professional or governmental organization regulating their profession.

A less obvious reason your attorney should be the first member of your team is that a well-established entertainment lawyer can often introduce you and your music to major executives in the music industry, important decision makers and power brokers whom you would normally be unable to meet. In addition, an entertainment attorney can usually get your demo to a manager or label A(rtists) & R(epertoire) executive more easily than you can. Remember, though, that attorneys with these types of professional connections are unlikely to circulate your demo unless they believe you have potential. If, on the other hand, your attorney believes strongly in your talent, he may be willing to call and send your materials to a few contacts.

What to Look for in an Attorney

In seeking legal representation, it is important to find an attorney who has specific expertise in the entertainment field. Entertainment law is extremely complex and quite different from other areas of law in commerce. You may know a great real estate attorney who says he or she knows about the music business, but it pays to use the same logic when selecting your attorney that you would use if selecting a surgeon: go to a specialist. When no entertainment attorney is available where you live, it pays to engage an entertainment specialist in a city that has a substantial amount of professional music activity, such as New York, Nashville, or Los Angeles.

Because attorneys most often charge by the hour to draft or review agreements, an attorney unfamiliar with entertainment law may spend many more billable hours than an experienced entertainment attorney to research this area of law and provide your legal counsel. Although the hourly fee charged by an entertainment specialist might appear high compared with a nonspecialist, a proven entertainment attorney will likely get the job done in less time and save you money in the long run.

One thing that makes it difficult to find an entertainment attorney who is experienced and capable in the music industry is the lack of certification for "music" or "entertainment" law by any state bar association. To exert some control over how attorneys advertise their expertise, the American Bar Association (ABA) recognizes each state's right to develop and govern "specialty certification" programs unique to attorneys practicing in their state. However, areas of specialty vary by state. Even the three states where music centers New York, Nashville, and Los Angeles are located have yet to certify a specialty called "Entertainment Law" or "Music Law." Although there is no certification of entertainment law as a specialty, the ABA and several states have formed groups to help entertainment attorneys meet and discuss issues of common concern.

Entertainment attorneys working in any of the three major music cities have state or local groups, like the ABA divisions, to help attorneys keep abreast of issues in the entertainment industry. The Beverly Hills Bar Association has an Entertainment Law section and a Committee for the Arts section. The Nashville Bar Association lists "Field of Practice Categories" that include both Entertainment and Publishing. The New York State Bar Association has an Entertainment, Arts, and Sports Law Section. But attorneys who become members of these entertainment law "sections" are self-identified and do not hold bar association certification. Be cautious, therefore, when reading directories in which attorneys indicate "areas of practice in entertainment law" or other music industry specialties, because these listings point to no certification of specialized skills. You can assume, however, that an attorney who is a member of ABA and state groups that focus on entertainment law is at least making an effort to learn and keep up with entertainment law.

If you need an attorney to help you find a manager and shop a record deal, you will have better success with one who has a strong track record in these areas. Conduct research to create your list of prospective attorneys, because lawyers customarily will not publish their current client lists. It is easy to ask professionals at record labels, music publishers, booking agencies, and management firms for recommendations of attorneys active in the music industry. It is always surprising how eager industry professionals are to offer names of lawyers they respect. Industry attorneys themselves can be good sources of recommendations. Because lawyers working in the legal affairs departments of record labels deal with the attorneys of many artists to negotiate recording contracts, they are knowledgeable about other practicing entertainment attorneys.

What to Be Beware of in an Attorney

It is a good idea to steer clear of attorneys who love the excitement of shopping recording, management, and publishing contracts so much that they want to branch out from legal counsel. Those who enter into management, recording, or publishing deals with their own clients create a *potential* conflict of interest— such as when an attorney manages an artist and also owns a portion of the artist's publishing rights. They believe an attorney should have the sole mission of making sure the artist gets the best publishing deal possible. It pays to be cautious of any potential conflict of interest when your attorney does things for you aside from providing legal counsel.

What to Discuss with a Prospective Attorney

When first meeting with your prospective attorney, be sure to discuss how he or she expects to be paid. Although some fee structures among attorneys are similar in general, others are unique to entertainment attorneys. And because attorneys often represent aspiring artists, they sometimes have trouble collecting their fees, so don't be surprised if your attorney asks for a *retainer*—money you pay upfront to create a fund from which your attorney charges. Some attorneys will request a monthly retainer if you ask them to do your legal work on a continuing basis.

It is important to understand the different options for paying your legal representative, because most attorneys are sympathetic to developing new artists and will consider various payment methods. The most common fee structure is hourly rates, called *billable hours*, for work performed on your behalf. Hourly rates vary by size of firm, reputation of the attorney or firm, and city in which the law firm is located. While a small firm in Nashville might charge $70 an hour, a large, prestigious firm in the same city might charge $300 an hour, and a major entertainment law firm in Beverly Hills might charge $400 or more an hour. Keep in mind that a large firm will charge you a lower rate if a paralegal or associate of the firm does some of the work on your project. A solo practitioner or small firm may not have paralegals or lower-paid associates on staff, so you will always pay a higher rate for all work done on your behalf.

An attorney may also agree to a fee arrangement based on a percentage of your gross income in much the same way managers do. A common rate is 5 percent of gross income, although some powerful attorneys ask for as much as 10 percent. While not as common, an attorney who actively puts together profitable deals for an artist, rather than merely negotiating contracts, can ask for an even larger percentage.

Still another creative billing arrangement is called *value billing*, in which your attorney charges a flat fee based on the value of the deal being negotiated. This works best when your attorney is negotiating a specific document, such as a recording or publishing contract, rather than providing ongoing legal counsel. Before accepting this method of payment, get an estimate of how much the total might be so you are not shocked.

A further question should regard what expenses the attorney will incur that require reimbursement. Typically these expenses include postage, courier service, and long-distance calls, as well as research and work done by paralegals, legal secretaries, and associates of the firm. This question will not only give you a better understanding of the work your attorney does, but also will alert you that these incidental expenses will be incurred.

How to Begin Working with Your Attorney

After you select an attorney, and he or she agrees to represent you, insist on a letter of engagement, even if it is not a state requirement. The letter should explain the scope of legal services your attorney agrees to provide. It should also describe the fees agreed on for various services and how often you will receive a bill. This will typically be monthly, but it should not go beyond two or three months. The letter should also explain that you have the right to discuss and dispute charges. An arbitration clause should be included, as well. In basic terms, an *arbitration clause* is a clause in the letter of agreement which requires the parties to engage in some kind of quasi-legal proceeding (mediation, binding, or nonbinding arbitration) prior to, or in lieu of, proceeding to court in the event of a dispute.

When you begin to work with your new attorney, send or bring a copy of each contract you have signed that relates to your career in the music industry. If you have formed any business entity, especially a partnership or corporation, with others, have your new attorney review the business formation documents and keep a copy of them on file. You should also deliver a typed list of all contact information for all industry professionals—managers, agents, music publishers, producers—who have encouraged you to keep in touch.

It is important not to "bother" your attorney unless you truly need his or her legal advice. It helps to create a list of questions or issues to discuss, then have a good solid meeting or phone discussion instead of numerous calls. If you constantly phone your attorney, you will more than likely be billed for each time you call.

ARTIST MANAGER

The individual who serves as your primary adviser, called an *artist manager*, a *personal manager*, or simply a *manager*, will influence your career decisions more than anyone else.

Your manager will help you select your agent, music publisher, and record label. When you begin to tour, your manager will be instrumental in hiring your tour manager, production manager, business manager, and the many other members of your touring staff. Your manager will also help you with creative decisions such as selecting a producer and songs for your recordings; assist with hiring session singers and studio musicians for recording sessions; help you hire musicians and backing vocalists for your tours; and work closely with you while you develop your performance. You and your manager will discuss your major career decisions, such as when to tour, what label offer looks strongest, and what publishing deal is best, and you will trust your manager to handle much of the day-to-day decision-making.

What to Look for in a Manager

A common mistake that unsigned artists make is engaging a friend, spouse, or ex-band member to assume the role of manager. A manager whom an unsigned artist hires solely based on friendship often does not have the expertise or industry contacts necessary to launch a career in music. Your manager should have a strong knowledge of the music industry and have good personal contacts at vital industry enterprises such as record labels, booking agencies, and music publishing companies. An often overlooked quality of a good manager is a clear understanding of your genre of music. Although a potential manager may have been successful in developing pop artists, he or she might not understand the idiosyncrasies of genres such as urban, contemporary Christian, country, or jam bands. For this reason, a close friend who is an avid fan of your music may seem attractive to you even if he or she has no industry experience. But their friendship and love of your music, along with their lack of experience and a desire to be "in the business," can seriously cloud their judgment. The question to ask yourself is, "Should I risk delaying my career development in exchange for having my friend manage me?"

Jeremiah "Ice" Younossi, a respected urban music agent, has worked with many emerging acts, some of whom, like 50 Cent, have become superstars. Describing new urban acts, Ice says, "Usually the groups have someone we call the 'best friend besides family' manager." Because urban artists often have a mistrust of mainstream industry executives, they have a higher level of trust for friends. As Younossi points out, then the question is, "Does this person have any experience? How aggressive are they? And are they really willing to learn about the business, not just help out."

An important characteristic to look for in a manager is good communication skills. Remember that your manager will, as a rule, be the first point of contact for many industry professionals. Your manager will spend many hours on the telephone with your agent and label executives. Anyone calling about potential tour sponsorships or product endorsements will contact your manager first. A communication weakness, such as not returning calls promptly, can cause someone to take their offer elsewhere.

The ideal manager will work with you to develop a career plan specific to you and your ambitions. He or she will also oversee your business needs so that the plan unfolds as intended. This allows you freedom to focus on more creative activities. While you are developing your music, your manager should aggressively be pursuing recording contracts, booking agency agreements, and publishing deals on your behalf. When you get ready to tour, your manager should also help you to hire everyone necessary to produce and present your show.

If you and your manager work well together, you will develop a career plan that helps achieve your goals. Therefore, before entering a long-term agreement with a manager, consider your eventual goals and think sensibly about how your manager can help you reach them. The adage, "Any map will get you there if you don't know where you're going," is especially true in the music industry. It is common for unsigned artists to have a vague mental image of the stardom they so desire. However, when they are asked what goals—short-term, five-year, long-term—they have, few can articulate anything more specific than "I want a record deal" or "I want to go on tour." Although it is your manager's job to help you develop concrete career goals with sensible milestones, you need to translate your dreams into terms he or she can understand.

Finding a manager is not difficult; finding a proven manager is. There are more emerging artists looking for managers than there are successful managers looking for new artists. Artists who aggressively search for a manager are more likely to find one then artists who sit back and wait to be discovered. One strategy is identifying managers of recording artists whom you admire.

Directories, such as the *Billboard Talent Directory*, list artists alphabetically and include managers and agents for each artist. This directory also has a separate list of managers and their artist roster. It is worth noting that any act creating a buzz that does not already have management will find potential managers coming out of the woodwork.

It can be difficult to get a face-to-face meeting with a prospective manager even after you have their contact information. Therefore, another strategy is to secure the services of a successful entertainment attorney who will help you find a manager. A manager is more likely to take a phone call from a well-known attorney than from an artist he or she has never heard of. Again, keep in mind that attorneys are paid by the hour for their services, so if you are able to do some research that helps narrow the field of prospective managers, your attorney will not have to spend as many hours working for you. Note that a reputable attorney will not risk his or her reputation by shopping an artist whom they do not believe is ready for professional management. An attorney may refuse to shop a management deal until he or she hears you perform live.

If a record label offers you a recording contract before you have a manager, it has an interest in whomever manages you. Label executives want artists on their roster to have professional managers who will work with them to develop your career. Your label may offer you some suggestions for management if you request their help. But don't forget that you need to make the final decision as to whom you ultimately hire. Regardless of the manager's pedigree and rave recommendations, you must feel comfortable with this individual. It can be a nightmare if you are unable to develop a good working relationship.

In legal terms, your manager accepts a fiduciary responsibility when he or she agrees to manage you. This term stems from *fiducia*, Latin for *trust*, something essential to a good artist-manager relationship. Like marriages that end in court, manager-artist teams sometimes end in litigation. You should be leery of any potential manager who makes grandiose promises such as, "I can guarantee you a record deal." Legitimate managers offer more practical predictions like, "I'll do my best to find you a good recording contract."

The relationship between you and your manager is like a marriage, built on trust and understanding. Anyone considering a field in artist management should understand that this is a "24–7" job, and 4 AM phone calls and "putting out fires" are not uncommon. Generally, when things go wrong, an artist's first call is to their manager. If a manager is not 100 percent committed to you, then you need to find someone who is.

KEY ELEMENTS OF A MANAGEMENT AGREEMENT

When you get to the point of negotiating a management agreement, it is essential that you have your own attorney to advise you and to protect your interests. If you use the same attorney as your potential manager, which you might be tempted to do in order to save money, a blatant conflict of interest will exist. The same attorney cannot vigorously negotiate deal points for a manager while representing you in the same negotiations. An ethical attorney representing an artist manager will most likely not want an artist to enter into an agreement with their client without satisfactory legal counsel of their own. From a business standpoint, it can provide the artist with potential grounds for ending the contract in the future should there be a dispute with his or her manager.

Although an artist-manager agreement is conceptually simple, it often becomes a complicated legal document written by attorneys in such a way that only they and other attorneys understand it. You need an attorney familiar with this type of agreement to represent your interests during negotiations with a prospective manager.

We should mention that while most managers create a written management agreement, some have had nothing more than verbal agreements, sealed by a handshake, with major artists they represent. There have been cases where this relationship lasted for years, as when Merle Kilgore managed Hank Williams Jr. until the former's death in 2005, and there have been cases where the relationship ended in a tangle of lawsuits. Once again, this goes back to the issue of trust, but agreements made over a beer following a particularly great show may wither several years later when millions of dollars are at stake.

Entertainment attorneys usually have standard contract forms they use as templates for management agreements. They then take the basic form, tailor it to the needs of their client, and present it to the manager's attorney for review. The manager's attorney returns it with comments and both attorneys have a discussion of deal points during a telephone call. The following deal points are ones you should think about before meeting with your attorney.

Identification of Parties Entering into the Agreement. It is important to begin the agreement by clearly identifying the manager, or management firm, and the artist. If you belong to a band, your manager will expect each individual to sign a separate agreement in case the group breaks up. It is also helpful to include the complete legal address of each individual and company entering into the agreement.

General Breadth of the Agreement. This section typically grants the manager exclusivity for all areas of the entertainment industry. This means no other manager may provide you the same managerial services as your exclusive manager. Occasionally, a manager is exclusive for a specific area, such as music, but not for other areas such as film or literary work. In these situations, the manager would be restricted from representing the artist in those stated areas.

Manager Duties. Although it is difficult to stipulate everything you expect from your manager, your agreement should detail important, specific duties you expect your manager to handle. For instance, you should state that you expect your manager to be available at reasonable times to provide you with advice about decisions affecting your career. You should also state your expectation that your manager represent you in negotiations with agents, label executives, music publishers, and other professionals in the industry. Your agreement should include a general statement that you expect your manager to do those tasks necessary to further your career. Your manager will, in all likelihood, want a statement in the agreement indicating that you will procure the services of a booking agent to secure performance opportunities. State labor laws, especially in California and New York, require anyone who procures engagements for artists to be a licensed talent agent.

Power of Attorney. If you grant your manager limited power of attorney, he or she can sign specific documents for you. You must specify what types of agreements your manager is allowed to sign on your behalf. For instance, artists usually give their managers authority to approve and sign performance agreements. It is also a good idea to state a limit for expenses, weekly or monthly, that your manager is approved to pay. In addition, you can list specific expenses—such as telephone long-distance charges, postage, and travel expenses—for which your manager will get reimbursed.

Compensation. Most artists pay their manager or management firm a commission rather than a salary. The rate of commission is a major deal point in a management agreement. This section of the agreement should clearly provide the percentage rate of the management commission and what income is considered commissionable income. Most managers are paid a percentage of the artist's *gross* income. However, you might exclude specified income from the commissionable income. For example, an artist who is an established songwriter may engage a manager to help launch his or her recording career. The artist would, in this case, exclude income from songwriting royalties from the manager's commissionable base. Because managers work on behalf of their artists, it is reasonable for them to expect to be reimbursed for reasonable expenses.

The rate of commission a manager can demand is based on his or her experience and bargaining power. Although some powerful managers are able to negotiate higher commissions, rates usually range from 15 percent to 20 percent, with 15 percent being the most common rate. An interesting variation on a fixed commission rate is one that varies according to your income. This method of determining your manager's commission rate might grant your manager a commission of 10 percent of your commissionable income up to $100,000 and then increase it to 15 percent when your income exceeds $100,000. If the agreement has a third tier, when your commissionable income reached the third level, for example $500,000, your manger's commission would jump to 20 percent. This method of calculating the commission rate, called an *escalating commission rate*, creates an incentive for your manager to improve your income from music as quickly as possible. Some managers prefer a descending commission scale, one that has the highest commission rate in the beginning. The rationale for this is that the manager needs a higher percentage when the artist's gross is lowest to earn significant commissions.

Duration. Because managers usually do not see much income from new artists during the first several years, the duration of a contract is a sensitive issue for them. No manager wants to spend several years helping an artist get established only to see him or her move to a new manager after the money begins to flow in. Management agreements typically have an initial term, ranging from one to five years, with several one-year renewal options. Your manager will likely want as long an initial period as possible plus several options to renew. If your manager controls renewal options, he or she can bind you to a longer obligation. It is best to negotiate a shorter term agreement with the option of not renewing it. If you are not satisfied with your manager, you can then escape the agreement at the end of the initial term.

A good tactic for artists is to tie options or extensions of the management agreement to performance standards such as getting a recording contract, continuing an existing recording contract, or reaching a minimum gross income for the artist. For instance, you can require your manager to get a recording contract from a major or major distributed label within the initial period or you will have the choice to dissolve the contractual agreement. This escape clause, often called a *kick-out clause*, encourages your manager to aggressively hunt for a label deal.

Sunset Clause. If you terminate your contract with your manager and hire a new manager, you might be responsible to pay double commissions unless you anticipate this possibility in your agreement. A *sunset clause* states the commissionable income and commission rate your manager will continue to receive if you end your agreement. This clause should indicate that the manager is only entitled to commissions on income you receive from performances, tour sponsors, recording contracts, publishing, and other income the manager helped negotiate on your behalf. The clause may indicate that your old manager will continue to earn the full commission—for example, 15 percent—on all recordings released and concerts booked before you ended the contract. You might further promise to pay a reduced commission, perhaps 5 percent, on recording contracts he or she negotiated, but have not yet been released, before the contract ended. You should also try to dovetail the sunset clause with any new management agreement, so you are not paying double commissions when your new manager takes over. For example, you could ask that your new manager receive reduced commissions on income for which you are also paying commissions to your old manager.

Key Person Clause. If your agreement binds you to a management firm, you should consider what would happen if the person who handles your day-to-day management leaves the firm. A *key person clause* gives you the option of dissolving the agreement if the primary person you work with leaves the firm. This is especially important if you first signed with a manager who was a solo practitioner, but later merged with a firm and brought you to the firm as a client. If you successfully negotiate a key person clause, you have the choice of staying with or leaving the firm if this person exits. This puts you in a great bargaining position if both the firm and the key person want you as a client. At the time you negotiate this clause, ask if the firm has bound the key person to a "noncompete" clause. If the key person has a noncompete clause in his or her contract, the firm can prohibit them from managing any artists for a named period of time or, at least, from managing any artists signed to the firm.

Breach of Contract. Although no one likes to think that a breach of contract will ever be necessary, it is good to hammer out the manner in which you and your manager will handle contract disputes. *Breach of contract* means one of the parties to the agreement—either you or your manager—have failed to fulfill promises stated in the agreement. It is worth noting that this may only be the *perception* by one party that there is breach. Typically, one party asserts breach and the other claims the allegations are false. In these instances, a third party must help decide who is right.

A practical first step to avoid breach is a clause that requires the party making allegations of breach to present a written description to the other party explaining what needs to be done. There should also be a stated period of time in the clause which allows the breaching party to fix the problem. A requirement that both parties will undergo binding arbitration is another way to avoid litigation. Although arbitration has associated expenses, it is usually less expensive than civil lawsuits.

Severability Clause. The *severability clause* simply states that if any clause in the agreement violates laws, removing it will not affect the rest of the agreement.

Acceptance. It is wise for both you and your manager to show your acceptance of the agreement by printing and signing your legal name, date, and the county and state in which you created the agreement. Although all of this information is not always included on management agreements that are drafted to resemble letters from the artist to the manager, it is best to include it.

BOOKING AGENTS

Finding and routing live engagements, especially for an organized tour, is a time-consuming activity. Because your manager needs to focus his or her attention on many other matters important to your career, finding and negotiating live performances, called *bookings*, has evolved into a specialization performed by agents. If you hope to become a touring artist, you need to acquire the services of a booking agent in addition to a manager.

The term *talent agent* refers to any agent who finds work for creative artists. Talent agents who concentrate on finding live appearances—bookings—for music performers have traditionally been referred to as booking agents. We will, therefore, refer to talent agents who concentrate on locating and contracting live performances for artists in the music field as booking agents. Large, full-service talent agencies have many divisions in addition to their music division, such as film and television and literary. We will refer to these companies as *talent agencies*. We will refer to companies whose sole focus is finding live appearances for artists as *booking agencies* or, more frequently, *agents*.

WHAT AGENTS DO

In basic terms, the agent/agency loosely routes a tour based on parameters set forth by management and assumptions as to where the act can or should play. In the traditional model, the agent then goes back and firms up each market, cutting deals with buyers and/or venues in each city. Again, in the traditional model, the talent buyer generally pays the act a *guarantee* (a minimum amount the act will be paid), often referred to as the *front end*, versus a percentage of ticket sales (the gate, the door, et cetera), often referred to as the *back end*, with the artist to be paid whichever is greater. (We will discuss fee structures in greater detail in Chapter 10.)

The more popular an act is, the more likely the agent will be to structure a back end deal and the larger the act's take will be. The percentages paid in the traditional model are typically 85 percent of gross ticket sales to the act, 15 percent to the promoter/buyer/venue, with each party's expenses to be paid out of their gross. While most acts have a starting guarantee in place, these fees are highly negotiable based on what the buyer brings to the party in terms of promotion, marketing, assumption of costs, ancillary revenue opportunities, and other factors. Once a deal is negotiated, contracts are signed, a deposit is paid, and the date is firmly added to the route.

REGULATION OF BOOKING AGENTS AND AGENCIES

While most vocations in the music industry, including managers, are free from outside regulation, booking agencies are regulated by both state laws and entertainment unions. Because booking agents find and negotiate employment for creative artists, a role similar to employment agencies, some states regulate them through labor laws. Although most states have general laws for employment agencies, several states, including New York, California, New Jersey, and Texas, have developed labor laws specific to the entertainment industry. New York and California have developed the most rigorous licensing laws governing talent agencies. California's laws fall under the California Talent Agencies Act; New York laws govern what that state calls theatrical employment agents through the Consumer Protection Law.

In both California and New York, anyone who wants to "find, procure, or attempt to procure engagements for artists" must apply to the commissioner of labor to obtain a license. One exception is anyone working in New York City, who must apply to the city commissioner of consumer affairs. Both states require many steps, including completing an application form that reveals the names of all owners of the agency and examples of each contract form to be used by the agency—exclusive agency agreement and performance agreements—relating to the artist. The office of labor, or consumer affairs, launches an investigation of the each agency owner's character. Besides application and license fees, both states also require each applicant to post a $10,000 surety bond to use in case the agency refuses, or is unable, to pay money owed artists they represent. Applicants must also state the commission they will collect for booking artists. New York places a ceiling of 10 percent on booking agency commissions except for orchestras, operas, and other fine art music ensembles, for which booking agencies can charge a 20 percent commission. California does not have a cap on commissions, because lawmakers there believe that entertainment unions adequately regulate rates of booking agent commissions.

The two unions that work most closely with the music industry—the American Federation of Musicians (AFofM) and the American Federation of Television and Radio Artists (AFTRA)—have set up maximum rates of commission for franchised booking agencies. The commission schedule for AFofM allows a booking agency to earn *up to* 15 percent of the artist's gross payment for steady engagements, ones that last more than two days at the same location. Agencies are allowed to earn up to 20 percent of an artist's gross income for single engagements. Keep in mind, though, that these are *maximum* rates and are developed more for gigging local musicians than artists on national tours. The AFTRA maximum commission is 10 percent for any engagements.

Because all major labels and most nationally distributed independent record labels have agreed to release recordings of only AFofM and AFTRA affiliated artists, it is essential for an agency to be franchised by these two unions if they hope to book signed artists. It is important to remember that an agency agrees to be bound by all rules and regulations of the union when it becomes franchised. If an agency does not follow the published rules of AFofM or AFTRA, it is placed on a list of unacceptable agencies, called the *unfair list*, of one or both of the unions. Union members are prohibited from working with nonfranchised agencies or agencies placed on the union's unfair list. If a union member ignores this rule, he or she can be brought up on charges by the union and possibly lose membership rights.

WHAT TO LOOK FOR IN A BOOKING AGENT

When beginning your search for a booking agent, you and your manager should decide what services are needed before contacting any agency representatives. The first consideration should be the reach—local, regional, national, or international—of your intended tour. For example, if you have just inked a label deal with an independent (indie) label and plan to tour clubs as a headliner, you will need a local or regional booking agency that specializes in clubs or a national one that has an aggressive club division. A relatively small, well-established regional booking agency might be better at getting you established in the region's clubs than would a large national talent agency. On the other hand, if you have a major label deal and are planning a national tour to coincide with your single and album releases, you need an agency that has contacts throughout the nation.

A second consideration should be the sizes and types of venues an agency books. Because they have more booking agents, talent agencies and large regional booking agencies are able to spend more time developing relationships with talent buyers for large venues and events than small booking agencies. Since local and small regional agencies have fewer booking agents, they tend to focus on local clubs, parties, and festivals. Also, note that national talent agencies have club booking agents who work with smaller venues, and have agents that specialize in booking private dates, fairs and festivals, conventions, and other niche areas.

It is common for an agent to book an act beginning at the club level and move with them as they graduate to larger venues, using caution, one hopes, with each step up the venue ladder. "We're here to build careers, and that's not a line," says William Morris agent Kirk Sommer, responsible for such acts as the Killers and Louis XIV. "It doesn't do me any good to sign something I believe in and exploit it to the fullest to the point where the act is not able to return on the same or a higher ticket price and step up into larger venues."

Yet another consideration is to find an agency that is active in, and understands, the music you perform. If you are an independent label rock band and plan to tour rock clubs, you will need a booking agency that can book you into the clubs that have the right "vibe" and present artists who are known as "cutting edge." You don't want to pull up in the van and find you have been booked into Joe Bob's Beer, Ammo & Music.

There are many different models for booking agencies, generally defined by size and geographic range. Some are small, owner-operated agencies with a limited roster of artists. Others are slightly larger regional agencies with a few agents, some of whom might be part-time employees. And some are national or international in scope with dozens of artists and agents.

Small or "boutique" booking agencies often stress that they are able to give more personal attention to their artists than agencies with a large number of acts. They tend to be adept at booking developing acts for small clubs, but there are also agents with this expertise at large agencies. Some small and/or regional agencies make a large percentage of their commissions booking cover bands and show bands for lounges, wedding receptions, and parties.

Agents who work for small agencies might be paid a flat percentage of gross bookings they bring to the agency. For example, an agent might receive 4 percent of gross bookings they contract for the agency. This makes it difficult for agents to have any month-to-month stability, so an established booking agency might offer their agents a draw against commissions. As an example, the agent might be paid $2,000 a month as a draw—advance—against his or her monthly commissions. If this same agent's total commissions were to exceed $2,000 in any month, he or she would be paid that additional amount. However, if the agent's commissions are lower than the draw for more than a few months, the agency owner will likely reevaluate the agent's performance.

A regional agency typically has more agents and a larger roster of proven acts. It competes mainly with the full-service national agencies that have several regional offices in addition to other regional agencies. The job of a regional booking agent is to form effective working relationships with talent buyers in their region in hopes that the buyers will develop a sense of loyalty to the agent. Some regional booking agents work so well with club operators that they become house agents, sometimes called *in-house bookers*, for one or more clubs. Although not common, agencies sometimes pay their booking agents a salary plus a percentage point or two. For example, an agent might receive a monthly salary of $3,000 plus 1 percent of all their gross bookings.

Large agencies offer clout and the leverage that comes when dozens of superstars are on the roster. A promoter might be more willing to cut a favorable deal with act "A" if he thinks act "B" will play for him or her next time around. The toughest competition is among booking agents who work for national full-service agencies, ones that represent signed artists, many of whom are gold- and platinum-level artists. A large, full-service talent agency often has several divisions, each of which handles different types of talent placements. For instance, William Morris Agency and Creative Artists Agency, both with offices in several cities and an international scope, have departments for film, television, music, speaking engagements, literary, commercials, and other areas. Each division is available to support the careers of music artists, so an artist who hopes to eventually break into television or film after they become successful in their music career should consider a full-service company.

The key in any situation is for an artist to find an agent with whom they form an honest and mutually satisfactory relationship. Trust is a key element when an act is traveling 500 miles overnight to a new venue in a market the artist has never played.

In 2006, 70 percent of the top 100 tours reported to *Billboard* Boxscore were represented by these eight agencies:

- Creative Artists Agency
- William Morris Agency
- Artists Group International
- Monterey Peninsula Artists
- The Agency Group
- Agency for the Performing Arts
- Howard Rose Agency
- Marsha Vlasic Organization

More than half of these 100 tours were booked by William Morris or CAA. But, interestingly enough, six of the top ten tours, including the Rolling Stones, Madonna, Cirque du Soleil's Delirium, Barbra Streisand, U2, and Kenny Chesney, did not make use of a booking agent, but rather handled tour routing either in-house or through their promoter.

HOW BOOKING AGENTS WORK

Because regional agents in national agencies have assigned geographical territories, they are able to spend a great amount of time cultivating relationships with talent buyers in their territory. Of course, they also have large artist rosters and must keep more artists busy. Most of their artists are signed to major labels and have charted records. But in some cases, the agent comes on board with an artist before a manager is in place, and invests "sweat equity" in an artist's career from the beginning.

A large office in the music division of a full-service agency usually has specific career stages that employees go through as they climb the corporate ladder. The entry-level job is often the mailroom, where new employees learn about the different agents and divisions of the particular office. The next job is likely to be an assistant for a club agent. From there, the person might be promoted to assistant to a line agent. A *line agent* is a full-fledged booking agent who books the agency's roster of artists. Line agents who have a specific territory are also called *territorial agents*.

If the assistant shows promise and the right position opens, he or she might be promoted to a club agent. The next likely stage is territorial agent. The highest level of agent is a *responsible agent*, or RA. This is an agent who brings a new artist to the agency and is considered responsible for their success in the agency. Once an agent becomes an artist's responsible agent, line agents must submit all contract offers for that artist to the responsible agent for review. If a line agent becomes the responsible agent for many artists, he or she might only review offers for his or her artists and no longer book other artists.

Pay structures for agents in large agencies are, as you might expect, slightly different from those at smaller agencies. Agents in large agencies typically are paid a salary plus an annual bonus. Their bonus is not a percentage of gross bookings, but bookings are something an agent's supervisors looks at each year. In addition to gross income from bookings for artists they booked, responsible agents often get credit for gross bookings of all income for their artists. As a general rule, agencies expect each agent to bring the agency commissions that equal three times his or her salary for the year. Some agencies even tie bonuses to a specific percentage of bookings that exceed three times an agent's salary.

Finding an agency that will help you move your career forward can be harder than finding a manager or any other member of your basic team. Because booking agents work on commission, they are interested in signing artists who have marquee value, ones whose name recognition alone will help sell tickets, or acts who they believe have this potential. If an artist has not gotten significant radio airplay or has not established a large fan base in cities with large venues, he or she will be less attractive to talent buyers. Because they must sell their acts to talent buyers, booking agents look for artists whom they can book for the largest number of dates at the highest fees. This creates an unfortunate paradox for artists: those who need a booking agent the most often do not have the drawing power to attract the major agents and agencies, while successful acts can easily find a booking agency.

The good news is that a manager's good reputation in the industry can sometimes help convince a booking agency to represent their artists. But keep in mind that booking agencies are generally not in the business of discovering and developing talent, although there are agents who pride themselves on spotting acts with the potential of developing into consistent touring artists. For an agent, a dynamic live performance is the key aspect of an artist's total package.

Key Elements of a Booking Agent Agreement

There are two types of business relationships you can have with your booking agency: exclusive or nonexclusive. If you sign an *exclusive booking agency agreement*, you cannot use other agents. An exclusive agency agreement prevents other agents from booking you without permission from your exclusive agency. This agreement does not prevent you from booking yourself, however. In reality, though, if you and your manager worked hard to secure an agency deal, you would not want to risk it by taking commissionable income from your agent.

A *nonexclusive booking agency agreement* is simple: You, as an artist, can work with as many agencies as you want and accept or reject each offer. Because a nonexclusive agreement allows you to consider offers from more than one agent, you have no real contractual commitment until you sign a performance agreement presented by an agency. A nonexclusive booking agency agreement—often a handshake or verbal agreement—seems intuitively attractive, but in practice, most large, powerful agencies insist on exclusive agreements, while smaller agencies are more willing to accept artists on a nonexclusive basis. Keep in mind that an exclusive agent feels more pressure to keep their exclusive artists busy, while nonexclusive agents may not feel this same duty.

Exclusive booking agency agreements are made more complicated by union restrictions and state licensing regulations. If an agency offers you an agreement, it is a good idea to have your entertainment attorney and manager review it. If you are a union member, you will have to work with a franchised agency or risk running afoul of the union. And each union has its own contract, or contracts, that you and your agent must sign in addition to your exclusive agency agreement. Here are some of the points you should consider when you negotiate your exclusive booking agency agreement.

Duration of the Agreement. An exclusive booking agency contract usually ranges from one to three years. Because your agency will spend a lot of time and resources launching your first tour, they will want to bind you to as long a contract as possible. The agency will press you to sign with them for at least three years, maybe longer. You, on the other hand, want to commit for as short a time as possible, preferably one year. In addition to the agency agreement, though, you and your agency will have to also complete standard artist-agent agreements for AFTRA and AFofM if you are a member of one or both. AFTRA has an interesting statement in its exclusive agency contract: "The initial term may not be in excess of eighteen months. A term of up to three (3) years may be entered into after one (1) year's representation." If you plan to work in the film industry, you will need to affiliate with the Screen Actors Guild (SAG) and complete one of their standard contracts.

Rate of Commission. Booking agencies earn a commission based on a percentage of the gross income from *each engagement booked*, unlike managers, who receive a percentage of an artist's *total earnings* as defined in their agreement. This creates a simple, but intense, motivation for an agency to keep the artists on their roster working. If the artist does not have bookings, the agency will not earn commissions. Consequently, successful booking agents must be great salespersons. Their product is their artists; their talent buyers—concert promoters and venues—are their customers.

Theoretically, booking agencies can fix their own commission rates. In reality, performing arts unions and state labor laws limit rates that licensed or franchised booking agencies can charge. The typical rate for agencies that book touring recording artists is 10 percent. This is because New York allows booking agents to charge no more than 10 percent unless they book fine arts ensembles and artists. AFTRA has a simple commission ceiling, and they make it quite clear: "No franchised agent may charge a higher rate of commission than 10 percent." Even if a platinum-level artist wants a lower commission rate, large agencies are reluctant to negotiate. Their major fear is that other artists on their roster will learn of it and want the lower rate. However, most agencies, when faced with a real possibility of losing a superstar client, will calculate potential commissions from a tour and decide to negotiate with the artist.

Agents who specialize in classical music usually charge 20 percent, the highest commissions allowable, because many of the artists and large ensembles on their rosters do not have managers, and thus out of necessity, they must offer some management services in addition to booking. Note that neither union rules nor state regulations of talent agents prohibit agencies from providing advice that might normally come from a manager. Agencies that specialize in booking artists for the college market are also likely to charge a 20-percent commission, because the contacts at colleges constantly change as students graduate.

Commissionable Income and Extent of Representation. Be aware of income that your agent is entitled to commission. As you should do in your management agreement, define commissionable income in your agency agreement. Your agent should get a commission from live performances they book, but usually not from your publishing or recording income. Pay particular attention to the AFTRA contract you sign, because it has a list of areas in which you authorize your agency to represent you. For instance, you and your manager should not check, or allow your agency to check, "sound recordings" or "CD ROM/Interactive." If you want your agency to help you land roles in film, television, or commercials, mark those as areas of representation and, thus, commissionable income. Full-service agencies typically ask to represent artists in all forms of entertainment. But, if you sign with an agency that has weak, or no, departments in fields other than music, specifically limit all areas outside music. By doing this, you can engage a different agency to find you employment in non-music areas of the entertainment industry.

When you define commissionable income for your agency, make sure that the agency does not plan to deduct any of their operating expenses from your income. Unlike your manager, the agency should not expect to deduct long-distance phone charges or postage, because these are the agency's cost of doing business. If you have formed a corporation for your business entity, be sure to state in your agreement that you or your corporation can be charged a commission, but double commissions are not allowed. Also, any fees you receive that include payment for support acts or travel should not be commissionable.

Geographic Limits. If your agency is one of the few that has international booking agents, they will understandably want world rights for representing you. If the agency does not have a strong international presence, limit the exclusive agreement to the United States or North America. It is not uncommon for major artists to have an overseas agency in addition to their U.S. agency. However, because many U.S. artists release recordings and tour in Europe before getting recognized in the United States, this concern should be discussed with your domestic agency before you sign an agreement.

Key Person Clause. If you are brought to an agency by someone you expect to be your responsible agent, ask to be released from your contract if that individual leaves. This clause is often difficult to negotiate in a booking agency agreement, because of something called a *noncompete* clause that agents are often asked to sign when they are hired. A noncompete clause states that an agent agrees to not book or sign any acts from the agency, or work for another agency, for a stated period of time if they leave the agency. Some noncompete clauses restrict the employee from even working as an agent for the agreed-on period of time. If your responsible agent has a noncompete clause that prevents them from booking you for six to twelve months after they leave the agency, a key person clause might not be effective.

Bottom line, an agent will be one of the most important professional relationships an artist forms in his or her career. The key asset an agent brings to the equation is the agent's relationships with promoters, venues, managers, and other artists. Such relationships help form creative tour packages, lead to profitable bookings, and build loyalty from all involved. The same can be said for the rest of an artist's team of handlers.

THREE MORE KEY REPRESENTATIVES

There are three more key players that need to be part of any discussion regarding assembling a touring artist's team: the business manager, the touring manager, and the production manager. When a tour is being planned, and particularly once it is up and rolling, these three people will be among the most important on an artist's team. Because these jobs are covered in more depth in the chapters that follow, we will provide only brief discussions of their duties in this chapter.

BUSINESS MANAGER

A business manager works closely with the artist manager in establishing budgets, regulating income, weighing in on various deals, and running the artist's career as a "business." If the artist is the Chief Executive Officer, then the business manager is the Chief Financial Officer. A manager may explain the artist's vision of touring with Bengal tigers, pyrotechnics, and 60-foot video walls in the production, but the business manager may come back and say maybe they should consider a smoke machine—unless a tour sponsor comes on board with deep pockets.

"I would sum us up as the financial watchdog for the artist," says Jamie Cheek, a business manager with the prestigious Flood, Bumstead, McCready & McCarthy firm in Nashville. "We work closely with the management team, giving them the tools to help make financial decisions for the artist. We're the accountants, the tax preparers, the financial planners, the business structure advisers, and constant financial forecasters."

Cheek says most artists find business managers through recommendations from managers and attorneys. Most, but not all, business managers are certified public accountants or have CPAs in-house with their firms, and are counted on to bring financial discipline to the table. "Managers, the label, and everyone else on the team are sort of the cheerleaders trying to grow and market the career," Cheek explains, "and our sole job is to, from day one, sit down with the artist and say, 'What is your financial goal?' Then our job from that point on is to be on the watch for financial threats and opportunities to that goal."

Tour budgets are a particular area where business managers offer input. "Part of that is because most business managers in this industry will have the experience of working with a variety of artists, so we're one of an artist's best resources for putting together a budget and understanding what are the best and worst deals out there for buses, trucks, sound and lights, et cetera," says Cheek.

TOUR MANAGER

When you take the giant leap into a structured tour, you first need to hire experts who know the touring world. These professionals include your tour manager and your production manager, and their key asset is experience. If your tour has limited production—sound, lights, and stage set design—and is playing small- to-medium-sized clubs, these might be your only two touring employees. The title *road manager* was commonly used for many years, but it has generally been replaced by *tour manager* for organized tours.

Your tour manager must manage the day-to-day needs of you and your entourage while communicating frequently with your manager. Your entourage might include musicians' families, a publicist, security personnel, one or more tour accountants, a tour caterer, merchandise managers, and anyone else who attends to your needs while you are touring. Another important responsibility, and headache, that the tour manager assumes is coordinating transportation and lodging for you and your entourage. In many ways, the tour manager baby-sits the artist on the road.

If your tour does not have a tour accountant, your tour manager must represent you at *settlement*, a meeting at each venue when the promoter gives you your agreed-upon fee. In the absence of a tour account, the tour manager will pay touring personnel per diems and salaries.

A tour manager typically coordinates any publicity activities, including telephone interviews, radio on-air appearances, retail in-store appearances, media interviews, and all meet 'n' greet events. The tour manager is also responsible for all ticket requests from artists and media.

PRODUCTION MANAGER

The technical side of your tour, called *production*, includes sound, lights, staging, and any other technical elements you use in your show. Artists usually prefer to transport their own production in order to have consistency from city to city throughout their tour. If you cannot afford to carry your own show production, you still need someone to coordinate your production needs at each location at which you perform. A production manager is someone you should hire to be responsible for all technical aspects of the tour.

Your production manager begins by helping you, your manager, and your business manager develop a realistic production budget based on the size of venues in which you plan to perform. The production manager then coordinates the design of sound, lights, and stage set. In order to make the design a reality, the production manager contracts with vendors for production equipment including lighting, instruments, sound systems, and staging. The production manager hires technicians to operate and maintain the gear throughout the tour. A critical job is leasing trucks and buses, and hiring drivers, to transport production equipment and techs.

It is well worth noting that the tour manager and production manager are always on the road with the artist, while all the other key representatives mentioned in this chapter are taking care of matters on the home front. If something goes wrong, which in the Murphy's Law world of touring is almost a given, then it is most likely the tour manager or the production manager who will deal with it. Because they manage the logistical, technical, and business needs of the tour, the production manager and tour manager keep the artist from worrying about the frustrating aspects of touring, allowing the artist to focus on the music.

CHAPTER 2

**Making Money
on the Road**

Beyond the pure love of performing—the value of which should never be underestimated—artists tour to make money. To approach touring with any other objective can lead to a short career. While music is art, touring is business.

The opportunities to make money on the road are many, first and foremost selling tickets, as well as selling tour merchandise; garnering sponsorship dollars; and getting label support. Before a tour ever begins, an act's handlers need to have a firm grasp on how many tickets the act can sell in a given city and at what price, as well as what type of other revenues may be available.

Given the amount of time, resources, sweat equity, and financial investment involved in mounting a tour, it is paramount that artists capitalize on all of the financial opportunities on the road, which may be the difference of a tour finishing in the red or the black. When artists are performing, they command their fans' attention.

There is never a better time than at your live shows to offer your fans new ways to connect with you as an artist. Fortunately, most of these ways provide revenue streams to the artist, primarily in the form of merchandise sales. But touring is also the truest form of "direct marketing" artists have, so in addition to bringing in revenue, live performance is how artists most effectively "market" themselves.

Finally, there is no purer way for fans to demonstrate they care about an act than to invest the time, money, and effort it takes to attend a concert. Advertisers, marketers, and brands are very desirous of reaching this type of "active" consumer, so artists should be aware of the type of clout they have in their fan bases.

In this chapter we'll analyze the three key revenue streams of touring: ticket sales, merchandise sales, and sponsorships. We will also look at label support, which helps fund tours for developing acts.

TICKET PRICING

Selling tickets is where the "rubber meets the road" in an artist's career. An act may have a radio hit and may have sold a few thousand albums, but until they can sell tickets as a headliner, they have not realized a fully developed career. And it is important to note that the overwhelming majority of ticket revenue goes to the artist.

Ticket prices are arguably the most controversial aspect of the concert business today. While the rapid rise in ticket costs during the past decade has finally slowed, promoters, artists, agents, venues, and managers all profess concern about the price of attending a live show, which, as any concertgoer knows, can soar far beyond $100 for top acts. Generally speaking, ticket prices for the average tour have doubled in a decade, while the price for the touring elite has gone through the roof. Tickets to "special" concerts like Paul McCartney, Madonna, or the Rolling Stones are now routinely priced at $250 to $450, and VIP packages for $1,000 and more are becoming increasingly common. At the same time, service charges, parking, and facility fees have been tacked on to the point where a $35 ticket can easily hit $50.

Some say concert pricing was due a restructuring a decade ago, when ticket prices fell far below what premier sporting and Broadway events were charging. Between 1975 and 1996, concert ticket prices increased less than 2 percent after adjusting for inflation. During that same time period, films increased 37 percent.

In many instances, concerts are still underpriced compared to other entertainment. But music fans often complain about high ticket prices. Those in the business maintain that the higher prices enable acts, promoters, and venues to reap the benefits that often go to scalpers, who for years have charged several times the face value for tickets while contributing nothing to the concert equation. Online resellers have only exacerbated this situation.

The ticket pricing dilemma is an ongoing debate in the touring business and obviously cannot be solved in these pages. Suffice it to say that, popularity being a given, ticket pricing is probably the single most determining factor as to whether a show succeeds or fails, so it should be approached with the utmost caution and with respect for the consumer.

Acts at different stages in their careers may approach ticket pricing differently. A band that has been on the road for more than three decades and knows that biology will eventually force them to park the bus has a totally different perspective than an act still building its audience and hoping to have a long and lucrative career. The main question is what the market will bear, as fans vote with their wallet. A band with much of its career still ahead would not be wise to sacrifice career longevity for short-term profits. In other words, just because an act *can* charge $100 a ticket does not mean it should.

Fortunately, the touring business is rife with examples of different ticket pricing strategies that worked—and some that didn't. Garth Brooks, arguably the hottest act on the planet in the mid-1990s, put together country music's first $100-million tour by charging about $20 a ticket when he probably could have charged several times that. The strategy of Brooks and his team was to play to as many people as possible and not let ticket prices determine whether or not someone came to the show. Brooks stayed in a market until demand was filled. And by attracting more fans to his shows, he sold more tour merchandise (which was also priced conservatively).

Conversely, during that same time period, the Eagles reunited after sixteen years for their "Hell Freezes Over" tour, which was met with huge anticipation. Realizing the demand, Eagles manager Irving Azoff offered up mainstream rock's first $100 tickets and sold out stadiums, amphitheaters, and arenas all over the world. Azoff was famously quoted at the time as saying the only people who complained about the price of Eagles tickets were members of the media who got their tickets for free.

Both Brooks and the Eagles gauged their markets correctly. While as of this writing Brooks has "retired" from the road, his still-strong album sales demonstrate ongoing popularity. The Eagles remain one of music's top draws at the box office, clearly having done no permanent damage to their fan base.

Right pricing benefits every party involved: the artist, the venue, the promoters, and the fans. And the "right" price can range from $10 at a club to $450 in an arena to charging zero and playing for a flat rate at a fair or casino that offers entertainment as an added attraction. The good news—or bad news, depending on one's perspective—is that fans always let the act know when a show is priced correctly. They either buy tickets or they don't.

Ticket prices are most often based on how much an artist wants to be paid and how elaborate a production the act wants to present. A minimum payment for the act is agreed upon, then the promoter and the act set a ticket price based on what it will take for the promoter to make money off the show.

It is worth noting that bands whose careers developed since the Eagles shattered the ticket price glass ceiling, including Pearl Jam, Red Hot Chili Peppers, Kenny Chesney, and Dave Matthews Band, have managed to establish longevity in no small part because they have approached ticket pricing conservatively.

With the exception of multi-act festival tours and packages, setting ticket prices is generally the responsibility of the headlining act, as support acts are usually paid a flat fee. When setting ticket prices, the entire "value" of the show should be considered. How many support acts are on the bill? Are there other attractions that are part of the show, such as exhibits or non-musical performers? Has the act been in the marketplace recently? Are album sales strong in the market?

Ticket prices are generally hammered out by a consortium of the act's manager, business manager, and agent. When a ballpark price is nailed down, the agent goes back to the promoter to make sure the price is not too high or too low for a given market, based on economic factors and market history. Trade publications such as *Billboard* and *Pollstar* publish weekly box office information that lists shows, venues, and ticket prices.

Once an act determines how much it can potentially make from a tour, then they must calculate how they can get to that level. The first consideration is what type venue will be played. While venues will be discussed in more detail in Chapters 3, 14, and 16, in basic terms, the venue hierarchy is as follows: small to large clubs (less than 100 to 2,000 capacity), ballrooms (800–1,500 capacity), theaters and performing arts centers (PACs) (2,000–8,000 capacity), auditoriums (5,000–10,000 capacity), mid-sized arenas (10,000–15,000), large arenas (15,000–20,000), amphitheaters (10,000–20,000 capacity), stadiums and grandstands (15,000–100,000), and motor speedways and other alternative venues (100,000-plus).

An act plays smaller venues for two reasons: that's how many tickets they can sell in a given market, or they want to provide a more intimate setting to command a higher ticket price. Most venues today above the club level also offer "gold circle" seating, usually less than 10 percent of the house, which are the closest and the highest-priced tickets available.

Beyond the venue's capacity, the configurations need to be considered as well. Theaters and performing arts centers are typically fixed-seat venues, but clubs and ballrooms can be set up as festival seating or general admission (GA)—when patrons are not assigned a specific seat—in part or whole. Most major arenas today have curtaining systems that can take capacity from a few thousand on up in graduated levels. Arenas and stadiums can also offer GA floors or mosh pits, if in accordance with local laws (of which the promoter and venue will be aware). Amphitheaters generally have about one third of the seats fixed and under a roof, with the remainder being GA on the lawn. Reserved seats, which give fans their own little piece of "real estate" for the entire show, are worth more than GA, hence arena grosses typically are higher than amphitheater or "shed" grosses. When an arena goes with a partial GA, as on the last two U2 tours, generally seating is removed from the floor.

When determining capacity, production is a key factor. In an arena, for example, the stage may be at the "end zone," seating may be 360 degrees around the stage, or just 180 degrees, or somewhere in between. These details are worked out by the production manager in accordance with what the artist wants to deliver aesthetically and financially. This will be discussed in greater detail in Chapter 4. Another factor is seats taken out of the manifest (available ticket pool) to be given away as "comps" to media, sponsors, friends of the band, et cetera. In most cases luxury suites and sometimes club seats—seats designated for sports team season ticket holders—are not part of the overall manifest.

"You have to figure out what the production limits are," says Steve Hauser, a former promoter and venue manager and now a VP at the William Morris Agency. "If you have a 17,000-seat arena and you're not selling behind the stage, that might cut capacity down to 14,000. Then you take the comps and production kills out and you end up with a capacity of about 13,000. Then you finalize what your ticket price will be."

For example, if 1,000 golden circle tickets are priced at $45 and the balance of tickets at $39.50, the act might achieve a gross potential of $519,000. "Then you take your taxes out and that gives you your net gross potential," Hauser explains. "That's the simplest way to figure out what your gross is and what your net is."

As ticket prices have risen over the last decade, some bands and promoters have tried to counteract consumer price resistance by offering multi-tiered pricing (also called *scaling*), thus letting consumers determine the price point that best fits their budget. In an arena, *gold circle* would probably be the best 800 to 1,000 seats in the building, with about 80 percent of those on the floor and the remainder on the second or mezzanine level affording a premium view of the stage. "Then you usually go back and do the rest of the floor and most of the mid-level at another price range," says Hauser. "Then you take the upper tier and charge another price range."

In smaller venues, particularly clubs, varied price points are less common, as all seats are fairly close to the stage. For a club date, ticket prices are generally $20 or less and may or may not include a seat. Theaters and PACs can be more expensive, particularly if the show is by a major headliner playing smaller venues by choice to create a more intimate experience, as did Bruce Springsteen on his 2005 "Devils & Dust" solo acoustic tour. Even so, Springsteen was relatively conservative for an artist of his stature and kept ticket prices under $75 to $85 for the most part.

Unless an act is a major superstar virtually guaranteed to sell out every show, a total gross potential is rarely looked at beyond deriving a ballpark figure for budgeting purposes. "We look at it as individual dates," says Hauser. "With our guarantees and pricing, even though it's pretty standard, each market has to warrant the price. Obviously, you might say, 'We think we can gross $600,000 a night and do forty shows,' but you're really looking at what you can do per market. A band may say, 'We want to make $25 million this year, what's the best way to go after that?' Sometimes it's adding more dates instead of charging more for ticket prices."

To summarize ticket pricing simply, to determine ticket prices an act needs to come to terms with how much it will cost them to tour, how much they would like to make, and then reconcile the two by tweaking every variable in a complex science.

When a band plays multiple venues on the same tour, scaling becomes even more complex. Canadian promoter Michael Cohl has produced every Rolling Stones tour since 1989, including the 2005–2006 "Bigger Bang" tour that is the most lucrative trek in history. Tickets on that tour (nicknamed TOAST—tour of arenas, stadiums, and theaters—by its crew) averaged $100 in stadiums and $110 in arenas, not counting the gold circle seats, which Cohl defines as the "5 percent or 10 percent where we try to get the high-priced-ticket people to pay for the tour." Those tickets were priced $250 to $450. Theater tickets were in the $50 range.

As has always been the case with the Stones in their latter-day tours, much of the media focus was on the highest priced tickets. "The mistake the media have made over the years in attacking that situation is that this 10 percent of the house allows the other 90 percent to be $99 or $60 in our case, or $75 or $90 in [Paul] McCartney's case," Cohl noted in a 2005 *Billboard* interview. "If you get rid of that golden circle and spread it over the house . . . then the punters everybody is trying to protect will end up paying 30 percent to 40 percent to 50 percent more."

For superstar acts at the U2 and Stones level, fans can pay extra for a shot at the best seats, in the Stones' case $100 for other perks and the opportunity to see the exact seat locations available before they join. These premium seating opportunities, along with VIP packages and other promotions targeted to passionate fans, allow artists to tap into another revenue stream associated with ticket sales.

MERCHANDISING

Outside of ticket prices, tour merchandise—commonly referred to as *merch*—is the most important revenue stream for touring artists. For superstar acts, merchandise sales can be worth millions of dollars on a tour. The Rolling Stones rang up merch "per caps" (short for per capita or per head spending) of about $18 on their most recent tour.

For baby bands traveling in a van, merch revenue is often what bankrolls the band in getting from point A to point B. As Drive-By Truckers frontman Patterson Hood puts it, "As long as our fans can't download T-shirts, we'll be okay."

Dell Furano, CEO of Signatures Network, is a pioneer in the world of concert merchandise. He says acts normally choose a merch company based upon of combination of factors, including relationships between management and the merch company principals, advance and guarantee available, royalty rates, and such company strengths as retail distribution and product line.

Competition can be fierce. "It is a marketplace," says Furano. "We constantly get calls from managers, attorneys, agents, et cetera, telling us that Meat Loaf is going on tour or Evanescence, John Legend, Black Eyed Peas, et cetera, and asking for a proposal."

Furano points out that these calls go both ways. "We merch companies are constantly calling the artists' representatives like we did with Kanye West, Christina Aguilera, and others, telling them that we want to submit a proposal," he adds.

Jeffery Bischoff, a former pastry chef who now runs merch company Cinder Block, agrees word-of-mouth often brings bands into the fold. "The most common scenario is when an artist or artist manager hears of Cinder Block, either by reputation or through an existing relationship," Bischoff says. "Occasionally, managers or attorneys will solicit bids from several companies."

Basic deal terms are fairly similar from act to act. Usually the term is the longer of one album or touring cycle or recoupment (payback) of all advances. "Many times at the end of a touring cycle the artist has a buy-out option," Furano explains. "This means if the artist is unrecouped at the end of a cycle [in the amount] of $200,000, they can terminate the deal by paying back the $200,000."

In terms of royalty rates, advances, and percentages of gross sales to each party, the terms can vary. If there is a large advance, the royalty rates to the artist are lower. If there is no advance, the artist usually requests a higher royalty rate. Some major artists don't ask for an advance, though most still do, according to Furano.

For most new artists with an album deal, merch deals are worth $75,000 to $100,000, he says. "If it's not worth this amount, [then there is] no reason to do a deal," he says. "But deals for a group like the Darkness can go much higher very quickly."

As to how the deal is serviced, including such factors as whether the merch company has someone on the road, how the merch is distributed on the tour, or whether there is a retail angle, the terms vary widely. "On the bigger tours we put two staff on the road, on a smaller tour just one, and many times he rides on the bus and the merch travels on show trucks," says Furano. He adds that offering retail sales as part of the deal has become more and more important to artists.

Most bands tend to carry at least one in-house person on the road who oversees the merch operation. That person works with the merch company to make sure the right amount and styles of inventory are at each date, and tends to details with the venue. For arena-level acts, the building often will supply personnel to man the merchandise stands for a negotiated fee. Bands must also pay the venue a percentage of gross sales for the right to sell merchandise on-site. That fee, also called the *house rate* or *hall fee*, can range from less than 10 percent to 25 percent or more, and remains a bone of contention for artists. The more leverage an act has, the less percentage they can get away with paying to the venue. Venues often use the merch percentage as a bargaining tool to convince acts to play their room or to add dates.

For most headliner acts, the royalty percentage is from 72 percent to 77 percent of the after-tax gross. The artist is responsible for paying the hall fees out of its share, which average 22 percent to 25 percent on a major tour, according to Furano. So the artist makes 47 percent to 55 percent of the after-tax gross. On mid-sized to small tours, artists take home 30 percent to 40 percent of the gross.

One option that some acts have chosen is to handle their merchandise in-house. This strategy should be approached with trepidation, though, as merchandising is a specialty requiring plenty of skills and manpower. "It looks easy, but it's much harder than it looks to do it correctly and maximize earnings," says Furano. "Each city has different sales patterns, making managing the inventory difficult."

Another factor to be considered when thinking of handling merch in-house is the investment required in inventory, staff, warehousing, and distribution. Acts can lose a lot of profits by ordering too much inventory or the wrong inventory. Additionally, each state requires the filing of state and federal income taxes, which can be burdensome and expensive.

"I can give you a list as long as a football field of the artists that at one time or another did their own merch and now use merch companies," says Furano, citing Aerosmith, Van Halen, Fleetwood Mac, Alan Jackson, the Rolling Stones, U2, and KISS as examples.

"A lot depends on the level of service you are getting from the merch company," adds Bischoff. "Cinder Block, for example, is full-service, with design, manufacturing, and distribution all under one roof. It's about economy of scale on every level, from shipping to retailers, to dealing with the buildings, to raw materials and design."

Another option is a firm called Music Today, based in Charlottesville, Virginia, and founded by Dave Matthews Band manager Coran Capshaw. In simple terms, Music Today's two hundred employees provide merchandising, ticketing, and Web-based fan-club services for some five hundred clients, including bands at all career stages and such entities as the Bonnaroo Music & Arts Festival and the Vans Warped Tour. In 2005, Music Today rang up gross sales north of $100 million from its ticket, merchandise, and fan-club operations.

For baby bands, Music Today will take the upfront risk associated with developing and launching a Web site and merch inventory, then work on a revenue-sharing basis on the back end.

Today, merchandise lines have gone far beyond the traditional concert T-shirt, ranging in price from $5 key chains to $500 leather jackets. The type of music an act performs can also be a variable, particularly if the merch company has expertise in a given area. Merchandise can be specific to a given event, and different lines are often available on the road or at retail.

"Genre—as well as fashion trends—have a lot to do with if a band or artist will do something at retail," says Bischoff. "Since youth culture is a moving target, you just do the research and make your best guess. It's kind of like playing the ponies."

The newest form of tour merchandise is the concert CD. Often, immediately after a show, fans can obtain a CD of the concert they just witnessed from an on-site kiosk, have it mailed them later, or buy it online or at a participating retail outlet. Some bands, including the Dead and Pearl Jam, handle live concert CDs in-house. But others, like the Allman Brothers Band, the Pixies, and the Black Crowes, choose to go with one of the two main firms offering this product, Instant Live and DiscLive.

The accounting details for live concert CDs can be complicated, with a revenue chain that includes such parties as the act's record label, the act, the venue, the promoter, and local unions. Under Instant Live's blueprint, labels and artists get 30 percent to 40 percent of a $25 Instant Live CD sale, which they typically split equally. The remaining gross receipts are broken down as follows: 5 percent to 10 percent to the venue; 10 percent for packaging; varying percentages for sales tax, shipping, production, and transportation costs; and perhaps 20 percent to Instant Live.

The future of this branch of the tour merchandise business is moving toward digital delivery of MP3 concert content to cell phones, PDAs, or some other device. Acts have found that sales of concert CDs have not cannibalized sales of other tour merchandise.

TOUR SPONSORSHIP

An artist being sponsored by a company was once considered a "sellout" by purists (remember the witty video for Neil Young's song "This Note's For You"? It parodied corporate rock, the pretensions of advertising, and Michael Jackson), but tour and event sponsorships are now ubiquitous. Corporate America bankrolls a wealth of tours in virtually every genre, and venues are adorned with signage and usually bear the name of a company.

Jay Coleman, founder and CEO of Entertainment Marketing & Communications International, was one of the earliest players in the world of tour sponsorships. Coleman's association with the touring industry dates back to the mid-1970s, and the executive has been involved in putting together the bulk of the Stones' landmark tour sponsorship deals.

As Coleman has watched the dollars available increase, he has also observed that sponsors expect a lot more for their money. "When I first started, if the CEO liked the band and he could bring a few customers back-stage to take a picture, sometimes that was enough," Coleman says. "Today, it's much more sophisticated. Companies are looking for a real return on investment."

As such, these companies are usually not willing to sink much capital into a band with a limited following. "Going into it, unless you just get lucky, the odds are that you're going to have to really bust your hump to go out and find a meaningful corporate partner to work with, especially when you don't have a lot of traction yourself yet," says Coleman. He suggests a band learn its audience completely.

"These brands want to connect with the consumer," Coleman explains. "If it's a beer company, they're trying to sell beer to the same people the artist is trying to sell tickets to. So you have to say, 'Who is my audience and what is my audience doing? Do they shop at the Gap or at Armani?'"

Rather than think about major Fortune 500 companies to approach, it is better for a band to approach a niche brand. Once you set your sights on a potential sponsor, you need to reach out to the decision makers. One approach is to go directly to the company and find out who the brand manager or promotion director is, or some other appropriate party.

"Maybe they have someone who does their music sponsorship and marketing," says Coleman. "Another way is to go in through the advertising agency. The biggest challenge is to get to the right person and to get them to give you a few minutes. And you're only going to get a few minutes, so you have to have your act together."

Even when a productive dialogue with a brand is established, only major acts should expect a cash infusion. More likely is marketing support, which can be equally important. "An emerging act shouldn't look at a sponsor initially as being a revenue stream, but more as someone who can provide them a marketing platform and visibility," advises Coleman.

Bands should also make an attempt to tap into endorsement deals that can help them save important money on instruments and other gear. Guitar ace Zakk Wylde of Ozzy Osbourne's band and Black Label Society, for example, has endorsement deals with such products as tuners, microphones, amps, guitar strings, wah-wah pedals, and speakers.

Wylde's manager, Bob Ringe, suggests acts be pro-active in reaching out to gear manufacturers. "Any act that has a solid touring base should be able to contact the artist rep at each gear company to find out what type of endorsements are available for up and coming or established acts," Ringe says.

One brand that has offered such marketing support to scores of developing metal bands is Jägermeister and its U.S. marketing arm, Sidney Frank Imports. Local Jäger reps often are involved in bringing bands into the Jäger family. "Usually our local reps get word that a band in the area is promoting Jäger through the bars," says Rick Zeiler, director of marketing and brand development for Sidney Frank.

"Otherwise, if the band is good at promoting or drinking Jägermeister, we always give them a fair shot at being a sponsored band," Zeiler continues. "We don't care if the band is local, regional, or national, bar band or Slayer, as long as they are cool and creative with the promotion of Jägermeister."

Jägermeister's primary support comes mostly in the form of customized "swag" to bands, such as giveaways like lighters, coasters, T-shirts, shot glasses, et cetera. "We understand that beer companies can write checks and be done with it, but Jägermeister is much more hands-on," says Zeiler. "We have a staff of people that follows the bands and works with them to build their fan base and try and make them successful."

Zeiler says most of the bands that are involved with Jäger have relationships that last five years or longer. "We do supply some bands a bottle or two if the situation warrants," he says.

Additionally, Jägermeister sponsors major club tours featuring headlining artists each year. "The bands on our tours do receive sponsorship money for their efforts, but the bands that we sponsor usually don't," says Zeiler.

Available sponsorship dollars basically depends on how many fans that band has. "The correlation usually lies with ticket sales and album sales," says Zeiler. "Bands like Nickelback or Metallica get millions for tour sponsorships. Big companies like Coke and Pepsi can afford this. Bottom line, the bigger the band the more people they can draw, the more they are worth to a sponsor."

But Zeiler says Jägermeister has a different approach. "We offer sponsorships to the bands we *know* like our product," he says. "Bands like Slayer, Slipknot, Disturbed, Drowning Pool, and others drink Jäger and like to talk about it. They may only sell 2,000 to 4,000 tickets but we know they are hard-core and really care about our image and brand."

An endorsement deal could lead to free or discounted gear, an important factor when every dollar counts. "Each company has a different policy regarding free goods or the ability to obtain items at wholesale," says Ringe. "These relationships are extremely important to a developing act, as they help the act expand its base." And when a band is just getting off the ground, every dollar and every fan counts.

LABEL SUPPORT

Record labels have historically invested significant financial resources toward new acts' touring efforts, whether it be $20,000 for a regional van trek or

$200,000 for a national bus outing. But in today's world of shrinking revenue and tight budgets at labels, tour support funds—though almost always recoupable to the label—are becoming harder to come by. If you are fortunate enough to receive tour support from your label, treat it as a loan that you pay back at the end of the tour, providing the tour finishes in the black.

Labels closely monitor tour budgets these days and are not nearly as free-wheeling with a checkbook as they once were. One business manager says a group he works with that is signed to a major label originally thought it would receive $75,000 for one month of touring on a bus. Later, the label came back with another offer: $30,000 and a van.

Still, labels realize that touring can spike record sales and many view tour support as simply a marketing expense. Artists should realize that tour support is something they can and should ask for contractually when signing a record deal. And, as label executives are quick to point out, there is more to tour support than just money. Maximizing an artist's presence at retail and radio when in a market is often part of the deal.

In one of the more controversial developments of late, labels have made noise about tapping into touring revenue. They say they are entitled to portions of that money, because they have invested heavily in developing a brand that potentially creates revenue that they never see. This philosophy, not surprisingly, has met with criticism by players in the touring scene like agents and promoters who are not interested in offering yet another slice out of the touring pie.

Other new deals see the promoter and label "investing" in a band, often to the tune of millions of dollars, so they can "buy in" to all revenue streams the band generates, including ticket sales, record sales, publishing, merchandising, et cetera. Critics call this tactic a glorified advance, but proponents say the strategy allows all parties to pull in the same direction in promoting a band's career.

Label support can be invaluable in getting a band's career off the ground and spreading the word beyond core markets. But the sooner a band can stand on their own, generating self-sustaining revenue on the road, the better for all parties.

When it is all said and done, there are numerous revenue streams an artist can tap into while touring. How involved the artist is in orchestrating these financial matters depends on the act. Some are very hands-on, others not so much. Tom Petty would fall under the latter category, and John Mellencamp the former.

"I'm not really involved in the business," Petty told *Billboard*. "I'm fortunate—I've been with the same manager since I started out thirty years ago, and he has always been very good at looking after our tours and things."

Mellencamp, on the other hand, is very aware of how his tours are booked and strategized. "I try to be hands-on in anything I'm involved with," he told *Billboard*. "The worst thing I could do is sit back at my house here in Indiana and have somebody hand me a tour schedule, then go out and be unhappy. I would only have one person to blame for being so lackadaisical, and that's myself."

CHAPTER 3

Why, When, and Where to Tour

Touring that is not strategically planned can be an exercise in futility. The earliest plans for a tour—the *preproduction* phase, before capital is invested in production gear and other costs—help the artist's team avoid costly mistakes and backtracking, literally and figuratively, once the tour is underway. The preproduction phase is when the benefits of touring can be maximized. Any time an act hits the road to play a series of dates, the tour should be carefully mapped out to most fully realize revenues and exposure, and to help meet objectives for career longevity.

Before the tour bus or van hits the freeway, several major decisions need to be made. These include determining tour objectives (why to tour); creating a timeline of proposed activities, including coordinating the tour with album or single releases, if necessary (when to tour); and considering potential cities and venues in which to perform (where to tour).

Plotting a tour is a process that usually begins with a meeting between the act and its team. These first meetings can take place as long as a year prior to the first date, particularly with major bands. When all these key personnel are in place on an artist's team, plans and objectives for a tour are coordinated by management, the label, the booking agency, and sometimes a publicist. A strategy is laid out, with such key factors to consider as album release date, targeted television exposure, tour announcement, an advertising and/or marketing campaign, when tickets go on sale, tour launch, routing East to West or vice versa, and the tour's conclusion. Many of these topics will be discussed in future chapters, but here we will analyze why to tour, when to tour, and where to tour.

WHY TO TOUR

An ideal tour should promote album sales, make money (sell tickets and merchandise), and put the band in markets they should play and in venues fans like to patronize, which will, ultimately, build the fan base. This is accomplished by putting the artist in the right markets and buildings at the right time and for the right reasons. By the right reasons, we mean that if an act knows its fans prefer to see it play in Theater X, but Theater Y offers more money, the act still plays Theater X because the fans like it.

Some bands, particularly in the early stages of their career, tour constantly, especially if they are not signed to a record label. They do this because this is where the greatest opportunity to create new fans lies, as well as the opportunity to build a "buzz" that may attract the sort of attention from labels and industry power brokers that can lead to a recording contract.

In other situations, a band may only tour every few years or, as has been seen in recent times, the band may reunite for only one "farewell" tour. Of course, as savvy concert fans know, one-off tours or farewell tours can stretch into years, if market demands. The Who's first "final" tour was in the late 1980s, yet the band has toured well into the new millennium. The Eagles have slyly toured the last few years under the "Farewell, Part I" banner. The reason bands tour beyond their album-selling or radio peak, one can assume, is primarily for the money. Professional musicians also play because they enjoy it and are gratified by time spent in the spotlight.

For most acts signed to a record label, touring is tied into the release of an album and is designed to capitalize on media exposure, radio airplay, and the record company's marketing muscle. Other acts who may not be signed to a label but can still tour find live shows the best place to sell their wares and to promote their latest recording efforts. In this case, they treat CD sales as another form of concert merchandising, a tactic also used by label acts.

Creating a successful touring strategy works best when all of the primary stakeholders are involved. With so many agendas to be served by touring, what is the "hierarchy of needs" here? Professional opinions vary on this topic.

Scott Siman, manager of Tim McGraw, says that touring behind an album is a given. "It probably sounds a bit corny, but the biggest priority is making for a great concert experience. With Tim, he has developed a reputation as a great live performer—we have set a high bar each time out and we want to continue that tradition and build fans for the long term. Once the tour is announced, our major goal is selling the tickets and maximizing the revenue for all sources given the tremendous cost of touring."

In a nutshell, Siman believes the priorities are rather simple for McGraw: "Create an event. Make money. Have fun. Tim really thinks like a fan and I think it shows when he performs."

Fun is one thing, losing money quite another. If a band should not be touring at all, ticket sales—or the lack thereof—will soon demonstrate this lack of demand.

TOURING TO PROMOTE ALBUM SALES

There is a general consensus among music business professionals that touring helps sell albums. Even though touring is a "parallel" business to selling records, artists generally attempt to maximize both simultaneously. Tracking figures have demonstrated time and again that album sales for an artist spike in a given market when the artist plays a concert in that market.

"There are many priorities [in touring], but the most important, in my opinion, is the proper setup of the album," says Michael Arfin, agent for such acts as Linkin Park and Sevendust at Artist Group International. "This would include a two- to three-month campaign to promote a single at radio and video, a full push at all press outlets, Internet promotion, guerilla marketing, and countless other traditional and nontraditional ways to do this."

The primary way touring helps sell albums is by creating exposure in the marketplace. When a band comes to a given city, there will likely be advertising to promote the concert, songs from the new record will be performed on stage, and there may be reviews in the local newspaper touting the new material. Additionally the artist can promote the new record through live radio performances and retail *in-stores*: when the act shows up at a record store, promotes both the concert and the album, and possibly offers a brief performance. These types of activities are typically coordinated by label marketing personnel and/or a *tour publicist*—a public relations professional hired to maximize exposure.

Arfin says that if the promotion or set up of an album is executed successfully, then other priorities such as selling tickets and bringing in sponsors will all follow naturally, as the chance for greater success on the road is usually dependent on the success of the album. "If the act has already proven their success over the years, then sponsorships can be secured well in advance of the album release," he explains. "The goal would be the sponsor becoming an actual partner who will work hand-in-hand with the artist to not only sponsor touring activities, but also to help set up and contribute to the promotion of the forthcoming album."

TOURING TO MAKE MONEY

All tours should be set up to be profitable, but for many acts touring is how they make their living. For acts that do not have a wide range of revenue streams available to them, touring and its ancillary profit centers are the primary source of income. The most successful of these artists have built up enough equity with fans from shows over the years that the sheer power of their history can sell tickets with or without a hot-selling album or radio airplay. Acts that fall into this category are arguably the largest segment of touring artists today. If they are prudent about when and where they play, these artists can continue to tour successfully well into their retirement years.

Touring is hard work and touring to make money is a worthy pursuit. There is no shame in playing for the money. Nevertheless, few artists ever admit publicly that the reason they hit the road is to make a buck.

TOURING TO BUILD THE FAN BASE

While the act is attempting to build album sales, they are also trying to build their fan base and, ideally, a long career that will see ticket sales continue for many years. Some artists benefit from a debut hit that instantly makes them a household name coast to coast. But more frequently, bands build their fan bases one market at a time, strategically targeting regions where they are strong and where they need to grow. Artists can do certain things to help grow their fan base, with the use of the Internet being one of the most useful tools available. A user-friendly Web site with a healthy database of fans can let them know each time the act visits their market. Word-of-mouth is still the best way to create a buzz.

For artists that may not have a current album or whose record selling peak is behind them, the top consideration should be "how much demand is there?" *Heritage acts*—acts whose biggest hit-making days are behind them—that consistently play the same cities and venues year after year often see their ticket sales dwindle through the law of diminishing returns. Others, however, have been fortunate enough to become staples for a given season or venue, like James Taylor in the summer, the Allman Brothers Band at New York's Beacon Theatre in the spring, or Jimmy Buffett anytime, anywhere.

WHEN TO TOUR

Once an artist has a reason to be touring, the next step is to decide when to tour. According to Kirk Sommer at the William Morris Agency, determining when to tour "really depends on what your objectives are. Are you expanding your business? Are you promoting new product? Are you trying to maintain your business? Are you rebuilding?"

Among the determining factors as to when to tour are the availability of the artists to be involved, the release of a new recording, when the artist is getting radio or television exposure, and how recently the artist has played a given market, as well as who else may be touring in that window. Also important are coordinating single performances when an entire tour is not planned, and the timing and execution of when tickets go on sale.

TOURING WHEN THE ARTISTS INVOLVED ARE AVAILABLE

Obviously there is no tour without the artist. Up-and-coming acts make themselves available when there is demand. But superstar acts have enough leverage to control when and for how long they will tour. This was true for the 2006 Madonna "Confessions" tour, when tour producers had to work around Madonna's schedule when trying to set up a tour that visits North America, Europe, and other international markets.

"The 'when' is certainly her call," tour producer and Global Chairman of Music for Live Nation Arthur Fogel says. "[Her] time frame is pretty consistent, late May through early September. That's the time that works for her."

The reason that time works for Madonna might seem strange for the once self-described Material Girl. "Madonna's family commitments are a priority," says her co-manager Angela Becker. "Specifically, her children's school versus vacation schedules needed to be factored into the tour plans."

The timing of a tour is most often dictated by the top act on the bill or the *headliner*. Taken into consideration to a lesser degree is the availability of the support acts, and at which level in the show's lineup they are to appear, whether first, second, et cetera. This is referred to as how the acts are *billed*.

The headliner is the act at the top of the marquee and the act that closes the show. Under the headliner come the varying levels of support. For example, on the first leg of the 2006 "Kenny Chesney: The Road & the Radio" tour, the billing was Kenny Chesney with Dierks Bentley, and Sugarland. Chesney was the headliner, Bentley was the support, and Sugarland was the opener or "third billed."

Support acts that want to be on a tour headlined by another act are generally at the mercy of when and where the headliner's handlers choose to play, although the supporting act or acts' needs are often taken into consideration. The lower on the totem pole an act is, the less input it will get, but this must be weighed against the benefits of exposure.

Sometimes there are co-headlining situations, as in the 2006 "Lynyrd Skynyrd/3 Doors Down" tour, or the most successful co-headlining tours of all time, the "Billy Joel and Elton John Face To Face" tours. In co-headlining situations, each act's handlers work out who will open, who will close, and how the tour will be promoted and advertised, right down to the size of the typeface. Both artists' priorities are considered in creating the touring timeline.

Touring When a New Recording Is Released

Michael Arfin is a firm believer that, "The release of the album dictates when the band tours. That's not to say that the band would not tour without a release or do isolated dates, but the touring cycle for a band is planned very well in advance with the specific goal of promoting that new album through touring."

Coldplay manager Dave Holmes agrees that the priority in determining when to tour revolves around the record and efforts to promote sales and, indeed, Coldplay has only toured when the band has a record to support. But the importance of growing the band as an entity that can sell tickets is also important. "The second priority is to try and expand the touring base as much as possible by going deep into secondary markets," Holmes observes. "This in turn helps drive record sales."

Recording schedules and delays can hold up a tour's launch indefinitely. In these cases, the touring timeline is totally dictated by the album's release and marketing efforts. This benefits both the label and the touring concerns, as the tour draws attention from the album's promotion as much as the record benefits from the tour exposure.

Touring When the Artist is Getting Radio or Television Exposure

For a band that receives ample airplay on the radio, timing around a hit's rise and fall on the charts can be crucial. "The normal process has been to allow the single to penetrate at radio for a few months prior to the album release, and allow the release to saturate the market and be exposed to new fans before launching a proper headline tour," says Arfin. "In certain situations the band will do underplays (playing small venues, known as *buzz plays*) in select markets to promote the launch of the album prior to or in conjunction with release of a single."

A growing trend among rock bands is to set up a new release and/or a major tour by underplaying markets in limited tours of small venues. Audioslave, Weezer, and System of a Down are among the latest bands to use such a strategy.

"This sort of under-play is absolutely a smart thing to do," says Andy Cirzan, VP of concerts at Chicago-based promoter Jam Productions. "It's a way to tell America, 'We're back and ready to climb in the ring again.' Rather than be presumptuous and say, 'Here's our tour,' you play some club dates and kick up some dust."

Coldplay manager Holmes is also a believer in the buzz play. "We have generally done buzz gigs or club shows around the world to coincide with the single release and left the actual tour to happen when the album is out," he says. "On the last two albums, I timed the on-sales to run concurrent with the first single going to radio. This is a good way to get exposure for your single by combining the marketing efforts of the [ticket] on-sale and single launch."

A band may also begin a tour following a major awards show or television experience. For example, if a band is to perform at the Grammy Awards in Los Angeles, it may also route in an appearance at that city's Wiltern Theatre, followed by a West Coast run, taking advantage of both economics and exposure.

Arfin says choosing markets begins when management presents him with a calendar of planned events. "The calendar includes tentative release date, dates for adds at radio, key awards shows, et cetera," says Arfin. "Then both management and agent will start to fill in the gaps in regard to touring in a perfect scenario."

TOURING TRAFFIC (AND OTHER CONSIDERATIONS)

Just as too much traffic on the highway can create problems, too much "touring traffic" can also be problematic, forcing consumers to make choices as to which acts they will see. One tactic more bands are realizing is to tour when most other bands are not. About seventy percent of all concert activity takes place between the months of April and September. "Regardless of the cities, one of the best times to tour in the United States is during the months of late January, February, and early March, as there is usually the least amount of traffic," says Arfin. "Not many bands are touring and therefore there is less to compete with."

As far as specific dates, experience has taught booking agents and promoters that some dates work better than others. Sometimes it's "just plain timing," according to R.E.M. agent Buck Williams. "These are generalities, but you know that it's bad to play around Memorial Day, around Labor Day, before Christmas, after Thanksgiving," he says. "Maybe one week after Thanksgiving is okay, but then Santa Claus comes along and nobody cares."

Acts should be cognizant of how often they play a given market. While Jimmy Buffett could likely play Cincinnati every year for the rest of his career (for whatever reason), most artists have to be careful of "beating up" markets, or playing them too often. A general rule of thumb for repeat plays in a given market is sixteen months to two years between engagements. Even if an act thinks they can sell out Dallas every year, it is wise not to kill the golden goose. Of course, some acts are "bulletproof" in given markets, meaning they can sell out under any market conditions. Examples would be Bruce Springsteen in New Jersey or Billy Joel in New York City.

TOURING IN THE RIGHT VENUES AT THE RIGHT TIME

Sometimes the type of venue the act wishes to play dictates timing of the tour. Obviously, outdoor venues like amphitheaters, stadiums, city parks, and festivals must take place when the weather is warm. Similarly, fairs tend to take place in the August through November time frame.

Arenas, theaters, and clubs tend to be more busy when the weather is cooler. But arenas are often busy in the fall/winter time frame due to sports team tenants, whose schedules take precedent over concert bookings. Many acts that tour in the summer have found success in playing arenas or theaters, with air conditioning offering fans a respite from the heat.

Acts can find success in playing tourism hot spots when in season, like playing Daytona Beach, Florida during Spring Break, or Las Vegas around New Year's Eve. These bookings can be in demand, so it behooves agents to let talent buyers be aware of their acts' availability in the given time frame and region.

PLAYING ONE-OFFS

Given the huge expense of touring, single dates or *one-offs* are rare because the idea is to amortize the expense over several shows. Sometimes, however, an act will play a show that is not part of an organized tour. The most common of these types of events is the radio show, which tend to be concentrated in the spring and holiday seasons, such as the KROQ Weenie Roast in Los Angeles in June, or the Z100 Jingle Ball in New York in December. A *radio show* is a concert organized by a radio station to either reward listeners or generate revenues. Acts, particularly developing acts, are often asked to play these shows for a reduced fee, or even for free. Given the leverage that radio stations hold in regard to coveted airplay, these shows remain a source of controversy in the industry. Federal investigations and charges of "payola" have added fuel to this fire.

Acts also will play one-off dates for private or corporate events. These tend to be among the highest paid gigs for artists, and mostly go off under the public radar. The talent buyer almost always covers production and travel expenses for these type shows. For most large agencies, booking corporate and private events is a big area of focus.

THE ART OF THE ON-SALE

When planning a tour, the timing of the *on-sales*—an industry term for when tickets first are available to the general public—is another crucial element to consider. Promoters and agents must take into consideration what else is going on in a market on that particular day—not only what other acts are going on sale, but what else is happening. The opening day of deer season in Wisconsin or a major football game day in Knoxville, Tennessee, would not be a good time to put a show on sale.

The on-sales, or "going up," is a key part of an overall promotional plan. "We control the on-sale process, the marketing of the tour, and provide materials to local promoters," says McGraw manager Scott Siman. "We work with each promoter and try to tap into their vast knowledge of their local market to make the right call on when to put a show on-sale, ticket scaling options and when you roll into multiple shows."

With so many tours jammed into the April to October time frame, the tight squeeze forces promoters to follow one of two strategies for putting tickets on sale. One strategy is to put the show on sale months before the actual concert date and try to make as much money as possible before markets are drained of discretionary income for concerts. The other strategy is to wait until only a few weeks out to create a sense of urgency for the show. Historically, the latter was the prevailing logic, as much a function of economics as human nature, because promoters did not want to budget more for promotion than absolutely necessary.

But increasingly, promoters and agents are more apt to "go up" early to get their financial licks in first. Some find this strategy inefficient. "This whole strategy of rushing to get the first dollars has dramatically altered the dynamic of promoting," Arthur Fogel says. "How can you reconcile going up three or four months out with the same ad budget as three or four weeks out?" Fogel wonders. "The logic escapes me. It's like you put a show on sale, and then you forget about it for a period of time."

In most cases, on-sales are rolled out in markets at staggered times to take advantage of local market opportunities inherent in announcing each show and the attention that attracts. At other times, most often with blockbuster tours, the entire tour is put on sale at the same time.

When the planets are aligned correctly, the result can be astounding. The Dixie Chicks' national on-sale in March 2003, geared to take advantage of tremendous media exposure for the group in the wake of the Grammy Awards, paid off over one weekend with the sale of 867,000 tickets, valued at about $49 million. "We were trying something that's never been done before: putting a million tickets up in one day," Chicks agent Rob Light said in a *Billboard* interview at the time. "It's so rare to get the Super Bowl, a *People* magazine cover, *Saturday Night Live*, and the Grammys in a five-week span."

WHERE TO TOUR

When determining where an artist will tour, the main factors are nailing down which markets should be played, given time and geographic constraints (including international opportunities); where an artist is most popular or where would they like to build their popularity; and which venues are available and most appropriate for the tour. In this section we will also take a look at the process of how a tour is routed.

DETERMINING WHICH MARKETS TO PLAY

For acts with widespread popularity that are willing to tour only for a limited amount of time, as on the previously discussed Madonna tour, the top-40 markets are the first to be booked. Major cities, with their population, media exposure offered and wide range of venues, are always a top choice to play when a tour is planned. But cities off the beaten, major-market touring path have proved fertile ground for agents and promoters willing to give them a shot. The assumption is star power increases in markets unaccustomed to national touring acts, and the plethora of new buildings that have cropped up in secondary and tertiary markets makes routing less challenging.

Particularly for country artists, the smaller, more rural markets are often the lynchpin for building careers with "legs" or longevity. "Nashville agents, by necessity, do a better job of recognizing this than the East and West Coasts, which I think are missing the boat," says promoter Brad Garrett of Police Productions. "I look at the Kenny Chesney model. He honed his craft and worked his butt off playing two hundred dates a year," Garrett continues. "So when the record stuff caught up, he was ready. He had a core fan base of five thousand in markets where we were doing dates with him, and those were hardcore Kenny fans."

Cher and Rod Stewart are examples of more mainstream acts that have found secondary and tertiary markets to be fertile ground. Garrett admits it can take a lot of extra effort to play outside the major-market circuit. "It just depends on if management wants to work that hard; if they're only going to play fifty to sixty dates, they're not going to go into a lot of these places," he says.

Several strategies can be applied in touring the United States. Michael Arfin says with a major arena act, "We usually start a headline tour by playing the biggest thirty cities in the country a few months after the album has been released to make the most impact," he says. "We will then look at secondary and tertiary markets as part of another leg, either a few weeks later or months later, and we may also play a mix of major and secondary markets in the summer with a festival package."

A well-plotted tour includes *anchor dates* and public appearances. Anchor dates are appearances that are important enough to route other stops around them. For example, if an act wants to play Lollapalooza in Chicago in July, it is logical to schedule other markets in the Midwest around the July Chicago date.

As in most aspects of touring, there is no substitute for history and experience when choosing markets. "Having been over ten years into this, you get a feel for each market and what makes sense," says Siman. "But you also have to be willing to challenge conventional wisdom—it was suggested back in 2000 that Tim and Faith couldn't sell out Madison Square Garden. Well, they did, and [next] time around they sold it out twice!"

PLAYING MARKETS BASED ON POPULARITY

Certain acts may be extremely popular in some parts of the country, but far less so in others. For example, some acts may be able to sell out 3,000-seaters in twenty to thirty cities in Texas and Oklahoma, but may have to play small clubs in the Northeast, or skip that region entirely.

If an act can sell out Minneapolis any time but is still largely unknown in Cleveland, then the act should logically play Cleveland at least once a year until they are as big in Cleveland as they are in Minneapolis. This is called *building the fan base*, and the process is aided when a local promoter supports the band and is willing to invest in growing the band in that particular market. The agent's relationships with promoters often come to bear in this situation. An act should always be looking to break new markets.

If an act is trying to become more popular in a given market, they can boost their drawing power by touring with similar acts to create more value for the customer. The inverse is also true; if an act is very popular in a city, they would not need to spend the extra money to partner with other acts but rather sell tickets on their own drawing power. An example of this would be the previously mentioned co-headlining tour by Lynyrd Skynyrd and 3 Doors Down. Neither act played their best markets as a part of the package, preferring to keep them "fresh" and then coming back later and playing those cities as a sole headliner.

Touring Internationally or Just Domestically

There are numerous factors that dictate how to reconcile geography and time in both international and domestic markets. If an act has international appeal, it only makes sense to play the markets where the act can sell tickets. For U.S.-based artists, touring internationally usually requires a commitment of time and money before it becomes profitable. But acts that make the investment in international touring can often tour overseas when domestic markets have been tapped out.

For acts with record deals, "Once again, in my opinion, the most important guide is the release date of the album," Arfin maintains. "Specific territories such as Europe traditionally need to have an artist touring right on top of the album release."

In the United States and Europe, there is more impact if touring begins after the album has been released for a few months and creates strong awareness, but this is less important in some foreign markets. "There's a bit more flexibility when dealing with Asia, South America, and Australia," Arfin says, "but the biggest consideration and priority is given to the United States and Europe when planning, as they normally make up for the largest album buying markets."

Time is budgeted for each territory, or for a domestic tour, each region of the country. In R.E.M.'s case, Bob Gold of Gold Artist Agency handles Europe and Buck Williams handles the rest of the world. "I'll say, 'Okay, Bob, you've got the summer, you route around the festivals, and I'll look at what's in Africa or South America' and we tie that in and then when's the best time to be here in the United States,' says Williams. "And it's all tied around the release of the record. After that meeting, when a template is set, then we put together options."

Determining Which Venues to Play

The type of venues an act plays is largely dictated by the number of tickets it can sell. The basic types of venues were discussed in Chapter 2, and other venue issues will be discussed in Chapters 14 and 16. As noted earlier, the standard graduated scale for venues is as follows: small to large clubs (less than 100 to 2,000 capacity), ballrooms (800–1,500 capacity), theaters and performing arts centers (PACs) (2,000–8,000 capacity), auditoriums (5,000–10,000 capacity), mid-sized arenas (10,000–15,000), large arenas (15,000–20,000), amphitheaters (10,000–20,000 capacity), stadiums and grandstands (15,000–100,000), and motor speedways and other alternative venues (100,000-plus).

Besides drawing power, a major issue for artists with regard to which venues they play is aesthetics. A rule of thumb is that production elements tend to work better inside due to controlled light levels and better acoustics. In addition, some acts prefer a "tribal atmosphere" that comes from an enclosed venue, while other acts prefer a party atmosphere, and for them, outdoor venues are often best.

Another consideration is the desired intimacy of the show. While modern videoboards bring the action to the farthest nosebleed seats, there is no substitute for the intimacy of being close to the artists on stage. Theaters, ballrooms, and performing arts centers offer this intimacy. Unless ticket prices are raised, gross revenue potential suffers when capacity is lowered, but fans of many artists have proven time and again that they are willing to pay top dollar for an intimate concert experience.

Certain acts work better outside. The Dave Matthews Band and Jimmy Buffett, for example, have parlayed their musical styles and a party theme into becoming "lifestyle" events that play well in outdoor amphitheaters, commonly referred to in the industry as *sheds*, stadiums, and festivals.

Other acts, particularly those that appeal to an older, less price-sensitive audience—such as Madonna, Bruce Springsteen, Billy Joel, and Elton John—play much better in an indoor arena or a theater. Not only do fans paying more for tickets appreciate having their own piece of "real estate" in a seat, but often they are adverse to a lawn or general admission situation. These fans like to know exactly where they will be and do not find sitting or standing in the grass appealing.

Both arenas and amphitheaters typically have capacities in the 15,000 to 20,000 range, but two-thirds of the capacity of sheds generally consists of lower-priced lawn seating. Because they are designed specifically for concerts, sheds often have more favorable sightlines and offer more seats at premium prices. In fact, for arenas to reach full capacity, seats behind the stage have to be sold. But selling 360 degrees only works with the biggest acts and requires additional production elements.

On the other hand, most modern arenas have the capability to reconfigure from theater size to full capacity via curtaining systems or elaborate theater configurations. Such a strategy allows shows to start with a lower capacity and increase as ticket sales warrant. Utilizing all reserved seating, arenas are able to charge more for each seat than amphitheaters because reserved seats are worth more than general admission. The top-grossing tours each year are almost always arena tours.

Some artists actually prefer outdoor shows. "There's an energy outside that you can't capture indoors and I think it's because of the people on the lawn, the party atmosphere, summertime, I don't know, it's just a feeling that's unparalleled to anything else," Rascal Flatts' Jay DeMarcus tells *Billboard*. "So

I think if I had my choice, I'd play outdoor amphitheaters all the time."

Other artists enjoy performing either indoors or outdoors. "We'd play in someone's backyard if they'd have us," Rascal Flatts' Gary LeVox says. "The sound is always better indoors. Outside is kind of like a party. Inside is a party [too], but a little more tame than some of those amphitheaters and fairs and things."

Ultimately, an artist's particular preference often determines the types of venues booked. Asked if he has a preference for venues, Cross Canadian Ragweed (CCR) frontman Cody Canada tells *Billboard*. "Clubs. Definitely a bar. Those outside, big gigs, they're great, don't get me wrong—we've been trying to sell out those places forever. But the clubs are just more personal. And they're rowdy. We like the rowdy crowds."

Canada thinks CCR fans also prefer club shows. "Those big [outdoor venues], you can't see somebody that's a football field away from you," he says. "Most of those people out there in the cheap seats—what we call the 'pot-smoking seats'—they're the ones that really, really live and breathe your music. Not taking away from the guys upfront, but the ones that are camping out on the lawn all day are always the ones that are upfront in the bars."

Fairly or not, for some there is a stigma attached to playing certain venues. Fairs have a reputation as hosting primarily country or oldies acts. Casinos have a stigma of the lounge-type performers. And amphitheaters, or sheds, have often been characterized as primarily hosting acts past their commercial prime. In fact, one promoter was famously quoted as saying, "When the career is dead, they play the shed." It's worth noting that the promoter in question had no access to promoting concerts in amphitheaters. But a quick look at schedules for all of these venues shows that these perceptions are not wholly valid. Superstar acts play casinos, hard rock acts play fairs, and hot pop acts play amphitheaters.

ROUTING THE TOUR

Assembling the complex puzzle of routing a tour is both time consuming and detail-oriented. Agents not only are looking for the right venues, they're looking for the right days of the week and separation from other entertainment events. "As I do R.E.M. basically by myself, it takes about a month of pretty focused work," says Williams. "If you have a team of agents working territories, you can put it together more quickly than that."

In routing the tour, the agent calls venues and promoters in various markets to determine available dates, known as *avails*. If a desired date in a given market in the appropriate venue is available, the agent will put a hold on the date to let the building's booking manager know they are interested. Sometimes another act or acts may also have a hold in place for that particular date, so the agent gets a "second" or "third" hold until one of the three acts firms up the date with a contract.

When calling buildings searching for avails, the agent is also calling promoters. While there are a lot of exclusive venue/promoter arrangements today that limit options, it behooves the agent to check in with the building and the promoters. "I do like to talk to the buildings directly," says Williams. "You can get a real deal sometimes when you start talking about what you can do for them, and you can find out what they're holding besides your date."

A promoter may only know what his or her firm is taking into a given building or market, "but if you go into a market where you have multiple promoters, like Chicago, one promoter might not necessarily know what the other promoter is bringing in," says Williams, "so if you talk to the building you'll have a better shot of finding out what else is coming in so you don't play heads up against someone else."

Siman says that on the 2006 "Tim McGraw/Faith Hill Soul 2 Soul II" tour, "We had buildings on hold for months in advance to guarantee we could get into the major venues. Also, this year in particular, we [were] doing a number of multiple shows in single markets, so it was important to hold multiple nights. Cities vary for a number of reasons. Generally we go to the bigger markets based upon the size of our production and the grosses we need to achieve."

Williams offers his bands several touring scenarios, with cities and dates in place. "These are workable dates," Williams points out. "They're not all first holds, some are second or third holds, but you can't challenge the holds in place until you know the band wants to work these options.

Then, in Williams' case, the band will choose the touring option they like. "They'll say, 'This is the tour we want to happen,' and it may not happen that Pittsburgh and New York are on those exact dates because they're only second holds and somebody firms them up," Williams explains. "But you know the buildings and you know the time frame and you know the basic routing of where you're going and the general revenue potential."

The process is much more streamlined when the act is in its early stages of development and/or is booked in a supporting slot. A smaller band can move more quickly, and a supporting slot is "the easiest thing in the world," according to Williams. "If a support slot comes up, then you're basically just issuing contracts. You don't have to go through the routing and all."

Production and distance between markets are huge factors in routing. "Sometimes the production itself will only fit into certain venues," says Siman. "There is a limit on how many miles you can move down the road—based upon load out and load in requirements. Building avails can become an issue when there is a lot of touring going on."

Routing is an imperfect science. "You get the tour almost exactly done and you may find out there's not a single building in Dallas that'll work and you have to have Dallas," says Williams. "So you throw it away and you juggle and something else doesn't work or fit in. And me being kind of a routing nut, sometimes my routing is really weird. But when it is weird, there's always a reason for it to be weird. It has to be worth it."

CHAPTER 4 Budgeting the Tour

When preparing to tour, the band needs to create a plan, and a tour budget is one of most important parts of that plan. The band's team of representatives will help develop accurate projections of income and expenses for this budget. It may sound simple—debits and credits—but the budget must be created carefully to ensure that the band will generate enough income to design and rehearse the show; to "make payroll" throughout the tour; and, theoretically, to realize a profit at its conclusion. If a budget is thought of as a planning tool rather than an arithmetic assignment, its importance can better be appreciated.

PROJECTING INCOME

As previously mentioned in Chapter 2, the most common sources of income for a touring band are ticket sales, merch sales, and sponsorships. Other financial backing the band might receive includes tour support from their record label and production reimbursements from talent buyers. Not all bands are fortunate enough to earn substantial revenues from each potential income source. Acts that play before large audiences throughout their tour are more likely to land lucrative sponsorship deals than those playing small clubs. While it is not impossible for acts playing small venues to get sponsorship deals, it is more difficult. And because merch revenue is tied to attendance, bands that play in smaller venues earn less merch income than those that tour large-capacity venues. The goal, of course, is to try to tap as many potential revenue streams as possible.

Projecting tour income is typically more difficult than estimating expenses, because there is less control over income than there is over expenses. After an agreed-upon tour budget has been created, the tour manager and production manager should stay within that budget. Income, on the other hand, is often beyond the band's control. There is no way that events—such as snowstorms, tornadoes, hurricanes, or cancelled shows due to illness, all of which can drastically reduce ticket and merchandise sales—can be anticipated. Lower-than-expected ticket sales can also cause merch sales to be lower than predicted. Consequently, it pays to be conservative in projections of tour income.

TICKET SALES
Fees paid to the band by talent buyers will likely be the biggest source of income for a tour. As mentioned in Chapter 2, the band might get paid a guar-

anteed flat fee, a percentage of ticket sales, or a combination of these two. Regardless of the fee structure negotiated, talent buyers base their offers on the number of tickets they believe they can sell for the show. Therefore, industry professionals have historically referred to this revenue stream as *ticket sales*.

Before income can be projected, the band and their team must make some important decisions. The types of deals the booking agency should aim for most aggressively must be decided. A minimum guarantee acceptable must be determined. Preference for a smaller percentage of gross or a larger percentage of net must be decided. If percentage deals are to be requested, the band will want their manager and booking agency to suggest realistic ticket prices when talking to talent buyers. If ticket prices are too low for a market, potential income will be forfeited; if they are priced too high, some potential ticket buyers will be discouraged. The most important decision that must be made is the size of venues in which the band will perform. The band's booking agency and manager will be the most knowledgeable advisers for all of these key decisions.

In projecting ticket sales it is prudent to consider different options for touring. "For R.E.M., what I've done is I make up a booklet with five or six different routing options with different buildings which create different revenues and different ideas," says R.E.M. agent Buck Williams. "One of them may be a small building tour, one will be an arena tour, one will be a hybrid of arenas and small buildings. One option will be six weeks, one will be four weeks. I have all these different scenarios that I present to them."

Production elements and configurations can impact revenues. "In 1995, R.E.M. didn't want to play in a 360 configuration, they didn't want to play with the audience behind them," Williams recalls. "So I went to the hotel room and did some math and came back and showed them that 3,000 added seats times $50 a head equals $150,000 a day times sixty dates. I showed them how much money they were leaving on the table and that's all profit. Then it was, 'Oh, I think we can design a set so we can turn around and play to the rear house.'"

Some tools booking agencies and manager use to help set ticket prices, pick venues, and estimate attendance figures are individual box office reports for recent concerts, artist tour histories, and venue prior event reports—called *priors*. Box office reports that reflect recent concerts by many artists are published weekly in such media sources as *Pollstar*, *Celebrity Access*, and *Billboard*. *Tour histories* are lists, sometimes lengthy, that include box office reports for one selected act dating back to when their information was first reported. (A tour history for U2 generated by *Pollstar Online* gave reports for a selection of more than 400 concerts since November 29, 1981.) *Venue priors* are data from all shows presented in the venue for a specified period of time. After identifying similar bands in terms of genre and level of development, the band's agency and manager can use these sources to note the capacities of venues the other acts performed in, what their ticket prices were, and what percentage of tickets they sold at each show. If the band has previously toured in similar sized venues, and their box office information was reported to the trade publications, their own tour history will be extremely helpful. If the band has had little or no touring experience, estimating ticket income will be more difficult. After working with one's team, an educated guess can generally be made.

After the band and their team agree on intended ticket prices, venue capacities, and intended fee structures, ticket prices can then be estimated. Projecting income from ticket sales is easier if the band's agency plans to negotiate flat fees—called *guarantees* or *flats*—rather than percentage deals from talent buyers. Although the band will likely earn more from each concert if they receive a percentage of ticket sales and the event sells out—the percentage the band gets being known as the *back end*—the risk taken in a straight percentage deal is that the gross ticket sales will be unknown. To remove some of the risk for their artists, most agencies try to negotiate a minimum guarantee versus a percentage of ticket sales. This fee structure provides the band a specified guarantee *or* an agreed-upon percentage, *whichever is greater*. This "best of both worlds" fee structure offers a financial safety net: the guarantee allows the projection of minimum tour income while the back end offers the potential for much greater income than the guarantee.

If the band's agency plans to negotiate percentage deals, it will first calculate the total amount of money, called *gross potential*, or simply *GP*, each venue would generate if it were a sellout concert. This can be calculated by multiplying the ticket price, or average ticket price, times the seating or standing capacity of each venue. However, GP is based on selling 100 percent of available tickets at each show, so it only offers an idea of the maximum income the show could generate. GP does not reflect deductions such as local tax on tickets or agreed-upon expenses. So it only provides "ballpark" estimates to help review tour expenses.

After the band and their team have made decisions on key variables—ticket prices, venue sizes, fee structures—their agency will begin routing the tour, meaning the agency determines the regions in which to book them during different time periods, as discussed in Chapter 3. Agents call talent buyers in different regions to discuss the feasibility of booking them at the predetermined asking price through the process discussed in Chapter 2 and to be further analyzed in Chapter 10. If the band is an in-demand act, word circulates throughout the industry and talent buyers call their agency to discuss dates and offers. After speaking with representative talent buyers in different regions, the band's agency can create more precise estimates of potential guarantees or back end income for each venue. If talent buyers think the band's ticket price and fees are unrealistic, the team will need to adjust them. Whenever this happens, the agency must contact any talent buyers who have made preliminary offers.

In the end, income from ticket sales is an educated guess. Pat Price, manager of the West Coast rock act Pico Versus Island Trees, explains the art of predicting tour income: "You can get an estimated guess by seeing what the artist has done in the specific markets the past few times. If it is a new market, sometimes all you will want to figure is the guarantee, because it's tough to know you will succeed if you haven't been there before."

Jason Pitzer, Senior Agent at Progressive Global Agency, a booking agency that handles bands such as Widespread Panic, R.E.M., deSol, and the Wailers, explains that it is never easy to predict how talent buyers will respond to a potential tour. "What it really comes down to is laying out a route, contacting talent buyers, and waiting for offers to come in." Pitzer says that it is not unusual to have more than one game plan for an artist. "We sometimes look at different sized venues and create different scenarios. An artist might want to know how they would do in arenas versus theaters." Even after he and his staff have worked many hours to solicit offers, a tour is not a sure thing. "We meet with the artist's manager and review all the offers before we confirm any of them. If the money doesn't work [relative to expenses], we have to shoot it all down and start all over again."

Flat guarantees can provide more predictable budgeting. If the band's agency plans to ask for flat guarantees, the number of shows they intend to play can be multiplied by the flat. For example:

$10,000 flat × 100 shows = $1,000,000 Gross Tour Income

If the band's agency hopes to get guarantee-versus-percentage deals, estimates will be less precise, but a general range of income can still be projected. First, the guarantee is multiplied by the number of shows. The result will be the projected minimum gross tour income. For example:

$5,000 guarantee × 100 shows = $500,000 Tour Guarantees

The next step in estimating income from guarantee-versus-percentage deals is to estimate income that might be earned if the band's shows sell well enough that their back end percentage exceeds the guarantee. This calculation depends on whether their agency will ask for percentage deals that permit the talent buyer to deduct expenses before that act is paid any percentage or deals that do not permit deductions. When the deal does not permit deductions, the percentage is earned before the promoter pays local show expenses. (A back end deal with deductions, something we will discuss later, is more complicated because it allows promoters to deduct agreed-upon expenses before providing the back end percentage.)

To calculate income for the potential percentage of gross ticket sales, the gross potential for each venue based on an average-sized tour venue must first be determined, and then that amount is multiplied by the expected percentage. That amount multiplied by the projected number of shows yields estimated gross ticket sales for the tour:

$18,000 gross potential per show × 75% = $13,500 per show × 100 shows = $1,350,000

In this guarantee-versus-percentage example, the projected ticket sales for the tour range from $500,000 to $1,350,000. If the band's agency has already received offers at this point in the planning process, they will provide more precise gross potential amounts for each venue, because venue capacities vary. Note that the major variables in all of these projections include the agency's ability to book the band for one hundred shows; back end percentages assume that each promoter can sell the estimated number of tickets for these concerts. In addition, these calculations do not consider the tax levied on tickets that will be taken off before percentage splits. The back end estimates are merely preliminary calculations that can be helpful in understanding the maximum income that might be earned from ticket sales.

MERCH SALES

Tour merch has evolved into a major profit center for touring artists. If an act is at the club or small venue level, income from merch is often what bankrolls that act in getting from point A to point B. A strong large-club band like Drive-By Truckers can earn $5,000 to $10,000 a night in merch sales. The Rolling Stones, the kings of merch, consistently earn $300,000 or more per show. Special events like Cream at New York's Madison Square Garden also generate excellent merch sales.

Manager Pat Price believes the age of audience members helps determine per caps. He feels "concertgoers under twenty-one (who don't spend money on alcohol) and those who are thirty-five-plus (who have more disposable income)" spend the most money on merch. He also recognizes that merch sales are hard to predict. "Sometimes you have big days, and sometimes a fight breaks out after the show and everyone is rushed out and you end up selling nothing," Price adds.

The average dollar amount of merch an artist sells is referred to as *per capita* or *per cap* merch sales. This ratio of ticket buyers to total merch sales can be helpful in projecting merch income for a tour. If the band's per cap has been six dollars in the past and it is expected they will sell 10,000 tickets during their tour, $60,000 in income can be projected from merch. If the band is trying to launch their first significant tour or is moving to larger venues, it will be harder to estimate tour income from merch, because their per cap might change as they move to larger venues. The good news is that if an act is moving up to amphitheaters or arenas from clubs, the professional merch salespersons at the larger venues will be helpful in selling more merch. If a merch company is used, they will help estimate merch income. In addition, large venues typically have a merchandise manager who can project a general range of merch per cap sales for similar artists. A general rule of merchandising is, the larger the crowd, the lower the per cap due to longer lines. But the increased volume can easily outweigh the decreased per cap, resulting in a larger gross.

Options of handling merchandising in-house or through a merchandising company are discussed in Chapter 2. Regardless of who is handling their merch—the band or a merch company—each venue in which they perform must be given a percentage of the gross merch sales. The idea behind this split is that a venue is like a store. If a band wants to sell their tour merch in the store, they must split the gross income. Each venue negotiates the percentage rate, called the *merch rate* or *house rate*, the act must pay. Because merch income for a venue can represent a sizable amount of income, venue managers negotiate these deals aggressively. Although venues had asked for merch rates as high as 40 percent in the past, rates are usually between 30 percent and 35 percent and less. Larger acts with more leverage can negotiate more favorable deals.

BUDGETING SPONSORSHIP DOLLARS

As discussed in Chapter 2, sponsorship dollars may have a significant impact on a tour budget. Proven acts playing large venues can land lucrative sponsorship deals. Acts doing arena tours can expect sponsors to offer $20,000 to $50,000 plus promotional support throughout the tour. Theater-level act sponsorships often range from $10,000 to $20,000. Although artists and sponsors tend to be tight-lipped about sponsorship amounts, it was rumored that Paul McCartney received $5 million from Lexus. Industry insiders said that the Black Eyed Peas landed a $1 million sponsorship deal for their 2006 Honda Civic–sponsored tour and the Goo Goo Dolls supposedly got $600,000 from Saturn Ion for their 2002 tour. Brooks and Dunn is rumored to have earned $1.6 million from their Toyota tour sponsorship deal in 2006.

Because tour sponsorship is a form of promotion, like advertising, it must offer companies a large number of "impressions" relative to the cost. An *impression* is each opportunity for a consumer to view the name or logo of the product or service. Since each local promoter advertises the concert, any tour sponsor will benefit from this "collateral" advertising. Paul McCartney even created a commercial for Lexus automobiles when they sponsored his tour. Although McCartney did not allow any commercial artwork during his show, he allowed the Lexus logo to be projected before and after the show.

Besides collateral advertising, companies offering sponsorships ask for several things in return. These can include:

- Including the company or product name or logo in all print advertising
- Mention of the company or product name in all electronic media advertising and on each ticket
- A specified number of free tickets for each concert
- VIP passes
- A "meet 'n' greet" with the artist at each concert
- Sponsor giveaway opportunities at each concert
- Company or product logo on the artist's merchandise
- One or more private concerts for sponsor employees and key clients
- Company or product logo on the artist's Web site
- Signage and booths at each concert site

"Sponsors play an important role of raising awareness for the tour and financial support to raise the level of production," says Scott Siman, manager for Tim McGraw. "Finding the right sponsor is a big undertaking. You are looking for that company that shares common audiences and buys into the vision of the artist—and hopefully shares the values of the artist."

LABEL TOUR SUPPORT

As noted in Chapter 2, label tour support is available to many developing artists, but not as easily nor in the amounts it once was. Labels view tour support as a marketing investment, much like creating a video, which must be repaid or recouped to the label. Bands should make use of label support if it is available and they need it to tour, but should always keep in mind that this is merely a loan that can delay artist revenues from any album sales that may come later.

PRODUCTION REIMBURSEMENT

If the band takes their own production on tour, asking for a *production reimbursement* should be considered in addition to their fee. The concept behind a production reimbursement is that each talent buyer would have paid local sound, lighting, and staging companies to provide production had the band not provided it. If they carry their own production, their agent reveals the total reimbursement amount in early discussions and includes it in each performance agreement.

Although it would seem like a good idea to include a hefty production reimbursement in each deal struck with talent buyers, it can make the band too expensive for some clubs or promoters, thereby pricing themselves out of a market. If local concert promoters are asked to pay a production reimbursement, they must add it to the other expenses they must pay, including the band's fees, local advertising, venue rental fees, insurance, and local crew wages. Although their production relieves promoters from the added work of contracting, paying, and supervising local sound and lighting contractors, it is a good idea to keep any production reimbursement to a reasonable rate. It's best to think of production reimbursement as a way to pay the rent on sound, lights, and staging rather than a profit center.

SETTING UP BOUNDARIES FOR EXPENSES

The band has more control over the expense side of their budget than the income side. After their team has developed and agreed on tour expenses, everyone should stay within their budget throughout the tour. Unlike the lack of control over income based on attendance and ticket prices, their team can control most of their tour expenses. But to have this control, a practical budget that considers all potential expenses must be created. Estimating expenses is, therefore, an exercise in detail. Each oversight the band's team makes in estimating show expenses is multiplied by the total number of shows. If the budget overlooks a $1,000 show production expense, it becomes a $100,000 expense by the end of a 100-concert tour.

The general expense categories that should be considered for a tour are startup costs and running costs. *Startup costs* include designing and building the show, band rehearsals, tech rehearsals, and launching the tour. Put simply, these are the costs that are incurred before a tour ever ventures out and before the first date is played.

Variable costs, called *running expenses*, include two general categories: entourage expenses and production/crew expenses. These are the costs that are incurred in moving the tour from point A to point B, and include travel, gas, lodging, meals, et cetera. These are harder to predict and contingency budgeting comes into play.

To estimate tour expenses, the band's production manager, tour manager, manager, business manager, and tour accountant will work together to estimate as accurately as possible tour expenses. (Their team of advisers may not include all of these individuals at this point in their career, but they might be needed soon.) As with all other aspects of the band's career, they should be involved with all major decisions about their tour expenses—especially production design, size of crew, and transportation—from the beginning. Keep in mind that everyone on tour gets paid before the artist.

The more elaborate the band's production, the more technicians (techs) will be needed on the road. As the number of techs increases, the number of buses and other crew-related expenses increase proportionately. In addition, catering, insurance, security, and lodging estimates are tied to the number of techs on tour. When their tour is taken to larger venues, production and techs will account for the largest percentage of tour expenses. Therefore, their production manager plays a key role in estimating tour expenses. After the band begins their tour, their business manager and tour manager will keep an eye on expenses and call their tour manager or road manager if any expenses exceed their budget.

In addition to touring techs, some sort of entourage will be needed. The tour manager will work closely with the band and their manager to decide who will be included in their touring entourage. Their entourage includes all non-production staff. Like adding techs, adding someone to their entourage also adds other expenses. The band's entourage might include their tour manager, backing road musicians and singers, and touring staff members for security, wardrobe, catering, tour accounting, and merchandise. It can also include friends, family, professional and personal acquaintances, and even press. Because veteran tour managers and production managers have created and managed many different types of tour budgets, their knowledge of tour expenses often saves money and alerts the band to potential oversights. A seasoned tour manager and production manager know where a budget can be reduced without hurting the show or compromising the band's health and safety.

TWO EXAMPLES OF TOUR BUDGETS

To better illustrate how to prepare a tour budget, we present the following two examples. The budgets are for a hypothetical six-member band that could be any genre—urban, modern rock, A/C pop, or country—with an added four side musicians and three dancers for the arena tour. These examples demonstrate that the band will get paid after, and often less than, anyone working on commission. Notice that the larger the band, the less each band member makes. We present these examples to demonstrate the budget process, not to provide actual budget figures. There are too many variables—genre, size of venues, extent of production, artist's level of success—in the concert industry to create a one-size-fits-all budget template that will work for all tours.

Club Act. The band in this example decided to tour as a headline act in small clubs rather than as an opening act for a tour playing larger venues. The band has an indie label deal and sells their CDs and T-shirts at shows. They will keep their costs down by touring with only a tour manager who also drives the van. This is a *backline tour*, one for which the local clubs provide sound and lights, so the band only needs to transport their own onstage instruments and amp cabinets.

INCOME	Guarantees	Merch Per Cap	Average Venue Capacity	100 Shows
Ticket Sales	$600			$60,000.00
Merchandise		$5	500	$250,000.00
Tour Sponsor				$0
			TOTAL INCOME	**$310,000.00**
EXPENSES				
Startup Costs				
Insurance				$5,000.00
Legal Fees				$1,000.00
Phones & Supplies				$3,750.00
Rehearsal Space	2	150		$300.00
Running Expenses	How Many	Unit Cost	175 Days–25 Weeks	
Passenger Van	1	900	25	$22,500.00
Merch Trailer	1	250	25	$6,250.00
Fuel/Oil		300	25	$7,500.00
Per Diem	1	35	175	$6,125.00
Salary: weekly	1	1,000	25	$25,000.00
Payroll Costs: 15%	1			$3,750.00
Hotel Rooms	4	75	175	$52,500.00
			TOTAL EXPENSES	**$133,675.00**
INCOME DISTRIBUTION			**PRETAX GROSS**	**$176,325.00**
			Agency Commissions (10%)	$6,000.00
			Mgt. Commission (15%)	$46,500.00
			Bus. Mgr. Commission (5%)	$15,500.00
			Artist Tour Income	$108,325.00
			Each Band Member Income	$18,054.17

Arena Act. This act has previously toured as a headline act in clubs and has been a support act for a successful platinum-level arena act. The band's second album and single will be coordinated with this tour. They will play 120 concerts during a 32-week period.

TOUR SUMMARY: Arena Act	Total Costs
STARTUP COSTS	**$4,142,250**
BAND AND STAFF COSTS	
Band and Staff Salaries	$1,442,571
Payroll Costs—15%	$216,386
Per Diems	$321,930
Hotels—Band & Staff	$996,000
Hotels—Band/Non-tour staff	$24,000
Hotel Gratuities	$32,571
Ground Transpot—Non-show	$234,657
Radio Rentals	$22,149
Charter Aircraft	$2,677,143
Commercial Air Travel	$616,000
Medical	$17,486
Miscellaneous Costs	$87,429
Sub-Total	$6,688,322
CREW/PRODUCTION	
Crew Salaries	$2,714,674
Payroll Costs—15%	$407,201
Per Diems	$523,300
Sound	$1,101,607
Lights	$1,655,357
Video	$1,839,286
Pyro	$367,857
Special Effects	$275,893
Barricade	$110,357
Rigging	$128,750

continued

Trucking: All In	$2,891,500
Busses	$1,083,086
Busses Tolls & Permits	$435,000
Passes & Itinerary Books	$119,000
Ground Transport	$301,000
Hotels—Crew (7 nts/wk)	$1,343,691
Hotels—Non-tour Staff/Crew	$55,268
Cell Phones	$147,257
Wardrobe & Makeup Supplies	$40,000
Road Supplies	$59,000
Air Travel—Crew	$580,000
Air Travel—Non-tour Staff	$31,500
Freight—During Tour	$54,000
Radio Rentals	$47,513
Miscellaneous	$6,000
Sub-Total Production	$16,318,097
VENUE REHEARSAL COSTS	**$387,425**
Sub-Total Crew and Production	$16,705,522
Band and Staff Costs	$6,688,322
Startup Costs	$4,142,250
Total	$27,536,094
plus 10% contingency	$2,753,609
GRAND TOTAL	**$30,289,703**

CHAPTER 5 Designing the Production

The design phase of preparing to tour is where the fun starts for the act. Like songwriting and performing, it is a creative venture unique to each artist and every tour. The collective technical components of the stage show, called *production*, require the efforts of several highly specialized designers to handle the stage set, lighting, and sound.

To pull together these collective efforts, a *production manager* must be secured to coordinate, and often hire, the production designers and equipment vendors necessary to creating the show. From the instant the design phase begins until the tour ends, the production manager is the communication link between the act and their team, the tour designers, and the equipment vendors.

Due to the complex production components and large numbers of designers and technicians involved in an arena or stadium tour, the act might also employ a *production director*, usually someone with success in producing large-scale tours, who hires a production manager with strong communication skills and large-scale tour experience to travel with the show. The disadvantage of this arrangement for the touring production manager is the lack of input regarding the design of the show and hiring of touring production personnel.

After the production manager is hired, the basic design team—the *stage set designer*, *lighting designer*, *front-of-house sound engineer*, and *monitor engineer*—is assembled. If a good working relationship with key designers from previous tours has been developed, the act will likely continue to hire those same individuals. (For example, Patrick Woodroffe has been lighting designer for the past twenty-four Rolling Stones tours.) Designers with this kind of relationship are usually hired directly by the act itself.

It is the design team's job to ensure that the production enhances the act's music and image, adding something to the concert experience that cannot be mirrored in video, film, or sound recordings. When fans leave a well-designed concert, they often talk as much about the stage set, lighting, and sound as they do about the actual performance. For this to happen, the production must fit the act and the genre of music being performed; poorly conceived production can be as harmful to a concert as poor studio production is to a recording. A huge theatrical production, with a complex stage set, pyrotechnics, and hundreds of lights, and visual effects would be quite fitting for a Madonna tour, but it would be out of place for a singer/songwriter such as Billy Joel.

One of the production manager's most important responsibilities is to develop a budget that includes all production-related design, construction, and staffing costs. Consulting with each designer, the production manager works through numerous drafts as the band and their representatives decide what expenses are justifiable relative to projected income. Although the band may initially ask for an elaborate production for its tour, after the preliminary cost estimates are developed, it may be determined that the show is too expensive. Three options will then be considered: increase ticket prices, earn less income for the tour, or scale back the production. The band's manager and booking agency would most likely recommend that ticket prices not be raised, as local promoters are reluctant to increase the cost of attending the show simply because the band wants a more powerful sound system and more dazzling lighting. Settling for reduced income is predictably not an attractive option either. The most likely decision is to scale back the production.

In addition to determining the cost of designing the show itself, the production manager must also estimate all production-related costs of touring technicians, including their salaries, lodging, per diems, insurance, and the cost of buses and drivers to transport them. These costs are directly related to the size of the production and must be calculated in cooperation with each designer. Chris Rabold, who has been production manager for several bands, including Widespread Panic, says that he is occasionally disappointed when his vision for production is affected by budget restraints. "I'm given a weekly touring budget of x amount," Rabold explains. As the scale of a tour's production increases, so does the number of touring techs necessary to operate technical gear throughout the tour. "It is a major juggling act, and sometimes I just do the best I can with the budget I'm given. I still try to put out the most creatively crafted, unique show that I can that satisfies management but also makes me proud and the fans happy. As you might expect, I always love to do magic."

If the act has a limited tour budget, fewer designers can be employed. One person can be hired to design lighting and the stage set and a second, an audio engineer, can be hired to design both the monitor and the front-of-house sound systems. The production costs of a tour can be kept down as well by contracting with a single production supply company to design the show and provide all technical equipment. Production-related expenses typically represent the largest portion of a tour's budget, and production design is the major factor that dictates all other production expenses.

STAGE SET

The stage set is the most critical facet of production, helping to distinguish one tour from another. Even if the act's song selections and sound system remain relatively unchanged from tour to tour, the stage set and lighting design routinely change for each new major tour. The stage set must accommodate the logistical needs of the show, including where to place equipment onstage, how much the act likes to move around during performances, and how to best provide unobstructed sight lines for all fans.

The *stage set designer*, sometimes referred to as *set designer* or *stage designer*, works closely with the band and their team, the production manager, and the lighting designer, and the sound engineers to create the basic structure that gives the tour its look and sound. The stage set designer for stadium and large arena tours is fittingly referred to as the *tour architect* because the enormous stage sets, including structural steel support towers, are as sophisticated as office buildings.

The set designer begins by working with the band and their team. As the design process continues, logistical challenges such as sizes of venues on the tour and limitations of transporting the set pieces on trucks, airplanes, or steamships must be considered. Finally, one or more set construction companies are contracted to create the stage set.

BEGINNING THE DESIGN PROCESS

The stage set design can begin one of two ways. The band might have a specific theme or idea for the designer to work with, or they may simply ask to see some designs. Whichever way the design begins, it ultimately moves to a review and discussion of the designer's sketches. Each time new sketches are presented, the act and their team identify the aspects they like and those they want changed and discuss them with the set designer. This back-and-forth process, which includes the lighting designer, continues until the act gives final approval of the set design.

VENUES

The size of venues in which the act will perform is a major factor in the stage set design. A club tour may have a small stage set designed to fit cramped performance space. Amphitheaters have a larger space in which to place a stage set, but typically have much less lateral room than arenas. Arenas offer a large, open space on a solid floor that offers the stage set designer a large "canvas" for the show. Arenas are built to be multipurpose, with music and sports being the two main uses. Although they are large enough to hold enormous stage sets, stadiums and other outdoor venues are the most challenging venues for stage set designers because they do not have a solid, flat surface on which to assemble the set and require the act to provide structural support—a basic metal stage—in addition to the artistic set.

CONTAINERS AND TRANSPORTATION

Concert stage sets differ from those designed for television, film, and Broadway theatrical shows in one important way: the entire production for a concert tour must be assembled and disassembled many times. The stage set designer meets often with the production manager to decide how the completed set will be built in modules for transport. If it is an international tour, the production manager helps determine whether all equipment crates and set pieces will fit into large sea containers, aircraft pallets, and trucks. Because trucks in the United States are typically wider than those in other countries, stage set modules designed for the U.S. leg of a tour might not work as well in Europe or Asia.

In addition to transport concerns, the stage set designer must be practical when selecting materials for use in building the show. Dazzling, illuminated panels for floors might be perfect for permanent installations at theme parks or casinos, but may not hold up to the constant jostling of assembly, disassembly, and transportation during the tour.

STAGE SET CONSTRUCTION

After the act and their team approve the design, the stage set designer, in consultation with the production manager, sends the design illustrations and technical specifications to several set construction companies who specialize in building sets. Based on cost estimates and the reputations of the companies invited to bid, the set designer and production manager select a vendor. The set builder, also called a *set vendor*, is awarded the contract and immediately begins to build the set because they are given a deadline—which can be anywhere from a few weeks or several months—to complete it. Designers of large, complex sets might use more than one vendor or several subcontractors, each fabricating a different component for the show. When completed, the stage set modules are shipped to the location where technical rehearsals will be held.

LIGHTING

While the basic physical form of the stage set remains fairly constant throughout the show, its visual elements change to capture the mood and message of each song. The lighting designer helps the production flow by varying the visual aspects of the show in response to the music. As lighting and other visual components of concerts have become more sophisticated, the lighting designer has taken on more responsibility. Patrick Woodroffe, who has designed lighting for tours by Bob Dylan, AC/DC, Cher, Elton John, as well as the Rolling Stones, explains, "The role of the lighting designer is often that of the *show designer* or *show director*."

The lighting designer cannot work in isolation. "The lighting in the shows that I do is so integrated with the set design, the visuals usually come from the set designer after the two of us have worked together on the ideas," says Woodroffe.

Woodroffe goes on to explain that the lighting designer must coordinate all visual ingredients of the production, even those not historically associated with traditional stage lights. Therefore, in addition to considering conventional lighting equipment, the lighting designer seeks advice from department heads who help design and supervise special effects—including pyrotechnics, atmospheric media, and confetti cannons—and video to "integrate their contribution into the show."

According to Woodroffe, "The manager and the set designer might also take an interest as to the way the show looks [during the performance], but generally it is the lighting designer, along with the artist, who decides the look and the shape of the performance itself. Finally, like the stage set designer, the lighting designer works with the production manager to hire vendors for all equipment to assemble the visual components of the show.

LIGHTING EQUIPMENT

Since the 1960s, concert lighting has become increasingly important as bands have moved from relatively small venues to larger venues. As bands began to play on larger stages, lighting designers were forced to find better equipment and create more innovative visual concepts to mold concerts into "an experience" in addition to music performances.

Individual lights, called *lighting fixtures* or *lighting instruments* in the concert industry, are the basic tools of the lighting designer. Until the 1980s, their fixtures could be divided into two general categories: *floodlights* and *spotlights*. Generally, floodlights illuminate a wide area and are less expensive. Spotlights, on the other hand, are easily adjusted to focus on a narrow space, but tend to be more expensive. Both types of lighting fixtures require operators to adjust them manually. For example, the spotlight most visible to audiences is the *follow spot*, a light operated by a technician and used to focus attention on one or more band members.

A new category of lighting fixtures, called *moving lights*, *automated lights*, or *intelligent lights*, emerged in the 1980s. These lights, unlike existing spotlights and floodlights, could automatically move and change color during the show. VARI*LITE, the company that developed the prototype moveable light, patented its system in 1983. Since then, many other types of moving lights, most of which are computer programmable, have been developed and marketed. Steve Powell, Project Manager with Bandit Lites, a company that has provided lighting for tours including Linkin Park, Jewel, Reba McEntire, and String Cheese Incident, says, "There are moving lights on every tour we do." Although expensive automated lights are the instruments of choice for lighting designers in the touring industry, fixed position lights have not disappeared. Powell explains, "It is a budgetary matter and some tours mix-and-match the 'old-school' lights with computer-controlled moving lights."

VIDEO

Video has become an increasingly important aspect of the overall visual design of a concert. In the 1980s, concert video production was less spectacular than it is today because the technology necessary to produce and display images in large venues was not well developed. It was often nothing more than simple live camera images of band members shown on a single screen throughout the show.

As the sophistication of video display and production techniques for large format videos has evolved, video has almost eclipsed more traditional visual effects in the design of arena and stadium tours. Video incorporated into concert lighting design now includes computer generated graphics, animation, prerecorded video and film clips, and novel live camera images. Because it has taken on a vital role in the overall production design for a major show, the lighting designer will likely hire a *video director* or *video producer* to help design and supervise all video elements of the show.

SPECIAL EFFECTS

Like lighting fixtures and video, special effects are an integral component of lighting design. Some increase the effectiveness of lighting; others create a totally different visual event. The most commonly used special effects in the touring industry are pyrotechnics, atmospheric media, and confetti cannons.

Pyrotechnics. *Pyrotechnics* (also known as *pyro*), is combustible material that creates a flame, flash, or explosion when ignited. The fireworks used in Fourth of July celebrations are an example of pyrotechnics. Although pyro adds an exciting dimension to the show, it also presents safety and liability concerns. Metallica's James Hetfield received second-degree burns from an onstage pyro accident during a show on their 1992 tour. One of the most tragic events in the history of the touring industry occurred at the Station concert club in West Warwick, Rhode Island, on February 20, 2003, when a fire, ignited by the band Great White's tour manager, killed 97 concertgoers and injured 187 others. As pyro is potentially dangerous, consultants and vendors work with the lighting designer to create safety recommendations, obtain appropriate permits, and purchase necessary liability insurance.

The most commonly used pyro effects for concerts are traditional explosions and brilliant flashes. This type of pyro is created with chemicals that contain an oxidizer and do not require air to activate them. Because they can explode while sealed in airtight containers, extra precaution must be taken when transporting these materials.

Another type of pyro includes flame-like effects that use a common fuel, such as propane, and oxygen from the surrounding air. Although these effects are less likely to explode, flames that shoot long distances are difficult to control, especially if caught in strong drafts or fanned by wind gusts.

Despite the hazards pyro brings to a tour, it is often a staple of some acts and genres. Doc McGhee, manager of heavy metal band KISS, says that "Pyro has been a part of KISS since the beginning of time. It's a big part of the show because it's over-the-top, it's exciting, and it has audio and visual impact with the explosions. A KISS tour is like the Fourth of July every day."

Doug Adams, president and designer for Pyrotek, a firm that has provided pyro for tours by Metallica, Kid Rock, Limp Bizkit, KISS, and other bands, always considers the danger pyro presents, especially to audience members. Adams tries to keep in mind that audiences for concerts are much closer than they are to Fourth of July fireworks. He is also cognizant of the effect smoke and fumes might have on the band, crew, and audience and understands that safe pyro must be nontoxic.

Atmospheric Media. Although many people refer to the cloud hovering over the stage and seating area of a concert as "smoke," it is actually highly controlled *haze*, created using specialized equipment and nontoxic chemicals. A less expensive atmospheric medium is *fog*, generated by dropping dry ice into a container with an outlet that directs the fog to the stage set. The advantage of a fog machine is the low cost. The disadvantage is that fog settles and does not create the lingering haze needed for dramatic lighting.

Light beams from lighting fixtures do not resemble solid color unless the lighting designer uses some sort of atmospheric medium. The particles, suspended in haze or fog, glow as light beams pass through them. The combined effect of many lighting instruments traveling through haze offers the illusion of many illuminated "tubes." This is what gives concert lighting its iridescence, length, and depth. Without haze, each lighting fixture would send little more than a large "dot" to its end point.

Confetti Cannons. The lighting designer can add a festival atmosphere to special moments in the concert by causing confetti to rain down on the stage set and audience seating areas using *confetti cannons*. Confetti used for concerts is not limited in color, shape, or material. Designers can chose from myriad shapes, including butterflies, hearts, shamrocks, and music notes. Confetti made from tissue is less expensive and stays in the air longer. Metallic colored plastic is more reflective, but more expensive. The selection of colors is almost unlimited.

LIGHTING VENDORS

After the act is pleased with the proposed lighting design, the lighting designer develops specifications for potential vendors. The bid specifications, according to Patrick Woodroffe, include "contact details for the project, a full equipment breakdown by area and by type of fixture, the lighting plot [an overhead diagram indicating types and positions of all lighting instruments], a rigging plot [an overhead diagram that shows each point from which equipment will be suspended], and, if applicable, a weight and power requirement reference sheet." The lighting designer, working with the production manager and the band's team, sends these bid specifications to several vendors who specialize in concert lighting. After the bids are returned, the production team decides who will be awarded the contract.

If the lowest bid comes in at a higher price than the lighting designer initially estimated, the production manager and act's team must decide whether the extra cost is an acceptable expense. If not, the lighting designer must negotiate with the potential vendor to lower the asking price. If the vendor will not budge, the lighting designer must revise the lighting design and renegotiate with the selected vendor. Because they are eager to keep the potential client, the lighting vendor typically works closely with the lighting director and suggests ways to reduce costs. If all initial bids are substantially higher than anticipated, the lighting designer may revise the specifications and send them to all vendors in hopes of initiating lower bids.

Once the vendor is selected, it works with the lighting director to finalize details of the show. "At that stage you can then start working in more detail with the contractor to tailor-make the production to your ideas and his equipment," Woodroffe explains. The vendor and lighting director continue to work as a team as the show moves through the construction, rehearsal, launch, and touring phases.

SOUND

The one facet of production most critical to the success of a concert is the sound system that provides the amplified, modified, and mixed sound heard by the audience. In addition to the sound system the audience hears, the act needs a second sound system to provide the sound on the stage that is much different from that which the audience hears. The sound the audience hears comes through the *front-of-house* (FOH) system; the one the band hears onstage is the *monitor* system. After designing the FOH and monitor systems, the two engineers in charge of these systems hire a vendor to supply all live sound equipment.

THE FRONT-OF-HOUSE SOUND SYSTEM

The FOH system, like the monitor system, begins with the sounds created on stage. Each sound source—voice or instrument—is captured by a microphone, a direct input box (a device that connects directly to an electronic instrument or amplifier cabinet), or a combination of both, and is fed into the sound systems. Each sound source cable is connected to a *stage box* then to a device called a *splitter*, which divides each input into two or more equivalent signals and sends one to the FOH system and the other to the monitor system. If the act is creating a live recording, a high-quality splitter can create a third signal and send it to a remote recording truck or recording console in the venue through a third snake.

All signals, running through individual wires, are bundled into larger cables, called *snakes*, to organize the maze of wires coming from the stage. The FOH snake is stretched across the venue floor or suspended from the ceiling until it reaches the FOH mixing console, the heart of the system. After inserting each input into the FOH console, the touring mix engineer, often the FOH engineer who designed the system, operates this console, usually placed in the audience seating area. The FOH mix engineer blends sounds and varies their timbre and volume using the console and numerous signal processing devices. All the processed signals are then combined into one output (*mono*), or two outputs (*stereo*). The mono or stereo signals then travel to other processing devices, amplifiers, and, eventually, to the speakers directed at the audience.

FOH systems for large venues—arenas and outdoor stadiums—are generally mixed for mono rather than stereo output. If the signal is mixed in stereo, those audience members on the left side of the venue hear a much different mix than those on the right side. If the guitar is mixed louder on the left side of the stereo output, audience members sitting on the right cannot hear guitar solos well. Because clubs are not as wide as amphitheaters, arenas, and stadiums, they can usually accommodate a stereo mix. The FOH system has one mix for the audience, regardless if stereo or mono.

A vital role of the FOH engineer is deciding where the speaker enclosures will be placed. One option is to place the speaker cabinets on the stage or venue floor. This technique, called *ground support*, is the least expensive way to arrange speakers because it does not require as many technicians to assemble it. The major disadvantage of a ground support sound system is that it can result in obstructed sight lines for some audience members if speaker cabinets are placed on the stage. Ground support speakers placed directly in front of the stage are also extremely loud for fans closest to them, but more muffled toward the back of the venue because the bodies nearest the cabinets absorb certain frequencies.

Suspending speakers from beams, called *flying* the system, is most common for large-venue tours, but more expensive because more technicians are needed, including specialists in designing and operating flown systems, to assemble and disassemble the FOH system at each stop on the tour. Because the speakers are high above the audience, no sight lines are obstructed with a flown system. In addition, flown systems allow the FOH engineer to configure many speakers so sound is evenly distributed horizontally and vertically. The FOH engineer often uses computer-generated diagrams to determine the ideal array of speakers for a flown system. This helps create an even distribution of speaker output. Hanging thousands of pounds of equipment above the crowd places tremendous responsibility on the FOH engineer designing the system to insure it is safe as well as great sounding.

THE MONITOR SOUND SYSTEM

Unlike the FOH system, the monitor system is designed for band members. In an ideal monitor system, each performer has a separate mix he or she hears through speakers placed on stage or through ear-worn monitors. Because band members routinely want frequent changes in their respective monitor mixes during the show due to onstage sound levels that change and crowd noise that varies, the monitor engineer's job includes paying close attention to, and communicating with, each musician on stage. To help facilitate this communication, the monitor engineer works with the stage set designer to place the monitor mixing console as close to the musicians as possible. Veteran production technicians refer to the area where the monitor console is located as *monitor world*.

Although it is possible to have the FOH mix engineer also create a monitor mix as a way to save money, it is better to have a separate console and engineer for the monitor system. It is difficult for the FOH engineer to listen to and concentrate on both systems, and if a band member needs to communicate with the sole mix engineer positioned at the FOH console a long distance from the stage, visual communication is difficult. Manufacturers have recognized the unique needs of the two different types of systems, and have developed consoles that are specially suited for either monitor systems or FOH systems. If the budget allows, a two-way system—FOH and monitor—with two engineers designing and operating their respective specialized systems is best.

While the band has a general sense of what the FOH system sounds like, they have a better knowledge of the monitor system. If the vocalist cannot hear his or her voice in the monitor mix, they will have trouble singing on pitch; if the bass player has difficulty hearing the drums in the mix, the rhythm will not sound as it should. Consequently, they are likely to have strong opinions as to who will design the monitor system as well as who will operate the system when the tour begins. The band should make sure the monitor engineer has excellent communication skills in addition to technical expertise. The monitor engineer must also have a temperament necessary to accept criticism about the monitor mix. The adage, "If it was a poor performance, it is because the monitor system was bad; if it was a great show, the band rocked," is accurate in the touring industry. Overstressed, angry band members have been known to throw items—microphone stands or chairs—at the monitor engineer to "get their attention."

SOUND VENDORS

Although bands are sometimes tempted to buy a sound system, this strategy is rarely cost effective. Audio equipment must be constantly repaired, maintained, and replaced throughout the duration of tour. The cost of storing the system when not in use is an additional expense. As a result, most bands that tour, especially those playing in large venues, lease their sound systems.

Because the FOH system and monitor system have many components that must be compatible, the FOH engineer and monitor engineer collaborate throughout the design phase. After assembling system specifications for both FOH and monitor systems, they, like the lighting and stage set designers, create bid specifications for the FOH system and monitor system. The engineers then send specifications to those who they, the production manager, and the act's team, feel are suitable. When bids are returned, the sound engineers meet with the production manager and the act's team and select the vendor who will serve as sound equipment contractor for the tour.

CHAPTER 6

**Developing
the Performance**

The actual performance is where the "rubber meets the road" in the touring game. Most artists will say that the two hours or so spent on stage is the payoff for the other twenty-two hours of the day spent getting to the gig.

For the artist, performance is the reward for the grind of touring. For the fans, it is the reward for their loyalty and the payback on their investment of time and money. When everything is working as it should, the live performance creates a deep and lasting connection between the artist and fan.

Singer/songwriter Livingston Taylor has spent time in front of an audience for the past thirty years, touring and performing with such acts as Linda Ronstadt, Jimmy Buffett, and Fleetwood Mac, as well as with his brother James. While he still frequently performs live, for more than a decade Taylor has stood in front of an audience of a different sort as a professor teaching the art and craft of stage performance at the Berklee College of Music in Boston.

"The core rule is that you have to watch your music land," Taylor explains. "It's not enough to just put the music out there, you have to watch it go out there and land. You need to see what effect your music is having on people."

In essence, what Taylor teaches is performance development, the importance of charisma and style, how to go about rehearsals and building set lists, tailoring a show to the audience, what to do when things go wrong, and other factors involved in the creation of the on-stage product.

PERFORMANCE DEVELOPMENT

The performance is what the artist is selling. A show that does not come off well can do serious damage to a tour. A tour rife with poor performances can derail a career.

Each date on the tour creates a "buzz" through reviews, advertising, promotion, and most importantly word-of-mouth. While good press and word-of-mouth can be hugely beneficial, negative buzz can be disastrous. The key elements in performance preparation are gaining experience and making use of charisma and style.

THE IMPORTANCE OF EXPERIENCE

It has often been said that experience is the best teacher, and nowhere is that more true than in the live performance world. "There is no substitute for experience," says Taylor. "Play live all the time."

Livingston Taylor feels artists should constantly be attuned to audience reaction and then tweak their performance accordingly. "When you do something that they like, do that again," he says. "When you do something that they don't like, don't do that anymore. It's always a fact-finding mission, where you're probing an audience to see what parts of you are attractive to them."

Audience reaction can vary from show to show and even song to song. "Sometimes, everything you do they love, sometimes everything you do they hate," Taylor adds, "but generally it falls somewhere in between."

Ironically, the larger the audience, the more the margin for error. "With acts like Sting or my brother James, they play in an environment where there can be 10,000 to 20,000 people there, and in the presence of this many people you can be predictable night after night because the average is going to be the same once you accumulate that many people. Some will have a wonderful time, some will have an awful time. But the average level of acceptance will be quite predictable, so you can slowly fine-tune your set."

A broad fan base widens the palette for the artist, particularly if that artist has enjoyed a long career. "I'm pretty sure that there are people that love *The Stranger* that might not love *An Innocent Man*, and there are people that love *An Innocent Man* that might not love *The Nylon Curtain*," Billy Joel tells *Billboard*. "But I've never written for the audience or radio, I've written for myself. And in a way, because of that, we've picked up a lot of different kinds of people along the way."

Taylor believes many young artists get their ideas as to what live performance should be from watching MTV. "The problem is, getting this information from an MTV video is like building a house because you've screwed in a light bulb. Trying to present ideas to people for the first time, that's what's tough."

Most artists with career longevity hone their *chops*, or performance skills, over thousands of live performances, from the club level on up, developing stage patter and crowd-pleasing moves along the way. But with the popularity of television shows like *American Idol*, young artists may embark on a national arena-level tour as their first live experience. The top ten finalists from the show soon go out on a major arena tour, before most of them have become adequately seasoned as live performers.

Taylor stresses that such an entry into touring is by far the exception to the rule. "There are people out there that are twenty-three years old who win the lottery, that's good for them," he says. "But that is not the norm. Winning the lottery is not having a career. *American Idol* is one person, not thousands of people. They may do a couple of tours with *American Idol* and then their career is through because there's nothing underneath it, no basic understanding of an audience you can take and work with the rest of your life."

CHARISMA AND STYLE

On-stage charisma can inspire passion in a fan base that leads to huge financial rewards. While much of charisma is God-given, artists can always learn "tricks of the trade" in how to work a crowd, again with experience being the best teacher.

"The great irony is we always thought that our job on stage was to put out, but actually the inverse is true," Taylor says. "How much can you take in? What do people love? They love to be paid attention to, so I don't care what kind of ugly urchin you are, if you can walk on stage and people get the sense that you genuinely see them and love them, they will respond. It is important to understand that the audience doesn't need you, you need them."

Obviously, looks are important. "When Jessica Simpson walks onstage, she's attractive enough that whatever she does is propelled by the fact that we love to look at her," Taylor observes. "And if Jessica Simpson were less attractive, she would have to make better music. On the other hand, Janis Joplin was a great musician, but while not unattractive, not Jessica Simpson's kind of attractive. And Janis had to fuel her career with great music."

The kind of on-stage charisma exhibited by such acts as Elvis Presley or Bruce Springsteen transcends mere physical attractiveness. "Ultimately, I don't think that kind of charisma can be taught," says Taylor. "I think Bruce was born with this amazing charisma."

Even without that type of charisma, or as it fades, there can still be a "love" relationship between the audience and artist. "It's like you have a spouse or significant other who, although they are not the best-looking person on the planet, you come to love them very much because of their attentiveness and their focus and their love of you and their attention to your needs and their kindness and decency as a person," says Taylor.

And, as in romantic relationships, the dynamics change over time. "The bond between a young performer and his or her audience is different than what it is for me," Taylor explains. "The bond with young performers is often nonverbal. Often it has a large sexual component to it. There's a lot of that nonverbal stuff that doesn't happen as you get older. But there's nothing like the attraction of passion and that then turning into the companionship of true love and mutual respect over time."

Style has always been a part of live performance, as well. Country singers wear cowboy hats, grunge acts wear flannel, metal guys wear black, rappers showcase urban style, opera singers wear tuxedos, and glam rock stars wear whatever it is they wear.

For singer/songwriters, style is less important. "I try to wear a clean set of clothes on stage," Taylor says. "Obviously, if you're KISS, your makeup is very important. If you are an image-based band, you be careful to have your image in place. That for me means caring about how I look, physical exercise, watching my weight, and being as attractive as I can reasonably be."

Of course, with rare exceptions, what the artist is wearing and how they relate to their audience cannot make up for a lack of talent or a poor performance.

REHEARSALS

Rehearsals are where bands devise the overall "vibe" of the upcoming tour, establish a *set list* or *set lists* (songs to be played at a given show), tighten up their chops or performance skills, and generally prepare to take their music to fans.

Artists approach rehearsals in different ways. For bands that tour on and off year-round, they are often not necessary. For acts that are touring in support of a new record, the touring band may be different from the recording band, and either way, on-stage versions of the new songs must be "worked up" to translate into live performance.

Some bands find little need to rehearse. "We don't rehearse," says Patterson Hood, frontman for the Drive-By Truckers. "We don't use a set list."

This, however, is the exception to the rule. Even bands as veteran and skilled as the Rolling Stones find the need to rehearse. Keyboardist Chuck Leavell has been a sideman for the Stones for more than twenty years, and says he keeps a "Rolling Stones bible" that proves invaluable when rehearsals begin. "Every time we have a rehearsal and work up songs, I keep notes on everything, from background vocals to different instrumental parts," he explains. "It's a huge catalog with a lot of information, and it's handy to have that."

Even the Truckers rehearse sometimes, Hood admits. "I know that right before our 'Southern Rock Opera' tour we rehearsed maybe four times because we had to learn how to play the thing live," he recalls. "The rest of the time we work up songs at sound check or in the studio, and we particularly have been trying to devote a little bit of time at each sound check to developing new things."

For Livingston Taylor, the rationale for rehearsals is simple: "The reason why we rehearse and practice is so we can spend less time concentrating on the physical act of making music and more time watching the music land."

When artists make a plan to rehearse, they need to find a space to do it, they have to work out technical requirements, and they must put together a set list.

Renting Rehearsal Space

Some artists own or have regular access to rehearsal space. Others must rent the space when preparing to tour. Generally, the idea is to rent the type of space that the band will be playing, be it clubs, theaters, arenas, et cetera.

For tours with extravagant production, choreography, and musical arrangements, the artist has several types of rehearsals, some going on simultaneously at different locations. The band might rehearse in a studio or rehearsal hall for a few days or weeks to hone the music. If there are dance numbers, the dancers will work with choreographers in a dance rehearsal studio. Using smaller, less expensive rehearsal rooms for the first few weeks of band rehearsals is more cost effective than renting a large venue for many weeks. When they are ready, the performers join the production staff in the large venue.

Florida venue manager Allen Johnson, general manager of the Orlando Centroplex, has a lot of experience in renting venues he has managed, as many bands rehearse in the winter months in preparing for spring or summer tours. This makes Florida a prime rehearsal destination. When Johnson managed the Lakeland, Florida Civic Center, dozens of tours rented the venue for rehearsals.

The person who first contacts the venue in regard to renting rehearsal space varies. "In some cases it was a promoter, agent, or manager, and sometimes a production company familiar with the venue," says Johnson.

Different factors go into determining the cost of renting venue rehearsal space. "I usually had two ways of doing this," he explains. "It is somewhat dependant on the number of days of rehearsal and whether or not we were the opening or 'kick off' of a tour date. Our published daily rate in Lakeland was rent of $2,000 per day. If they did a show, I would go as low as $1,000 per day plus the rent for the concert. Concert cap was $10,000 to 12,000."

Johnson says the length of time for rehearsal rentals in Lakeland ranged from as little as three days for Jimmy Buffett to as long as thirty days for U2's "Zoo TV" tour in 1992, and everywhere in between. "Usually it was a week to two weeks, depending on the complexity of the show."

Often Johnson has been able to nail down a tour date by offering up rehearsal space. "Most tours start usually at one end of the country or the other, so if they were starting on the East Coast we were in the running for the rehearsal as well. Would you rather have rehearsal in Lakeland in January or Bismarck, North Dakota?"

Tech Rehearsals

During tech rehearsals, the production crew breaks down and works out the various technical requirements and special needs of a show. The two biggest factors considered are *load-in*, when the show production is taken off the trucks and loaded in to the venue and set up, and *load-out*, when the show production is broken down and loaded out of the building and back on the trucks. The length of time for load-in and load-out is a key concern in setting up all other timing for the day of show. Tech rehearsals are also a time when the production manager works feverishly to be certain that all technical gear will fit in the estimated number of trucks.

In many cases, a tour's crew will conduct tech rehearsals independently of band rehearsals; in some cases they work together. "I have had tech-only rehearsals on some shows, and other times bands were there the whole time," Johnson says. "U2 did their rehearsals at night, as did Phil Collins, due to the time difference in Europe."

The band and crew generally don't require too much from the venue when conducting rehearsals. "They ask for the usual in electric and technical assistance, security, and then for us to just stay out of the way," he adds. "We always pushed for a show, but if that didn't work we would ask for a dress rehearsal where we could invite limited guests, two hundred or so. Some folks got to see some neat things and the band got to work out some kinks and didn't affect sales if they were playing nearby cities."

Building a Set List

Some artists stick with a very strict set list, with little variation from show to show, usually coordinated with elements of production like lighting and special effects. Other artists work up hundreds of songs and anything is fair game on a given night. Widespread Panic, for example, never plays the same song twice within a three-show span.

For bands with long careers and numerous hits, putting together a set list can be a challenge. Tom Petty and the Heartbreakers have been together for more than thirty years now, compiling a huge list of hit songs and fan favorites in the process. Such an arsenal of songs can make paring them down for a set list challenging.

"We have a set list, but we work up a lot more [songs] than we're gonna do," Petty tells *Billboard*. "That way we can throw things in and change it around, especially if we're in a place for two days. It's good to keep yourself interested."

Petty challenges his band by throwing a few curves into the set list, and his history with the Heartbreakers leads to an instinctive alchemy on stage. "The Heartbreakers are one of those rare groups [where] I can really throw them something and they'll go for it and they'll pull it off," he explains. "I have this really deep faith in them that they're gonna read me and follow me. That comes from all those years of playing together."

For veteran touring artist John Mellencamp, the challenge is "trying to come up with ways to present songs that are two and three decades old, keeping them fresh and combining the new songs with them."

Drive-By Truckers' Patterson Hood says the only time his band puts together a set list is when they are performing for television in a carefully timed and orchestrated production. "As far as our regular shows, as we're about to walk up on stage we decide what the first song is gonna be and whoever sings that song points to the next person when he's done, and it just goes from there. It keeps us all on our toes and keeps it all new."

For the Truckers, it's about finding songs that work well within the context of a given tour. "Some songs get put on a back burner or just don't fit with the new songs as well and they get left behind a while," Hood says. "Like the songs on [our new] record fit real nicely with a lot of the *Decoration Day* songs, and a lot of the songs on *Dirty South* fit better with the *Southern Rock Opera* songs. That probably makes sense in the way we zigzag from record to record anyway. It's probably something we got from growing up listening to Neil Young so much."

THE SHOW

The show is why artists tour. As Jackson Browne writes in his song "The Load-Out," the grind of touring is alleviated by the actual performance: "The only time that seems too short is the time that we get to play."

Artists should always approach their shows with their audience in mind. With rehearsals behind them and armed with a set list, their focus should be on tailoring the performance to the venue and audience, playing off audience reaction, using production technology, deciding the length of the show and making the most of an encore if the opportunity arises, as well as knowing how to react when things go bad.

TAILORING TO THE VENUE

By their very nature, different venues and crowds require different approaches from the act. Coffeehouses and songwriting showcases like Nashville's Bluebird

Café draw crowds that are very attentive and appreciative of lyrical content. In these venues, acoustic music is generally preferable, and such production elements as pyrotechnics and laser lights are out of the question. In these type of venues, the song rules.

Rock and roll clubs and country honky-tonks are smaller venues. Their clientele generally appreciate loud music and, in many situations, music that can be danced to. These venues can often "break" an act to the next level, so charisma and showmanship are highly valued. Sound checks help the act get it right, keeping in mind that the empty room at 2 PM may well be a seething, sweaty, raucous mass of bodies by 10 PM.

Larger venues like arenas, amphitheaters, and stadiums require an act to not only play to the front rows, but also to fans in the "cheap seats" a football field or more away from the stage. Video screens and public address (PA) equipment deliver the message to faraway fans, but it always behooves the artist to recognize these fans in one way or another from the stage. This includes an occasional nod to fans sitting behind the stage or in "obstructed view" seating. A simple "how are ya'll doing up there?" will often suffice.

Alice Cooper tells *Billboard* his "Dirty Diamonds" tour in 2005 was tailored to work in a variety of venues, despite the unique production elements. "We've done a lot of big outdoor shows on this tour, and then the next night we'll be in a small German town in a 2,500-seat theater, and we never change the show. I personally think this show works better in a theater because everybody can really see the details. They can pick up on Alice's claustrophobia in the strait jacket, and all the little facial things going on in the guillotine part."

Attendance also makes a difference, as Livingston Taylor points out. "When you're working in a club some place and there are twenty people there, your set can be very different from if there were five hundred people in the club, which there might be the next night. So this notion of watching your music land, practicing, and rehearsal should not be so you can play more but so you can play what you play more effortlessly."

Tailoring to the Audience

The classic scene from the original *Blues Brothers* film illustrates the importance of knowing the audience. When the band takes the stage at Bob's Country Bunker, their blues music is not well-received. But when the band showcases its flexibility by playing "both kinds of music"—country and western—they win over the crowd.

Some groups' music crosses over into different audiences. Cross Canadian Ragweed, for instance, is equally at home in rock bars and more country-oriented venues. The group is signed to a Nashville label, has taken a few marginally successful shots at country radio, and toured and recorded successfully with mainstream country acts. But when the members headline their own shows, they tend to lean more to the rock side of the country-rock equation. "There have been some gigs where people come out to see a country show and they realize it's not as country as they thought, but they don't walk away pissed off," CCR frontman Cody Canada says.

It is worth noting that contemporary music fans have more diverse tastes than did most fans a generation ago. That's why a country act like Kenny Chesney can successfully put rocker Uncle Kracker on his bill, and music festivals like Bonnaroo host rock, urban, bluegrass, folk, electronic, and many other genres.

Still, it's logical to assume that country music will not go over well in a hip-hop or metal club, and opera won't play in a honky-tonk. Artists should also consider the age and demographic of the audience. Fairs, for example, often have a large family contingent, and fair talent buyers often stipulate that the act must not use profanity or lewd behavior.

The Use of Production

Artists use—or depend on—production to varying degrees. "Of course we rely on technology," says Taylor. "We rely on amplification, lights, and all of those things. There is no such thing as acoustic. Realistically, we're all electrically fueled with the rare exception of the small house concerts."

Taylor professes to love technology, "But only if there are things that are basic to the human condition. The question is: Are you using technology to accentuate points about the human condition or are you using technology as a gimmick because you haven't observed enough of the human condition to be worth talking about?"

In other words, he believes artists should use technology and production to add to their shows, but should never be dependent on it or use production tricks to make up for a lack of performance chops. Production is a tool, not a crutch.

With some acts, such as KISS and Radiohead, production is a key element of the overall performance. Alice Cooper has had on-stage production bells and whistles for more than thirty years, so that now fans have come to expect these theatrics.

Cooper shows offer sensory overload, he says. "When you've bombard an audience with images—there's crutches, there's guillotines, there's strait jackets, there's manikins that come to life, there's garbage cans, there's swords, money, jewelry thrown in the audience—at the end of the show they'll tell you the most amazing story you've ever heard. And about half of that really happened."

Set Length and Encores

The length of the performance is usually dictated per the contract with the talent buyer and will be discussed again in Chapter 11. In general terms on a major tour, the headlining act performs for a minimum of ninety minutes, with each support act getting less time on stage based on their status. These times are rather strictly adhered to, because a show that runs over time greatly increases show costs.

Most headlining acts build an *encore*, when the band exits the stage and then returns for an additional couple of songs in response to audience demand, into their overall set length. This demand mostly consists of loud cheering, clapping, stomping, and, for rock acts, cigarette lighters or cell phones held aloft. Most artists tend to save at least one major hit for the encore, and often an obscure or rarely played song, or a crowd-pleasing *cover*, a song made famous by another act. Sometimes the audience response is so overwhelming that the act may return to the stage for several encores, an audience reaction all bands should strive for.

When Things Go Bad

Occasionally a performance does not go over well, despite the best intentions of the performer. When this happens, most veteran performers take a "the show must go on" mentality.

Any artist that performs live at some point has to deal with things going bad. "It happens at all performers all the time at all levels," says Taylor. "It happens to me, James Taylor, Jimmy Buffett, Bonnie Raitt, anybody you name. Sometimes you show up and things don't happen the way you had hoped."

Taylor takes a philosophical approach to this problem. "This gets a little bit Zen," he admits. "One could argue, how could anything in the passage of life be wrong? This is very important when you're on stage. If your instrument doesn't work, so be it. If your audience defines you, for whatever reason, a disappointment, that's their verdict. Things go wrong, and sometimes audiences don't like you."

The key, Taylor says, is how the performer reacts to adversity. "If they're booing, you continue to do your work. If they're being violent, you tell them it won't be possible to continue."

An artist can never "expect" to have a great show, according to Taylor. "Our disasters happen when we have an expectation of what should have happened. If you go up neutral, with no expectation, then whatever happens is fine. It's the course of the event."

Drive-By Truckers' Patterson Hood says that when things go bad, plunge onward. "If the string breaks, you keep playing with five strings until there's a chance to change it or grab another guitar. If the crowd boos, you turn up your amp so that you can't hear them—I came up with that one myself and had plenty of experience, as being one of the only 'punk rockers' in my small Bible belt North Alabama town. If the power goes out, grab an acoustic and keep playing. If that's not an option, throw your guitar down, cuss, and make it look like part of the show."

In general, concert performance is about being professional, but Taylor says it goes beyond mere professionalism. "The problem with simply saying 'be professional' is it's too nebulous, it doesn't give enough information," he says. "What I'm saying is, arrive at the intersection of the time and space in a neutral frame of mind, with the hope that the equipment will work, but no expectation; the hope that they will like you but no expectation that they will. Hope is fine, expectation is a recipe for disaster."

CHAPTER 7

**Finalizing
the Production**

The production is designed and the vendors are prepared to ship their equipment to the building rented for technical rehearsals. The act is developing the performance, anxiously waiting for their chance to rehearse on the set. Now the production manager must orchestrate the final phase of producing the show in preparation to launch the tour, basically fine-tuning the final product that will be presented to the public, along with the team that will "deliver" it night after night. This requires hiring the production manager's administrative and leadership staff, hiring technical specialists for each production department, arranging and supervising rehearsals, and creating the necessary paperwork to launch the show.

The production manager hires department heads, crew chiefs, and the stage manager to supervise the technical areas of the show and to help the production manager determine how many technical personnel, including the stage carpenters, the lighting techs, the riggers, the backline techs, and the audio crew, to hire for each production department. The production manager also consults with the production designers, the vendors, the tour manager, and the act's team, before hiring the production crew who will tour with the show. The lines of communication are understood: any questions regarding a department are directed to the appropriate department head or crew chief; crew chiefs and department heads report to the production manager.

Most employees on a major tour are *production technicians*, generally referred to as *techs*. Techs are the crew members who operate and maintain the stage set, audio systems, lighting fixtures, and other production equipment. The term *roadie*, used in the past to describe tour personnel, no longer reflects the level of technical expertise touring techs must have. Vendors often provide some or all of the techs needed to operate and maintain their equipment during the tour. The production manager, stage manager, crew chiefs, and department heads normally have input into these and other personnel decisions to ensure that each tech has the personality, in addition to the technical expertise, to work well with others involved in a stress-filled tour. Because techs spend many hours together—traveling and working—each needs to blend with the rest of the team. Independent techs, those not employed by the vendor, usually come by way of a previous relationship with the production manager, crew chief, or department head on previous tours.

After the production staff is in place and technical components of the show arrive from the vendors, the production team holds tech rehearsals, production rehearsals, and a dress rehearsal. The production manager must then finalize the *equipment manifest*, a detailed list of equipment the tour will transport.

Finally, the production manager creates a comprehensive *production rider*, an attachment to the performance agreement that includes all technical, hospitality, and security needs that must be provided by local promoters in each city.

THE PRODUCTION MANAGER'S STAFF

The production manager often needs one or more assistants, known as *assistant production managers* or *production assistants*, to help with the administrative duties of the tour. The responsibilities of this position include creating and distributing security passes, coordinating travel and hotel arrangements for production crew members, creating and distributing detailed schedules for each day, and setting up a temporary production office in each venue. If the tour does not have a tour caterer, the production staff must coordinate all production crew meals with local caterers as well.

If it is a stadium tour, the production manager also employs one or more *site coordinators*, who visit the venue several days or weeks in advance of the show to discuss the logistic needs of the act. These needs include the placement of the stage, the locations of dressing rooms, parking for tour vehicles, storage of cases and crates, and the location of the production office and management office.

In addition, the production manager usually hires a stage manager to assist with the hands-on work of coordinating technical departments and directing local stage crew employees, temporary workers provided by the local stagehands union or one of the regional labor contractors. The stage manager can be thought of as a "traffic cop," directing each local stagehand to one of the production departments. Under the direction of their assigned supervisor—crew chief, department head, or tech—each local stagehand works alongside the touring crew members throughout the day. When the local stagehand finishes his or her work in the department, he or she returns to the stage manager for a new work assignment. The stage manager is responsible, too, for the order in which trucks are unloaded and where cases, crates, and equipment are placed in the venue.

THE ROLE OF PRODUCTION TECHNICIANS

Production technicians are the "worker bees" of a tour, sometimes working from 6 AM until midnight after sleeping on their bus the night before. They are the employees who operate and maintain the equipment supplied by vendors or owned by the act. Each tech must understand the equipment well enough to quickly react to problems during the show and make minor repairs during the tour.

A tech must be willing to spend long periods of time away from home. Flory Turner, who has worked as a tech on tours of Bruce Springsteen, Madonna, Tina Turner, the Rolling Stones, and U2, admits that life on the road can be tough. "I really miss my family and my dog when I'm on tour. I wasn't even home to see my grandpuppies born," she says. When asked what she enjoys about touring, Turner responds, "The money is good and, if you don't waste money shopping too much, you can build a nice savings account.

The other great thing is touring has taken me to cities and countries I wouldn't have dreamed of visiting if I weren't in this business."

Because techs represent a large portion of the weekly budget for a major tour, the act and their team must consider all related expenses. Production techs for major tours are paid a weekly salary and a *per diem*, a small daily payment intended to compensate them for the higher cost of meals while away from home. A common range for per diems is $30 to $45. In an effort to cut touring costs, a few acts pay their techs a per diem only on non-show days. The rationale is that crew members can eat their meals for free in the venue on performance days, because the local promoter is typically required to provide catered meals backstage.

The act also provides transportation, usually tour buses, and lodging for each tech during the tour, as well as airline travel to the tech rehearsal site and from the final city of performance. Additionally, most major acts provide health insurance for techs and paid vacations while the tour has brief breaks. If the act or production manager is eager to keep a valuable tech committed to an upcoming tour, they will pay the tech a *retainer*, a modest weekly salary, in return for the tech's promise to remain available.

Acts that play larger venues are able to pay their techs better salaries than those touring small venues. Like other vocations, experienced techs are also paid more than entry-level techs. Another factor is expertise: If stage carpenters are in short supply, they will likely be paid higher salaries than other techs. The following are some general ranges of weekly salaries for touring techs:

LOW:	MID-RANGE:	HIGH:
Entry-level techs and others working small venue tours	Fulltime professionals touring larger venues	Seasoned veterans of the road touring arenas and stadiums
$1,000–$1,400	$1,500–$2,400	$2,500–$3,000

PRODUCTION DEPARTMENTS TYPICALLY INVOLVED IN TOURS

Because the staffing needs of each tour differ, it is impossible to create a "standard" production crew list. However, the production departments and crews likely to be involved in major tours include stage carpenters, the steel crew, the lighting crew, the pyrotechnicians, the video crew, the audio specialists, the rigging crew, and the backline technicians.

THE CARPENTRY CREW

The carpentry crew, the stage carpenters, assembles and maintains all stage set components that travel with the act's show. Stage carpenters build and dismantle the elevated stage floor, the scenery, and the moveable props. They are also responsible for carefully unpacking, hanging, disassembling, and repacking all of the *soft goods*, the curtains and other set pieces made of fabric that frame the stage and mask some areas of the set from the audience's view. Because they are responsible for ensuring that each part of the stage set is carefully packed into carts and crates before they are loaded onto trucks, the carpenters closely supervise any local stagehands assigned to the department.

THE STEEL CREW

Acts touring outdoor venues, such as stadiums, must have a basic metal stage constructed before the stage carpenters arrive to assemble the stage set. The stage is built by the *steel crew*, who arrive as much as three days before the rest of the techs. After the show, the steel crew then dismantles the stage structure once the stage carpenters and other techs have left the venue. Because the steel crew must travel to venues in advance of the rest of the touring crew, the act usually has at least two steel crews that "leapfrog" one another, alternating cities. Members of these teams are typically hired by the vendor that supplies the staging materials.

THE LIGHTING CREW

The lighting designer spends a great deal of time and energy creating the visual effects of a show and wants the lighting to be consistent throughout the tour. Some designers tour with the show and serve as *lighting director*, overseeing all lighting equipment and lighting techs, while others design the show and, in consultation with the production manager and act's team, hire someone else to be lighting director for the tour.

The lighting designer, lighting director, and production manager work with the lighting vendors to select *lighting techs* who are responsible for operating the lighting equipment. Because tours use many different types of lighting fixtures, and lighting techs must operate and maintain the equipment, vendors commonly supply trained techs. The production manager may hire all lighting techs from the vendor, or all independent techs, or a combination of both.

THE PYROTECHNICIANS

Experts in the use of pyrotechnics (pyro) for concerts, known as *pyrotechnicians* or *pyro techs*, are responsible for ensuring that all pyro displays are consistent and safe. Prior to the 1960s, when concert productions were much simpler, stage carpenters or lighting techs were responsible for any explosive charges used in shows. As pyro grew in size and sophistication, the pyrotechnician became a new job category in the touring industry.

Pyro techs work closely with the lighting director to ensure that the effects are consistent and safe throughout the tour. They are also responsible for obtaining the necessary licenses and insurance certificates required for the use of pyro in the production, working with local government officials and local pyro techs in each city to gain the necessary approvals.

THE VIDEO CREW

Adding a video component to the lighting design of a show provides a uniquely different dimension that many fans find captivating. However, the added cost of the staff, equipment, and preproduction necessary to incorporate video into the show is substantial. Therefore, video is generally not an affordable production component for most acts playing clubs, theaters, and auditoriums. And, for many acts, video does not fit the "vibe" and music of the act. Nevertheless, video has become a major part of many large venue shows that present dazzling productions.

As mentioned in Chapter 5, when designing the show's lighting, the lighting designer consults with the video director to create video images for the show. Consulting with the lighting designer, the video director hires all necessary video techs, including camera operators, for the tour. The video director and techs create a "studio" in the backstage area of each venue to coordinate prerecorded and live video images. Elaborate shows, especially those using video curtains, screens, and panels, require a video crew that rivals most local television stations.

THE AUDIO SPECIALISTS

Audio specialists are needed to operate the mixing consoles during the tour. The process, called *mixing* the show, is done by audio engineers. Unless they are touring small clubs, the act has at least two audio engineers: the *FOH engineer*, who mixes the front-of-house system, and the *monitor engineer*, who mixes the monitor system. They are sometimes referred to as *mix engineers* or *mixers*.

Dave Natale, who has been FOH designer and touring engineer for Lenny Kravitz, Prince, Tina Turner, and the Rolling Stones, explains that, "The person who designs the sound system for a major tour almost always wants to be the mix engineer for the tour." He adds, "The vendor that supplied the sound system might also send a *systems engineer* to set up and check out the system before each show. The systems engineer makes sure that the system is operating so that the FOH and monitor engineers can mix the show."

In addition to the mix engineers and the system engineer, most large venue tours employ *sound techs* to help set up and troubleshoot the system. The techs, whose responsibilities include placing microphones on the stage and assembling the massive arrays of speakers suspended above the stage or audience, may be hired by the vendor or they might be independent techs hired by the production manager.

THE RIGGING CREW

Instead of placing equipment for sound and lighting systems on the floor or stage, production designers usually specify that the tour's sound and lighting equipment be suspended from beams or other forms of structural support. The process of attaching equipment to the beams, called "flying" equipment, is the job of *riggers*.

Riggers work in teams of two: the *climbing rigger* or *up rigger*, who works on the beams overhead, and the *ground rigger* or *down rigger*, who stays on the ground and sends supplies to the climbing rigger. Riggers face significant occupational hazards. Climbing riggers are always in danger of falling; down riggers risk having objects dropped on them.

The production manager typically hires a *head rigger* to act as department head. The head rigger helps hire other riggers for the crew and supervises local riggers in each venue. The production manager can use vendor-supplied riggers, independent riggers, or a combination of these options.

THE BACKLINE TECHNICIANS

The instruments, amplifiers, and speaker cabinets the act uses on stage are referred to as the *backline*. *Backline techs* set up and maintain this equipment for the act. In addition to maintaining the instruments, these technicians often must play each instrument during *line check*, the point during setup when each separate instrument is fed through the sound system to ensure that all connections are correct. When the act is unavailable for *sound check*, several hours before the show when the act performs and the mix engineers adjust and test the sound systems, line check is the only chance for mixers to prepare for the show. Large tours employ a technician for each instrument: guitar, bass, drums, keyboards, percussion, and wind instruments. Whenever there are several backline technicians, one person is hired to serve as *backline crew chief*. Smaller tours may have one backline tech or have the audio engineers handle the backline.

REHEARSALS FOR THE TOUR

For a major tour, the production manager organizes all technical aspects of the show—equipment and crew—while the act is rehearsing the music. The production manager rents a venue, finalizes the hiring of crew members, and begins *tech rehearsals*, set up to give the techs an opportunity to learn to assemble, operate, and disassemble all technical equipment for the show. These rehearsals last from a few days to several weeks, depending on the size and complexity of the tour's design. While tech rehearsals are in progress, the act is often in a different facility rehearsing music and stage movements.

The production manager and stage manager use rehearsals to create a plan for arranging equipment in trucks. Vendors and the production crew often stencil the intended locations of the equipment—FOH, monitor, lighting, stage left, production office, dressing room—on the cases and crates to help the crew identify the equipment inside, thereby hastening the process of loading and unloading the trucks. Many vendors use color coding and numbering to distinguish cases and crates of different equipment. Because they only have a few hours to assemble the show after they arrive at each venue, the production crew rehearses unloading trucks, setting up the show, disassembling the show, and then loading everything back into trucks.

After all technical elements are in working order and the act has practiced the music, the act, their team, and the production manager arrange *production rehearsals*, several days or weeks after tech rehearsals, when the act practices on the stage set. In order to save money, the production manager might hold tech rehearsals in an inexpensive rehearsal facility and move to a more expensive

venue—one similar in size to those that the show will perform in while touring—for production rehearsals.

Production rehearsals provide the lighting director an opportunity to hear
each song and to program corresponding lighting cues into computerized lighting control consoles. During production rehearsals, the FOH engineer hears
any new songs or arrangements and learns the set list. The act uses this time to
become comfortable with the stage set and to refine any stage movements or
choreography.

Production rehearsals also help the production manager and designers see
how well all elements of the production work together and what the overall
"look" of the show is as it changes from the beginning of the performance to
the end. In addition, production rehearsals offer the act their first opportunity
to see the actual stage, having only seen design illustrations and miniature
models to this point. If all goes well, the stage, sound systems, lighting instruments, video, and special effects work as a cohesive unit and the act is pleased.
If not, this is the time for making design changes.

When production rehearsals are finished, the act and crew hold a *dress
rehearsal*, a simulated show. To create a live-show environment, the act invites
a small number of family, friends, and invited guests to watch the dress
rehearsal. The dress rehearsal provides an opportunity for the production
manager and act's team to spot any weaknesses in the show that require last-
minute attention.

THE EQUIPMENT MANIFEST

Among his or her duties, the production manager is responsible for creating an
equipment manifest, a detailed inventory of all equipment supplied by vendors—
lighting, sound, rigging, portable power—as well as all instruments and other
equipment owned or leased by the act. The manifest also includes the replace-
ment costs of all equipment. This helps the act's business manager purchase
insurance for equipment that may be stolen or damaged during the tour.

The manifest is also required in order to obtain the tour's *ATA Carnet*, often
simply shortened to *Carnet*, a customs document that can be thought of as a
"passport" for the equipment. In 1961, the Customs Co-operation Council, now
known as the World Customs Organization, created ATA Carnet to remove
some of the obstacles caused by varying customs regulations. (ATA is an acronym
based on the French terms "admission temporaire" and the English terms "temporary admission.") The International Bureau of Chambers of Commerce
(IBCC) designates and oversees Carnet-issuing organizations in each of the sev-
enty-five countries that participate in the Carnet system. The U.S. Council for
International Business manages the Carnet system in the United States.

The Carnet reduces the amount of time necessary for the act's equipment
to clear customs at each border because it allows the tour's freight company to
use a single document for all customs transactions. It also ensures that no participating country will charge import duties or taxes on the tour's equipment as

it would for purchases of tourists or other temporary visitors. If the tour originates in the United States, the Carnet expedites the tour's re-entry as well by eliminating the need to register all equipment with U.S. Customs at the time of departure.

The freight company hired for the tour works with the act's team to obtain the Carnet, which is valid for one year. The application includes a processing fee and equipment manifest, including model, serial number, and value of each piece of equipment. The freight company must post a deposit, usually in the form of a surety bond, obtained through a bonding company. The bonding company, like a bail bonding company, is a third party that agrees to be financially responsible for the promises made by their clients. In the case of a Carnet bond, the freight company promises to transport the same equipment out of each country that it brought in. The deposit is a percentage of the equipment's value, usually 40 percent, and is used to pay for any charges assessed the freight company by any Carnet country. When the tour ends, the freight company returns the Carnet document to the originating office and, if all paperwork is in order, the deposit or bond is returned.

THE PRODUCTION RIDER

Before the tour is launched, the production manager reviews all *riders*, attachments to the performance agreement that list everything each local concert promoter must provide in addition to payment of money. A major tour typically includes several riders, including technical, hospitality, and security. It might also create one general *production rider* which includes all rider requests. (We discuss riders in greater detail in Chapter 11.)

When the riders are finalized, the booking agency, production manager, or other member of the artist's team sends a copy to each concert promoter on the tour while the production manager begins calling each concert promoter to discuss the rider requirements, especially those contained in the technical rider. The process of calling each promoter, called *advancing the show*, does not end with one call. As the date of each concert gets closer, the production manager calls more frequently and discussions become more detailed. The production manager for a small venue tour that has fewer rider requests typically begins advancing the show closer to the show date—often three weeks prior to the concert.

THE CREW FOR THE U2 "VERTIGO" TOUR

It is unlikely that audience members know how large a group it takes to mount a major tour. The following crew list for the U2 "Vertigo" tour, which grossed $333 million from March 28, 2005 to March 2, 2006, illustrates the large number of specialists necessary to produce a tour of this magnitude. The "Vertigo" crew traveled to 100 global markets, including arenas in the United States and stadiums in Europe, Mexico, Brazil, Argentina, Chile, New Zealand, Australia, Japan, and Hawaii.

Steve Matthews: Director, Principal Management
Susan Hunter: Management Associate
Shan Lui: Management Associate
Suzanne Varney: Band Assistant
Dennis Sheehan: Tour Manager
Bob Koch: Tour Business Manager
Ben Schwerin: Assistant to Tour Manager
Bret Alexander: Band Advance and Travel Coordinator
Sharon Blankson: Style Consultant/Head of Wardrobe
Elizabeth Spencer: Massage Therapist
Jake Berry: Tour Production Director
Craig Evans: TNA Tour Director
Ian Jeffery: Production Accountant
Rocko Reedy: Stage Manager
Joe O'Herlihy: Audio Director
Wendy Overs: Production Coordinator
Dori Venza: Production Coordinator
Cynthia Oknaian: Tour Ticketing Manager
Jim McCafferty: Guest Ticketing Support
Alison Larkin: TNA Production Coordinator
Dana Walsh: VIP Project Manager
Clay Charters: VIP Project Assistant
Sam O'Sullivan Jr.: Backline Crew Chief and Drum Tech—Larry Mullen Jr.
Dallas Schoo: Guitar Tech—The Edge
Terry Lawless: Programmer/Keyboards
Stuart Morgan: Bass Tech—Adam Clayton
Rab McAllister: Tour Tech
Philip Docherty: Guitar Tech—Bono
Scott Nichols: Tour Security Coordinator
David Guyer: Security
Jerry Meltzer: Security
John Sampson: Security
Brian Murphy: Security
Karen Nicholson: Wardrobe Associate
Louise Kennedy: Wardrobe Assistant
Jay Maskrey: Makeup
Bart Durbin: Head Rigger
Chuck Melton: Rigger
Steve "Elky" Chambers: Rigger
Alan "Woody" Doyle: Head Carpenter
Adam "AJ" Rankin: Carpenter and Bono Stage Assistant
Heather Rogan: Carpenter
Flory Turner: Carpenter
Dewey Shepherd: Carpenter
JP Van Loo: Carpenter
Jon Boss: Power
Joe Ravitch: Audio Technician and Crew Chief
Niall Slevin: Audio Monitors
Robbie Adams: Audio Monitors

Dave Skaff: Audio Monitors
Tom Ford: Audio Technician
Rachel Adkins: Audio Technician
Alex Campbell: Audio Technician
Ben Blocker: Audio Technician
Bruce Ramus: Lighting Director
Garry Chamberlain: Lighting Crew Chief
Raffaele Buono: Lighting Tech
Craig Hancock: Lighting Tech
Matthew Hamilton: Lighting Tech
Russell "Bits" Lyons: Lighting Tech
Aaron Stephenson: Lighting Tech
Kester Thornley: Lighting Tech
Stefaan Desmedt: Touring Video Director
Stefaan Vanbesien: Video Crew Chief
Ed Moore: Video
Jason Lowe: Video
Gary Beirne: Video
Koen Lavens: Video
Sandy Hylton: Head of Catering
Felix Makin: Catering
James Jacques: Dressing Rooms
Andrew Johnstone: Furniture
Joshua Kapellen: IT Specialist
Robin Ball: IT Specialist
Thomas Whitelaw: De-lux Merchandising
Jamie Betwee: De-lux Merchandising
Dave Walters: Senators Coaches Crew Bus Driver North America
Joe Folk: Senators Coaches Crew Bus Driver
Craig Wall: Senators Coaches Crew Bus Driver
Dave Morgan: Senators Coaches Crew Bus Driver
Mike Mallatt: Senators Coaches Crew Bus Driver
Vince Grecco: Senators Coaches Crew Bus Driver
Steve Sallee: Upstaging Truck Driver
Richard Everit: Upstaging Truck Driver
Robert Frost: Upstaging Truck Driver
Kitzy Sallee: Upstaging Truck Driver
Kenny Rich: Upstaging Truck Driver
Theresa Everit: Upstaging Truck Driver
Scott McKeel: Upstaging Truck Driver
John Ferris: Upstaging Truck Driver
John Heeren: Upstaging Truck Driver
Dempsey White: Upstaging Truck Driver
Gail Gorby: Upstaging Truck Driver
Lon Simpson: Upstaging Truck Driver
Rodger Baughman: Upstaging Truck Driver
Ron Baidenmann: Upstaging Truck Driver
Chuck Lamb: Upstaging Truck Driver
Jody Winslette: Upstaging Truck Driver

CHAPTER 8 Launching the Tour

The tour is routed, the venues are booked, the production is built, and the rehearsals are planned or under way. Now it's time to kick this big machine that is a concert tour into gear.

While it may seem as though most of the groundwork has been laid at this point, there are still some key considerations that must be in place to get the tour off the ground and on the road smoothly and successfully. If a tour stumbles out of the gate, a bad tone can be set for the entire run of dates.

Among these considerations are laying out the lodging and the means of transportation for the artist, entourage, and other tour employees; choosing options for transporting equipment; hiring specialized personnel such as caterers and a tour publicist, and handling matters of tour security and insurance policies.

TRAVEL, LODGING, AND TRANSPORTATION

The main concerns of getting a tour down the road are travel and lodging for band, crew, and gear. Once a tour gets beyond the van stage, the former two are generally handled by entertainment travel agents and bus companies, and moving the gear is coordinated by trucking and freight-forwarding firms.

VANS, BUSES, AND JETS

One common denominator among all touring artists is the inherent need to get from point A to point B. But the comfort and style in which they arrive is, in most cases, in direct proportion to the commercial success they have achieved and the amount of money they are willing to spend.

The traditional touring artist transportation hierarchy often progresses like this: van, van with trailer, older model bus, nicer bus, still nicer bus, charter plane, and, later in the career, ultra-nice bus. However, that could be an oversimplification, as much depends on personal preference. What is important is that the band arrives ready to play.

On the club circuit, vans usually rule. "In situations where you're playing clubs and you don't have to be at the venue until 4 PM or 5 PM for sound check, you can afford to [take] the van, sleep in a hotel, and drive to the gig the next day," says Jamie Cheek, business manager at Nashville-based entertainment accounting firm Flood, Bumstead, McCready & McCarthy. "And the agent tries to route it so you can do that."

A major act with fifteen to twenty people on the road needs a bus, but sometimes downsizing the number of buses can save more than simply the cost of the vehicle. Cheek says he often tries to get acts to downsize their bus entourage. "The problem is," he points out, "an artist may have a couple hits and may be earning $60,000 to $75,000 a night, with major production and three or four buses on the road. Then two years go by, the money comes down a little, and the buses are the number one thing you look at for reducing costs."

According to Cheek, eliminating one bus can mean saving as much as $5,000 to $6,000 per show in costs. "It's not just the cost of the bus, but the crew and payroll that goes along with it," he says.

Some developing acts have shown a tendency to try to move to a bus after one hit record, but many rock acts are known for extending their van days well into their second or third albums, if they get that far. When the bus comes, even if it's an older model, the move is a big deal.

"A lot of baby bands will go from a van pulling a trailer to a mid-1990s Prevost brand of tour bus that is very plush. The typical setup is a front lounge, rear lounge, and twelve bunks in the middle," says Doug Rountree, president of Nashville-based tour bus leasing company Pioneer Coach, whose clients have included Prince, Disturbed, Mark Knopfler, and others. "When they go from a van to this, they think they've died and gone to heaven. It's a huge step up, but it's also a significant step up in expense."

Indeed, while leasing a van runs in the $50- to $60-per-day range, a five- to ten-year-old bus is more like $350 to $425. And costs only go up from there. A million-dollar, tricked-out Prevost tour bus can run more than $1,000 a day. Amenities include 42-inch plasma TVs, DVDs in the bunks, tanning beds, high-end stereos, satellite dishes, convection ovens, wireless Internet, master beds that rise with the push of a button, and any customization a star could want.

"Customizing is one of our fortes," says Trent Hemphill, who with his brother Joey owns Hemphill Brothers Coach Company, which runs a fleet of some eighty coaches. Clients include Tim McGraw, Faith Hill, Aerosmith, Kenny Chesney, and Beyonce. "Star buses are becoming hotels on the road."

Top-of-the-line band and crew buses can run as much as $500 a day, with star buses running up to twice as much per day, and big tours need a lot of buses to accommodate the band, production crew, management, and sometimes even the tour promoter. Stars will often take out separate buses for themselves, their band, security, production, promoter, and various entourage members.

When it comes to driving the bus, leasing companies generally keep a pool of drivers to pull from, and make strong recommendations as to which drivers go with which tour. Some artists enjoy having the driver as a late-night conversationalist; others desire absolutely no interaction with the driver. It is up to the tour manager to communicate to the bus company what they want from a driver.

All drivers must be U.S. Department of Transportation (DOT) qualified, drug-tested, and up to snuff on all current driving regulations. The perception of the partying tour-bus driver is incorrect, at least in the modern world. "They've got to be 100 percent legal because there's a lot at stake, including reputations and careers," says Hemphill. "We may love you like a brother, but if you're not drug-testing properly, you're outta here. This is big business."

CHARTER PLANES

Charter planes range from 8-to-12-person, mid-sized executive aircraft to large Challengers or Gulfstreams. Some superstar bands have leased 727 Boeings that seat up to forty people in an executive configuration. The cost is extravagant. Chartering a plane can run $25,000 to $50,000 a week, $200,000 a month, an expense only a handful of tours can accommodate. In most cases, an aircraft charter charges a minimum of sixty hours a month whether it moves or not.

If a charter doesn't make financial sense, sometimes it makes career sense, even when compared to traveling via commercial flights. With commercial flights, artists travel on the airlines' schedule; with charters, the artists travel on their own schedule. On a charter flight, a high-profile celebrity can be guaranteed security, avoid paparazzi, and conduct private business on board without being overheard. Artists may also bypass commercial airline terminals and use what is known as a Fixed Base Operator, or an FBO terminal, for private arrivals and departures.

Many stars have opted for charter planes over commercial flights as a reaction to September 11, 2001, and travel concerns and increased airline security have provided a boost to the private charter industry. Among the advantages to air charter are convenience, comfort, access to more airports, and better food. A round-trip charter flight from Nashville to New York, for example, runs about $8,000 to $9,000 for up to eight people. A short-notice commercial flight, if it could be arranged, would cost at least $600 to $900 per person.

For artists looking at buying their own airplane, the price tag starts at about $4 million to $5 million for a brand-new jet. A Boeing business 737, converted for corporate use and designed for the worldwide theater, runs about $45 million.

Like most things in life, the decision by an artist to travel with wheels or wings while on tour simply comes down to a matter of dollars and cents. "It's all about what kind of guarantee the artist is being offered," Cheek says. "Buses are three or four times the cost of going out in a van. And when it comes to flying, you just have to weigh the costs."

ENTERTAINMENT TRAVEL AGENTS

The world has no shortage of travel agents, but relatively few specialize in the business of concert tour travel. And those who work with the touring industry require skills that far exceed just getting artists and crew from one city to another. For entertainment travel agents, it's all about managing the *jump*—the move from one gig to the next.

The entertainment travel agent's primary point of contact with the tour is via the tour manager. "One of the best things you can do is hire a very competent travel agent," says John David Nixon, formerly a tour manager for such acts as Lynyrd Skynyrd, Patty Loveless, and Hank Williams Jr. "They give you an itinerary advisement based on the information you have given them."

Less than a dozen agencies handle 80 percent of all touring acts, estimates Nick Gold, president of Nashville-based Entertainment Travel. Among the major players in North America are Preferred Travel, Entertainment Travel, Tzell Travel, Pro Travel, Altour, and Linden Travel.

The travel agent takes the band's tour itinerary and coordinates travel, from booking hotel rooms to making sure limos are in the right place at the right time. "When you look at the routing sheet, the first thing you try to figure out is how long the jumps are and the number of rooms you'll need," says Gold. "Jumps are very important, because drive time will have an impact on whether a band will take the full complement of rooms versus a 'cleanup room'." According to Gold, production crews tend to only get a room on off days, while the driver always gets a room to sleep in. "It's a fairly standard crew travel pattern," he explains.

Once a show is concluded, it usually takes one to three hours to get production and crew on the trucks and buses and off to the next town. The tour manager travels with the artist or band, but the production manager is the first one in, last one out. "What really pushes my fun button is when we get to the next city at 8 AM or 9 AM, and they tell you they won't let you check in until 3 PM," says Nixon. "By 3 PM, you're already supposed to be at the venue."

Each tour has a travel budget, and a database of each band's personal requirements and preferences is kept by the agent. "We're selective in the hotels we use, and most of the time we've done our research to make sure they're up to the caliber of the band," Gold explains, adding that inexpensive doesn't mean cheap. "I'm not driven by what [each band] is spending; I'm driven by the fact that they're on tour and need comfortable accommodations."

Aside from national and international travel agencies, several independents also work the touring industry. "It's all about knowing the market, the venues, your bands, and the specifics of touring," says Janet Crowley, an independent travel agent specializing in the concert business. "You just need to understand the logical process that the touring business dictates. I don't know cruises or vacations in the Bahamas, so I would turn that over to someone else. I've put my knowledge and expertise into this market, and I know how a tour [should] function so everything goes well."

A key skill of entertainment travel agents is knowing which hotels are "artist-friendly." That can entail everything from having a place to park tour buses to being located near the venue where the act is playing. One of the biggest complaints tour managers have is when an act is booked at a hotel a half-hour from the gig and "when they get to the gig, there's a hotel next door," Gold says.

Beyond simple logistics, being artist-friendly today is also more likely to mean wireless Internet access than tolerance of TVs being thrown into swimming pools. A travel agent will meet with the tour manager to determine specific hotel needs, which could include proximity to shopping, exercise equipment, or allowing pets.

While Crowley has certain hotels she works with regularly, she says, "There's never one hotel in a given city that I send all my bands to. You change hotels based on the needs of the bands." Typically the travel agency staff will deal almost exclusively with on-site hotel staff, not national sales people. That way, if problems develop, there is a relationship in place.

But finding the necessary information for a tour stop in a given market is not limited to hotels. "We need to know about access to various vendors, limousines, high-end rental cars, private jets, and vacation places that are not run-of-the-mill," Gold says.

Another necessity of a tour travel agency is keeping travel data out of the wrong hands, for obvious reasons. Such information tends to be guarded at a level that rivals national security standards. "I would say that our industry is on par with lawyers and insurance companies in terms of confidentiality," Gold says. "If someone's wife calls me and says she's lost her husband, if I'm not convinced she is who she says she is, that information does not leave our office."

A travel agent can also help make sure the hotel in each city is in the touring loop. In a perfect scenario, the bus pulls up to the hotel, room keys for everyone are waiting at the desk, and the tour manager distributes them and gives everyone the day's schedule. "The bus driver is the first person you want to put in a room," says Nixon.

Some hotels are more up to speed for touring needs than others. "There are hotels in each city, part of a network the tour manager and travel agent get used to, that are near the venue and trained to cater to the touring business," says Nixon. "Like the Sportsmen's Lodge in Los Angeles. The location is great, it's got truck and bus parking, and they're used to early check-ins. There are hotels like that in every major market, and the experienced tour manager knows these places."

These hotels appreciate the business. "We have lucrative deals with a number of hotels in a number of towns, both major and smaller markets," says Gold. "The choice of which hotels we use is relative to three things: budget, location of the show, and availability of bus parking."

At times, different tour components have different hotel needs. "The truck drivers want something close to the Interstate, and the crew wants something close to the venue," says Crowley. "Sometimes you have to book three different hotels. It can be logistically challenging."

Tour managers don't crash at hotels, Nixon points out. "That's your office time," he says. "In all honesty, a tour manager averages about four hours sleep a day. Ninety percent of the time I'm in a hotel, the bed is never messed up. Some of the best five-star hotels I've ever been in, my head never hit the pillow."

Even with the best laid plans of touring managers and travel agents, sometimes people get left behind. "Truck stops are usually the places where that happens, and usually in the wee hours of the morning," says Nixon. "If you get off the bus and nobody sees you, you're supposed to throw a cap or something in the bus driver's seat. There's nothing worse than being left at a truck stop in your pajamas with no wallet and no cell phone."

MOVING THE GEAR

Even if the band and crew make it safely to the gig, the show will never come off if the gear is somewhere else. Tour cargo companies like Stage Call, Road Show, Horizon Entertainment Cargo, Upstaging, Janco Transportation, and Rock-It Cargo are prized for their ability to transport concert equipment from show to show. It's a niche business that requires touring expertise and specific know-how.

When a tour manager contacts a trucking company, the latter needs a copy of the itinerary. Once the trucking company knows when the tour is going where, they provide the tour manager with a per-truck price quote. The trucking company typically pays for everything (except the drivers' hotel rooms), including driver, truck, fuel, and insurance.

Rates have been pretty stable for the past few years, generally in the $375-to-$475-per-day range per truck, but the rapid increase in gas prices has had a dramatic impact on the cost of trucking. The number of trucks required has decreased as equipment has become more streamlined, and loading and packaging has gotten more efficient, which amounts to large savings on truck space. Trailers are bigger today than they once were, but still have to operate within DOT guidelines, which means they can only carry 80,000 pounds per load.

Concert industry truck drivers, like those in the mainstream transportation industry, rarely handle the load, but they understand the business and sometimes direct local stagehands in loading and unloading the gear. Once the stagehands get the gear inside, the band's production crew takes over. Post-show, the band crew tears down, and local stagehands get the equipment on the truck under the watchful eye of the stage manager and drivers.

Sometimes a jump is so far that standard ground transportation cannot get the gear to the next gig on time. That's when a company like Horizon Entertainment Cargo comes into play. Horizon's niche is under the "airfreight forwarding" banner. "We're the guys who come in, pick up the equipment, take it to the airlines, put it on pallets, take it through customs if necessary, and get it where it needs to be," says John Greenstreet, owner of Horizon. "We make moves that can't be done by truck."

Often freight forwarders will coordinate with local equipment vendors to make sure all the right production equipment is on hand for the start of a tour or rehearsals when trucking it in is inefficient for whatever reason.

SECURITY, INSURANCE, CATERING, AND PUBLICITY

For a show to come off at all, acts have to be safe and protected—both physically and financially—and they have to eat. Security and insurance take care of the physical and financial protection, and tour caterers—if a tour can afford them—take care of the food.

Additionally, a tour that nobody knows about cannot hope to do much business. Promoters use paid advertising to alert consumers to a show, but often a tour publicist can draw more attention to a tour by attracting media coverage.

TOUR SECURITY

While venues and promoters typically provide security on-site, many acts, particularly at the superstar level or those with unique security issues, carry their own security on the road.

Scott Nichols has served as security director for tours by U2 and the Rolling Stones, two of the most challenging acts for security due to their huge popularity. "Tour security includes protecting hard assets—instruments and production equipment—as well as all personnel," says Nichols. "I begin by submitting a security proposal that includes a risk assessment of the client. This requires a great deal of research."

The security director creates a security rider that includes detailed instructions, sometimes including a diagram of requested positions for local security personnel for the venue.

In some cases, security personnel must deal with issues that transcend strictly crowd control. "The security director must also consider any political or social viewpoints the artist has and their effect on the general public because these could affect the level of risk from agitators," Nichols says.

The major concerns in the security world used to be unruly fans, alcohol control, drugs, moshing, stage diving, and the occasional concealed weapon. Today, those concerns are still very much in place, but new buzzwords like "dirty bombs," "bioterrorism," and "profiling" have become top of mind for security professionals. Potential threats can come from anywhere.

"Obviously, everybody is a little more aware of what's going on," says Bart Butler, president/CEO of Nashville-based Rock Solid Security. "And more money is being spent on security. We're doing far more searching and actual profiling. If we see a suspicious person, we check it out a lot deeper."

Butler has provided tour security for such acts as Jimmy Buffett, Phish, Santana, Dixie Chicks, and Toby Keith. Duties range from simply escorting the artist from the bus to the venue to accompanying the artist on a night on the town. Butler says a traveling security professional can cost from $700 a week to $2,000 a day, based on experience and what their duties will be. In all cases, discretion is paramount for the security professional, and a unique skill set is required.

"Some people are a little sensitive to the positions they get put in, where I don't have those sensitivities," says Butler. "There are certain artists that like to do certain things and some people don't want to be around that. I keep my mouth shut about what takes place. The fact is, you see a lot of the private life of artists that does not need to be taken public."

The security director for a major tour often hires additional touring security: two for a solo artist, four to eight for a band, and as many as twelve for superstar acts. Planning for each venue and show is done well before the tour actually hits town. "I advance the show (discuss with local security in each venue) four months before the show. I talk to local security again two days before the show and one day before. I have a meeting with local police and venue security the morning of show day," Nichols says. "Our biggest challenges are coordinating arrival times, movement to the hotel, movement to the venue, and return to hotel, bus, or jet."

While security that actually travels with the tour is more akin to the traditional "bodyguard" role, venue security is generally more related to crowd management and will be discussed from that perspective in Chapter 16. Even so, the term "bodyguard" has largely been replaced in the industry by "executive protection," according to Butler, who adds that the job has become more professional over the years, with diplomacy skills generally preferred over physicality.

One of the key factors regulated by security professionals is access and the various credentials or passes that allow this access—the famed "backstage pass." The security director helps devise a credentials system to provide levels of access to areas restricted to the general public. Access is generally allowed to various tour personnel, crew, entourage, press, and guests based on their pass, which comes in the form of a *laminate*—a plastic-coated pass most often worn around one's neck—or a *satin* pass that is granted at a particular show and worn as a sticker on the clothing.

Tour managers or production managers usually contract with a graphics company specializing in the touring industry to supply the various passes necessary for a tour. The larger the tour, the more passes ordered and the more levels of security required. "Almost always ordered is All Access laminates and VIP laminates," says Seth Sheck, president of All Access Pass & Design.

According to Sheck, satins usually come as "Working" (for locally hired personnel), "Meet 'n' Greet" (a meeting between the artist with sponsors and/or fans, usually held preshow), "After Show" (for a party or reception after the concert), "Guest," "Media," and/or "Photo."

"Sometimes, as on the Vans Warped Tour, satins will be multi-purpose, with several categories printed on a single rectangle where the categories not used are crossed off," says Sheck. "Satins usually always have a white box for dates, codes, or other customization, and are usually shape coded for easy identification, where each category has its own shape. Also, they tend to be color-coded as well, so that multi-night dates can be changed up to avoid having people show up with the previous day's pass."

Laminates are typically for band and crew and their entourages to be used throughout the duration of the tour, unless a new leg mandates a design change. Satins are day of event only. Laminates average $1.50 each, where satins average 50 cents each.

Passes are usually ordered two weeks prior to the beginning of the tour. "I always encourage a larger order on the front end, because it is usually cheaper to end up with a few extras at a lower unit cost than to have to rerun a much smaller order midway through the tour," Sheck explains. "Additional orders almost always come in throughout the tour, however, as far more passes seem to be distributed than was anticipated."

INSURANCE

Just as most people would not consider driving a car without auto insurance, most artists, concert producers and venues would not consider playing a show without insurance, either. Most touring acts maintain a laundry list of insurance coverage, including general liability, workers' comp, hired-but-unowned-auto, equipment, crime/cash, non-appearance, and business interruption, "in case you can't perform and might lose tour income," says Peter Tempkins with

DeWitt Stern Group insurance company. Insurance professionals tend to deal mostly with an act's business manager.

High-profile terrorist attacks and well-publicized concert tragedies have led to an extremely difficult concert-liability insurance market. The insurance business in general is being hammered, a situation exacerbated by natural disasters.

Beyond terrorist concerns, high-profile club tragedies in Chicago, where twenty-one people were trampled at a hip-hop club, and Rhode Island, where one hundred concertgoers died in a fast-moving fire at a Great White show, have added to insurers' caution.

James Chippendale, president/CEO of CSI Entertainment Insurance, agrees the market is dicey. "We've seen more programs stop writing [concert insurance] than we've seen enter the market," he says. "That creates a supply-and-demand issue, so pricing is going up, and insurers are cutting some coverage."

Generally, the promoter is responsible for securing liability insurance for a concert or tour, but the venue is wise to make sure it is covered as well. Rates are usually figured on a per-admission basis, which can range from as low as 20 cents a head to more than $1 per head on a show deemed as a high risk. "An act should have their insurance agent review their [performance agreement] and any riders to address potential liability issues," says Tempkins.

When and if a lawsuit does erupt, trial lawyers tend to name any and all parties. In cases of multiple injuries, claims can quickly add up to millions of dollars. "What's happening now for all special events and concerts is everybody has insurance, including the booking agency, venue, promoter, and artist," Chippendale explains. "What you're seeing with the Rhode Island [club fire] incident is that everybody's being named in those lawsuits. They're looking for the deepest pockets."

Tempkins agrees. "The most common way an attorney approaches an injury to their client is what I call the 'shotgun approach': they sue everyone—the band, the venue, the promoter—and hope that one of them will offer to settle."

Such companies as Robertson Taylor and CSI act as brokers, finding insurance coverage from among a limited number of carriers willing to deal with musical events. Hip-hop tours are among the most pricey to insure, but Chippendale says caution is not limited to rap tours, and other genres are also considered a higher risk, among them heavy metal/hard rock.

"These insurance companies deal in facts. They look at the history of an event, the history of the artist, and the history of the concert, tour or festival," Chippendale says. "If an artist is going on tour, they look at what happened last time they toured. And if there were sixteen occurrences at fifteen venues, they'll probably pass. It doesn't matter if it's rap or heavy metal."

Tempkins agrees. "The act's history of claims and the genre of music can affect the cost of their insurance."

Still, Chippendale says, "the carriers still in this segment are the ones that know the business and have been doing it for years. They know how to underwrite it and rate it with a fair premium and coverage. We're able to place 90 percent to 95 percent of all concerts that come into our office, it's just a little more difficult."

CATERING

Most promoters and venues provide catering for band and crew, per the deal they cut with the artists. If an act cannot afford a tour caterer, they create a hospitality rider that lists food and beverage preferences that must be provided at the venue. However, many bands choose to carry their own caterer on tour.

Sandy Hylton is owner of Sweet Chili Catering, a company that specializes in tour catering. Hylton, who has served as catering director for acts including Paul Simon, Sarah Brightman, and U2, says a typical catering budget depends on how many people will be touring and what their specific dietary needs may be. "After I'm hired, the first thing I do is ask about any special diets, favorite foods and dishes, and nutritional concerns," she says. "My job is to keep the band fit and healthy."

Hylton typically travels with an assistant on tour and hires a local assistant and a runner in each city. On large tours like the Vans Warped Tour, which carries as many as 800 people from town to town, a larger staff of professionals travels on the road.

"We do all our own catering," says Warped producer Kevin Lyman. "There's no way a promoter would cater Warped. This catering bill, if you based it on a normal deal when you go into an arena, I think it'd be somewhere around $30,000 a day. Most people couldn't handle it."

Shelleylyn Brandler's Ta Da! Catering feeds the Warped tour. "We always say 90 percent of the people on the Warped tour will eat the best they ever do and the other 10 percent can afford to go out and eat somewhere else," Lyman says. In the egalitarian society that is Warped, bands, crew, bus drivers, and producers all stand in line for the same chow. The caterer must coordinate with local suppliers to make sure that fresh vegetables and other perishables are available in each town. Ta Da! carries eighteen full-time staffers on the road with Warped.

TOUR PUBLICISTS

A tour publicist's job is to draw media attention to an act that is about to tour and then to maximize exposure for a touring act when they come into a market. He or she also deals with the media when there are show cancellations or other unforeseen incidents. A tour publicist can be hired by a record company, a manager, a promoter, or sometimes the artists themselves.

The difference between publicity and advertising is that publicity is free news coverage and advertising must be purchased. Therefore, while the promoter buys advertising to promote a concert, the publicist leans on the media via *pitches*—solicitations for coverage. Mitch Schneider, tour publicist for such tours as Ozzfest, says it is best to have a tour publicist in place at least two months before the launch of a tour to maximize press coverage. "The publicist needs to start pitching monthlies in each market and then the weeklies and the dailies," says Schneider. "If you have a superstar, you'll be expected to deliver covers of entertainment sections. So you have to get your pitches in early as possible."

Schneider says the primary duty of a publicist is to produce interviews in key publications. "This is achieved by properly pitching the media by sending along music and a good press kit including the best clippings that exist on an artist," says Schneider. "Of course, the publicist needs to be persuasive in their pitch, whether it's via phone or in e-mail."

The publicist is often asked to produce TV coverage on the day of the show, so they'll have to send out a media alert to the local television outlets in each market. "You know you did your job to the max when all the local crews are positioned at the soundboard shooting the artist," says Schneider.

A tour publicist can also be asked to generate performance options on local morning TV and radio programs. "If you're a new artist with a day off in a city—and you don't mind getting up at the crack of dawn—performing acoustically on a local morning show is a good way to build a buzz," Schneider adds.

The tour publicist works with the tour manager in allocating press passes. "A sharp tour publicist will provide a guest list for the show the day before, encompassing which media are attending and which media passed on coverage," says Schneider. "If you're an artist, it is helpful to know that, say, the *Chicago Tribune* was unable to offer a feature or review because, for example, Aerosmith was being covered instead."

Every publicity firm charges different rates and every artist has varying levels of services they require. A band that is looking strictly for tour press as opposed to a national campaign can expect to pay anywhere from $2,000 to $3,000 per month, plus expenses (encompassing the cost of mailings to the media, printing costs for press kits, et al.). Superstars are known to pay more, as their needs and demands are greater.

Schneider says it is tougher than ever to reach writers, so e-mail has become more important. "The publicist better know how to pitch an artist with a concise e-mail. It helps, if you have a new artist, to send a link to the artist's [Internet] page so the journalist can easily hear what the artist sounds like," Schneider suggests.

With the increase in the value of tickets, tickets for the media are less available than they used to be, particularly with hot shows. Most writers (and guests, for that matter) don't want to attend a show alone, so they ask for a *plus one*, meaning their ticket plus one guest. Today, Schneider explains, publicists are often faced with the unenviable task of telling a reporter they must attend the show solo.

Schneider says that at his company, a tour publicist coordinates with the national publicist if an artist cancels a show. The national publicist then confers with the artist's management about issuing a press release regarding the cause of the cancellation. If there are other complications regarding a show—like a riot or injury—the national publicist will confer with the artist's management regarding making a statement to the media.

PART II

 **Types of Talent Buyers**

A talent buyer is the person or company who pays an act or artist to perform. The size and scope of talent buyers are nearly as diverse as the types of acts that can play for them. From independent buyers for a 300-capacity club to mega-promoters that bankroll multimillion-dollar world tours, there is a talent buyer for every type of show.

The basic types of talent buyers include concert promoters, national and international promoters, college buyers, club buyers, venue and performing arts center buyers, fair and festival buyers, casino buyers, and private date buyers. The objectives of the talent buyer can differ widely. A corporate promoter may seek to make money over the course of 100 shows, not panicking if a show in Cleveland does poorly because Philadelphia was way better than expected. An independent promoter may be motivated by not losing his house if a $100,000 act stiffs in his market. A club owner's objective may be to sell a lot of beer. A casino talent buyer wants to attract high rollers who will hit the tables. And a private buyer may want to throw the biggest birthday bash ever for a deep-pocketed client.

Though there is no strict delineation in types of buyers, for the purposes of this chapter we will divide buyers into hard ticket talent buyers, basically promoters whose primary goal is to profit from selling tickets; venue talent buyers like clubs or performing arts centers, whose primary goal may be to sell beer or keep the venue programmed with content; and fairs, festival and casino buyers, where the entertainment is free or an add-on to another major event or attraction. That said, it is important to note that many casinos, fairs, and festivals often do wish to turn a profit from ticket sales in addition to their other revenue streams. We will also include discussion of private date buyers in the latter section of the chapter.

HARD TICKET TALENT BUYERS

Hard ticket talent buyers are typically referred to as concert promoters. These buyers expect ticket sales to cover the cost of buying talent in a venue, with ticket revenue being the primary revenue generator in the business model. This is not the case with other talent buyers such as fairs, many festivals, or casinos, who have other primary revenue producers, and buyers for private dates, who do not sell tickets. Among the buyers covered in this section are national and international tour buyers, and college buyers.

But, in setting the stage, it would be impossible to discuss the modern day concert business without a brief history of how the business has evolved into today's concert industry.

THE EVOLUTION OF THE CONCERT PROMOTION BUSINESS

Americans have been paying and businessmen have been charging for some sort of live entertainment since colonial times. Venues, festivals, fairs, and special events paid for talent in pre– and post–Civil War eras through the Depression. The big band era was rife with live concerts, and crooners, country and western bands, blues, folk, and other musicians toured incessantly both before and after World War II. But for our purposes, the modern day concert business found its true beginnings when rock and roll matured from its origins in the 1950s to big business.

As the rock 'n' roll caravans—large package tours comprising the top hitmakers of the day—helped build stars that developed careers beyond one-hit wonders, these tours became increasingly in demand. By the time the mid-1960s rolled around, regional promoters began to have success promoting rock bands from the United States and the United Kingdom. Chief among these promoters was the late Bill Graham, who established his base in San Francisco promoting bands like the Grateful Dead, Jefferson Airplane, the Who, and the Rolling Stones. Propelled by creative promoters like Graham, the concert experience became more of a lifestyle event, and attending concerts became one of the primary entertainment choices for the youth culture.

By the time the 1960s became the 1970s, several regional promoters had developed successful businesses in their respective areas of the country. Among the concert promotion pioneers were Ron Delsener in New York City, John Scher in New Jersey, Jim Koplik in Connecticut, Larry Magid in Philadelphia, the Belkin brothers in Cleveland, Jack Boyle in Washington D.C. and Florida, Louis Messina in Texas, Danny Zelisko in Phoenix, Barry Fey in Denver, Irv Zuckerman in St. Louis, Dave Lucas in Indianapolis, Arny Granat and Jerry Mickelson in Chicago, Michael Cohl in Toronto, Don Fox in New Orleans, and, of course, Graham in San Francisco.

These young entrepreneurs were risk takers by nature. They built their territories by buying exciting talent from powerful agents like Frank Barsalona in New York, and they protected their fiefdoms fiercely. While many promoters started as club owners, as bands grew in popularity, these promoters established relationships with larger venues, including civic centers, auditoriums, arenas, and stadiums. While skittish at first, these venues soon began to welcome rock bands with open arms, relishing the revenue they brought in rental fees, concessions sales, parking fees, and other ancillary income.

The industry operated status quo throughout the 1970s and most of the 1980s, and promoters who did not make prudent talent-buying decisions soon found themselves out of business. In the mid-1980s, larger promoters like Cellar Door, PACE, and the Nederlander Organization began building and operating their own venues in what became the beginning of the amphitheater boom. Promoters, tired of watching arenas capture all the ancillary revenue from their own risk-taking, felt they needed to get into the real estate game themselves, and an amphitheater or shed could be built for a fraction of the cost of an arena. The primordial entertainment viewing experience became contemporized, as amphitheaters were opened in most of the top markets in the country over the next decade.

In the late 1990s, as all types of businesses including music began to consolidate, radio entrepreneur Robert F.X. Sillerman began, quietly at first, buying up regional concert promoters. In most cases, the promoters he targeted had some sort of venue commodity, either owning amphitheaters or long-term exclusive booking deals at other venues. By 2000, Sillerman had spent $2.5 billion buying up promoters and live entertainment producers, which he assembled under the SFX Entertainment banner and forever changed the concert industry. And in February of that year, Sillerman sold SFX to radio conglomerate Clear Channel Communications, which christened its new live entertainment division Clear Channel Entertainment (CCE).

With billions of dollars in debt and a questionable business model that drove up talent costs to control market share, CCE eventually became a drain on its radio parent, raising the ire of stockholders and the resentment of competitors. In December of 2005, Clear Channel spun off its live entertainment business, giving birth to independent, freestanding live entertainment giant Live Nation.

As of 2006, Live Nation owns, operates, and/or has booking rights for 153 venues worldwide and produces more than 28,000 events annually. Headquartered in Los Angeles, California, Live Nation is listed on the New York Stock Exchange, trading under the symbol "LYV." The company produced some forty tours in 2006, routing them both threw their own amphitheaters and other venues.

Though Live Nation is the world's biggest promoter, independent promoters have continued to thrive through innovation and creative talent buying.

CONCERT PROMOTERS

The basic concept of concert promotion is the promoter pays the act, usually through an agent, an agreed-upon sum to perform on a given date at a given venue. The promoter then agrees to "promote" the show through whatever means necessary, primarily paid advertising. Box office proceeds traditionally go 15 percent for the promoter, and 85 percent for the act, though that figure has tilted in favor of the artist in recent years. From his share of the box office, the promoter covers his expenses, including promotion of the show, some production fees, venue rental (if the promoter does not own the venue), catering, and any other costs incurred. Some have estimated a promoter's profit margin at about 1 percent, if he comes out ahead at all. It is easy to see why independent promoters must choose wisely and be judicious when buying talent.

The math is tricky, to say the least. "We have limited control because the artists establish the guarantee, then they want you to lower the ticket price, but they don't want to lower the guarantee," explains Randy Phillips, CEO of international promoter AEG Live. "So if they want $200,000 for a show and you want to have a high ticket price of $50 and a low of $25, then they want you to bring all the ticket prices down, but the guarantee will stay the same."

Setting ticket prices is a delicate balance, Phillips points out, aptly illustrating the thought process a promoter must go through. "You're not going to double your audience because you have a low ticket price; it's just not going to happen," he says. "But you will have a pushback from the audience if your ticket prices are too high. So if you think an artist, historically and in today's market, and in the package that's out there, should do 9,000 people, then you work your numbers up in a range of 8,000 to 10,000, which is a pretty good range of estimating what you'll do, and the agent is looking at 10,000 minimum and a low ticket price that would require 12,000 tickets sold to pay for the show. So you're in this nowhere land where typically we all must acknowledge that we really don't know how many people are going to buy the tickets at the end of the day no matter what the price is."

Then, armed with must-meet figures, artist history, and no small amount of instinct, "you have to acknowledge that, based on a certain amount of evidence and gut feeling that still plays a part, you think the show will do 'x'," Phillips says. "And then you build a model. It's very hard, because you could say in March and April the shows that have the most optimistic appearance. You can lose heat and you can gain heat. You start believing in everyone's optimism or your own taste in music, you're headed for trouble."

Obviously, some shows are going to lose money. "You sit back and say 'how did we make this mistake?' We either believed these three bands would make one-plus-one-plus-one would equal seven, or we were intoxicated by our love of the artist," Phillips adds. "You definitely have to love the music, artist and business across the board in order to do this, because it's a tough business when you're guessing what the consumer will do."

Selling tickets is unlike any other product, Phillips points out. "In manufacturing, the marketing team drives the business. They say we want the wrapper to be blue next year with red trim and a white splash. And the consumer wants more dark chocolate and less milk chocolate. Then you go out and advertise it and distribute it," Phillips muses. "But the talent buying team drives the concert business, and not by something we create. We do not create our own product. It's created by an artist, a band, a musician, a singer, a songwriter, a manager, and then an agent sells it to us, and we have to think 'well, this could be stronger if we wait until October,' and they say 'our tour is August and September.'"

NATIONAL AND INTERNATIONAL TOUR BUYERS

Beginning with the advent of deep-pocketed, corporate promoters with a presence in multiple markets, national and international promotion—where one promoter buys the whole tour instead of the agent and manager cutting individual deals in each market—first began to appear in the 1970s with Bill Graham and Concerts West. But the concept really began to take hold in 1989 when Toronto promoter Michael Cohl and his team at Concert Promotions International promoted the Rolling Stones' "Steel Wheels" tour worldwide.

Rather than break down each individual date, tour buyers look at the gross potential of an entire tour and try to build and advantage by *cross-collateralizing* the tour. This means that if a show in Cleveland, for example, does not meet projections, the money will be made up by big successes in New York, Boston, Philadelphia, and Los Angeles.

Sometimes the concept works and sometimes it doesn't. Proponents of the one-promoter model say the "one-stop shopping" aspect allows for consistency in production and promotion from market to market and maneuverability without having going through layers of communications. Those not in the national touring game say no one knows a given market better than the promoter on the ground year-round in that city, and problems can develop when a cookie-cutter approach is taken that assumes market conditions in one city will be the same as another.

"I make the case and the team that we have makes the case to agents and managers that there are certain liabilities to doing a national tour," explains Randy Phillips of AEG Live, which has promoted tours by Bon Jovi, the Eagles, Rod Stewart, and others. "If you establish an average price that is weighted too high for any reason, even if someone is willing to pay it, you set yourself up for difficult times in the medium and small markets. We make the case that the price of an artist should be determined city by city and that buying in bulk is not necessarily advantageous to the artist."

But when the Dixie Chicks' 2006 tour came out of the gate with lower-than-expected ticket sales, national promoter AEG Live, working with management and agency, were able to deftly reroute the tour into the group's strongest markets and put weaker markets on hold. "Only a national promoter could have moved this fast and responded to the tour's perceived strengths and weaknesses as evidenced in the initial public on-sales," says Phillips.

Cross-collateralizing and tour buying is about averaging out costs and maximizing the biggest markets, and it can be tough for all involved to lower prices in smaller markets. "Big-city markets pay for some losses and break-evens in the small-city markets, using the artists' overage earnings," Phillips explains. "Some say 'that's robbing from Peter to pay Paul and you should not be operating on an average price, you should be operating on a market-by-market price.' But when they total up their dates and it's one check for the whole tour, it's very intoxicating."

Arthur Fogel, Global Chairman of Music for Live Nation, has fine-tuned the original CPI international touring model, promoting global tours by U2, Madonna, Sting, and others. The first order of business in putting together a world tour historically was lining up investors to bankroll huge production costs and artist guarantees that could climb north of $100 million. With Live Nation's massive bank account, the financing is now in place.

"It's very different from how the normal [touring] business exists and operates," Fogel says. "We tend to have close relationships, partnerships, with the artists we work with. And when you come at it from that basis, it's really about strategizing first, putting together what they want to do, where we think they should play, putting all the pieces together, establishing an agreement on ticket prices, and sort of building the model from the ground up."

Then the variables come into play, most importantly "how much money is available, ultimately, for the producer and the artist," Fogel continues. "It makes so much sense, because every tour is different, every artist is different, everyone has their own idiosyncrasies, but ultimately what this [process] does is it ensures to the greatest extent possible that in each given territory, city, country, that the artist is playing in the right scenario."

An international tour promoter's duties are split between two sets of functions. The first is organizing promotion, putting together the routing, strategizing the marketing, and coordinating the efforts of local production staff and promoters. The second is putting together a production budget, contracting vendors, and hiring key personnel, who then go out and hire their own staff.

Even artists who have historically balked at a one-promoter deal have bought into the global touring model. "The concept of going on a world tour with only one promoter was a new one for me, but one that was extremely economically advantageous," Sting says, whose 2004/2005 tour was promoted by Fogel. As the tour shifted from theaters to amphitheaters to arenas to college venues, the promotional model proved flexible.

In some cases on a one-promoter tour, agent involvement is minimal, as the promoter brings an entire route and financial deal to the table. "My relationships are direct," Fogel says, adding that his approach is no indictment of the way others do business or of the agency system.

"This is one man's way of going out in the world and doing business under a different model, which works very well in a direct relationship with the management and the business people that represent that artist," Fogel says. "It's a model that doesn't work for everybody."

COLLEGE BUYERS

College students are some of the most passionate music fans there are, and music on college campuses at college venues has been a staple entertainment for decades. Students are particularly receptive to new and developing artists, with acts ranging from R.E.M. to Dave Matthews Band first gaining momentum at the college level.

Mainstream promoters are active at colleges, but most universities also have some sort of student-run campus entertainment buying association. In fact, many of today's top touring industry professionals first got their start by participating in these college concert committees. It makes sense for any student that is considering entering the entertainment field to play some role within their campus entertainment association, whether it's T-shirt security to ushering to booking talent.

But an act often does not want to risk its play in a given market to non-professionals, and conversely most schools cannot afford to lose thousands on a misguided talent buy. So, often college buyers are partnered with local professionals. "We try to strike a balance between buying shows directly and working to attract promoters by offering to co-promote or share revenues," says Marty Kern, director of major events for Clemson University. "The best-case scenario is an established promoter comes into our building and is wowed by the service and cost savings we can provide and we work together to market the show."

At Clemson, a full-time staff provides weekly advisement to the student committee directors. These student leaders learn the nuts and bolts of facility management, promotion, production, and talent buying. Kern says she and the students she works with stay active in the buying process.

"We can't wait for the phone to ring," she says, adding that renovations to the university's Littlejohn Coliseum has helped bring in bookings. "One thing we were smart to do here at Clemson is to house the university concert committee right here at the venue. That seems so obvious, but it is not common."

Student activity fees typically help fund the talent-buying budget, but campus buyers must keep the market at large in mind. "Rather than using the annual allocation to produce one or two big shows just for students, we use the money to invest in shows that are viable for the entire market and will give us a return on investment," says Kern. "We also work with area businesses, sponsors and investors to create a pool of risk money that we can utilize to fund shows."

LARGE VENUE BUYERS

In a large number of cases, the venue and the talent buyer is one and the same. The largest volume buyers in this segment are the club buyers, followed by venue talent buyers including arenas, theaters, ballrooms, and performing arts centers. We do not include Live Nation, the company that owns the overwhelming number of amphitheaters in North America in this section because at its core, Live Nation is a concert promoter.

Club Buyers

The American rock club is a venerated institution that has included such historical establishments as the Stone Pony in Asbury Park, New Jersey, Antone's in Austin, the Whisky A Go-Go in Hollywood, and Max's Kansas City and the former CBGB's in New York—venues that have played an undeniable role in launching such legendary careers as those of Bruce Springsteen, Stevie Ray Vaughan, the Doors, Aerosmith, and the Ramones, respectively.

While some of these rooms have survived and dozens of new ones have come and gone, the marquee rock club remains a vital developmental cog that serves to build a regional fan base and helps create sufficient buzz to attract record labels and bring mainstream press to the party. A widespread rock-club circuit still exists, and remains hugely important in artist development, and club talent buyers have been key players in developing rock bands well into the new millennium.

As national and international tour buying has increased, the club circuit remains an important vestige of the traditional touring model, where promoters take chances on acts at the club level with hopes of being involved in dates if and when the act breaks to arena headliner. Hopes are if a buyer loses a few hundred bucks at a 200-seat club, the act will remember that promoter if he or she breaks big.

Indeed, building bridges between promoters and baby acts may well be the most important role of rock clubs today. "As a promoter, I need to get in when the band's as small as I can and develop them every step of the way," Washington, D.C., promoter and I.M.P. president Seth Hurwitz says. Hurwitz buys talent and promotes shows both for his own 9:30 Club and larger venues in the market. "That part of the system still works, and on that level, clubs are as essential as they ever were. If you win that battle, you pretty much win the war. If as a promoter you don't do a great job at the smallest of levels, not only do you probably not deserve the history [with the band], you probably won't make as much money in the following steps."

For most rock bands, playing clubs is a crucial rite of passage and path to musical maturity.

Clubs are also the place to bring in fans at the entry level. Many of today's rock clubs have found that to be successful, the under-twenty-one crowd must be a part of the scene. That's why all-ages shows are an important part of almost every major club's monthly schedule. "The key element is rooms with [general admission] floors and all-ages concerts," Massachusetts promoter John Peters says. "If you only allow twenty-one and over, you can't develop concert acts in a room like that. Very few acts break to arena level that appeal primarily to people over twenty-one. You have to have all ages, and most clubs do."

With a sizeable impact on taste-making music fans, rock clubs and the promoters who buy talent for them are involved in a symbiotic relationship with acts and their agents and managers. For many acts, clubs simply offer a better payday, because the pie is split up into fewer pieces. For example, the 2,660-capacity Palladium in Worcester, Massachusetts is the size of a smaller theater, but promoter Peters contends both act and promoter can come out better in the club than the theater.

"In general, expenses are higher in a theater, including labor costs, base rent, and building fees—all these things that make it less favorable for the promoter," Peters says. "There are also certain acts, like aggressive rock bands, that can't play theaters, just like there are certain acts that shouldn't play in the clubs."

Peters says that if a promoter owns the club or has an exclusive booking agreement, he can often pay more than a theater because he has access to certain revenue sources. "I pay [acts] more than a theater of the same capacity would," he says, adding that his price for acts ranges from $5,000 or less to as much as $50,000.

Almost all acts have a "back end" or door-percentage opportunity in their major-club deal, but in most cases a club owner has different interests from a promoter, with the latter looking at club dates as an investment in the future of an act. For most promoters, promoting in clubs is not a money-making proposition on the door, while the club owner can hope to make money off the bar even if he does not on ticket sales.

Hurwitz says that unlike a promoter, a club owner who is not a promoter doesn't necessarily have an interest in seeing a band move up to arenas. "If you're simply a club owner, you're happy to keep a band for a few gigs after they get big. There is a ceiling on what the club owner can recoup from his investment. As a promoter, there's really no ceiling to it, unless an act goes with a national tour."

PERFORMING ARTS CENTER BUYERS

Arenas, performing arts centers, and theaters also buy talent in-house. We will discuss these larger venues' role in talent buying in Chapter 16. But in basic terms, these larger venues deal directly with the agent or talent seller in contracting the act to perform, and the venue takes the risk that the promoter would. Performing arts centers often buy talent, most often in the form of subscriptions for a Broadway series or local arts companies.

Arenas are the largest venue buyers of mainstream talent. For 2006 tours such as Mötley Crüe, the arenas came to the table to buy dates more readily than did a wary concert promoter base. Often, the arena must offer to take a risk in order to gain leverage in a highly competitive market. The typical tour will play 35 to 50 dates, and there are 130 to 140 legitimate arena plays in North America, so arenas have had to become more aggressive in attracting live entertainment.

Many public arenas, however, operate under tight budget constraints and often find difficulty in convincing public officials to risk hundreds of thousands of dollars to attract concerts. As stated throughout this book, it takes a lot of "winners" to make up for one "loser."

FAIRS, FESTIVALS, AND CASINO BUYERS

Among the major buyers of talent in North America are those that buy talent that is surrounded by ancillary events—events that also may produce revenue and often are the primary or at least equal attraction. Foremost among those buyers are fairs, festivals, and casinos. For example, at a fair, other ancillary attractions include a carnival midway. At the Garlic Festival in Gilroy, California, the primary attraction is garlic. In this section we analyze the similarities and differences among these talent buyers.

FAIR AND FESTIVAL BUYERS

Fairs and festivals are some of the most established talent buyers in North America, particularly the former. Such acts as the Beatles, Elvis, and countless country artists received their first major concert exposure playing fairs.

Fair talent buyers have objectives that can be different from mainstream promoters and venue owners. "We need to determine specifically what will do best in our individual markets," says Joe LaGuardia, director of booking for the New York State Fair in Syracuse. "I program eleven days at our 16,400-seat grandstand, and twelve days at our free stage, which holds around 10,000 with standing room. We need to be as diverse as availability will allow with the main regard of financial feasibility."

LaGuardia says his objective with grandstand acts is to buy talent that will sell at least 10,000 tickets, "first, to pay for themselves, and second to provide rain insurance and a built-in positive attendance for the fair. Basically, the need is to find entertainment that makes financial sense and that will bolster [fair] attendance and allow bragging rights and prestige in scheduling top name artists."

Some fairs go in with a strict budget they must adhere to and others have more flexibility. "I make decisions based on what I believe will sell in my market," says LaGuardia. "My ticket prices will reflect the cost of the show and what I feel will allow us to make guarantee and expenses so the show can be successful."

Fairs attract a wide demographic and ticket prices must reflect that, LaGuardia explains, but the perception that acts must charge lower prices at fairs is not always correct. "We have raised our ticket prices accordingly to reflect the cost of the guarantee and we have found no resistance in charging a fair and reasonable ticket price. [In 2006], our prices ranged from $40 and $35 to $54 and $49 for various shows. The higher ticket price reflected the higher show cost."

Most large fairs offer both hard and soft ticket (free) shows. Free shows are generally booked within a budget and programmed with "those acts that we don't feel can sell a hard ticket but yet provide an outstanding value of just the price of fair admission are the shows we go after," says LaGuardia. "That is reflected in the standing room only crowds we attract to our free stage."

Because they are held at a certain time of year, fairs are limited to buying talent available during the fair's run. "That inflexibility limits what we can present. Also, we lose buying power since we aren't in business twelve months of the year like the main promoters," LaGuardia points out. "Because our buying is limited to a short time period, we don't buy in volume, sometimes causing our guarantee to be higher than it might be if we had a year-round operation."

In the past, fairs have battled the perception that they are second-rate bookings, but today's top fairs offer production values and revenue potential in line with major venues. "If fairs run a tip top operation, they will get a crack at booking the top acts. If they don't measure up they run the risk of being passed over for consideration," says LaGuardia. "Fairs pretty much survive on their own merit and how they measure up by today's necessary touring standards."

While most major fairs buy talent in-house, there are companies that exist primarily as talent buyers for fairs. These companies, like Louisville, Kentucky–based Triangle Talent, or Hendersonville, Tennessee–based Jayson Promotions, buy talent for several fairs and are often able to offer a string of dates to agents in order to leverage more favorable pricing for talent.

While fairs offer entertainment as value-added to a multifaceted event, live entertainment at music festivals is obviously the main attraction. While such events as the New Orleans Jazz & Heritage Festival have been around for decades, music fests have enjoyed a true renaissance in the twenty-first century, with such events as Bonnaroo, the Austin City Limits Music Festival, Coachella, and Lollapalooza very high on the radars of music fans.

Festival talent buyers can take one of several approaches in putting together their lineup. One is to nail down a couple of major headliners then fill out the bill with smaller acts. In this type of top-heavy scenario, 10 percent of acts on the bill can take up 90 percent of the budget.

The more successful fests these days tend to be more democratic in how the money is distributed. Bonnaroo, held at a rural site on a 700-acre field about sixty miles south of Nashville, books nearly 150 acts that perform across a dozen stages and tents during the June event. From a talent budget *Billboard* estimates at around $3 million (the producers don't divulge that information), co-producer Jonathan Mayers says about 20 percent goes to about 65 percent of Bonnaroo's acts.

Distributing this wealth of talent across many stages and days is a rewarding challenge, Mayers says. "We have a real vision of what the whole experience is about. We're in the details business, and hopefully that's what makes us a little different and special."

Seth Hurwitz at I.M.P., talent buyer for the first Virgin Mobile Music Fest at Pimlico Race Track in Baltimore, says he was very concerned about putting together a talent lineup that resonates with music lovers. "I did not want to book every band I could find and put up as many stages as I could and do a smaller version of Coachella or Austin City Limits or these other great festivals," says Hurwitz. "My concept was to book the absolute best, most power-packed, quality-versus-quantity lineup I could. I wanted to make this the most prestigious festival to play on for bands."

Hurwitz says that when assembling the lineup he wanted to nail down the key anchor bookings first. "We booked it from the top down, and we did not agree to go ahead with the festival until I knew what kind of show we could put together," he says. "I was ready to walk away from it, I did not want to do a mediocre show."

The first act he booked for the 2006 event was the Red Hot Chili Peppers. After the Peppers came the Who, a "dream booking" for Hurwitz due to the group's popularity with kids, half of whom, Hurwitz says, listen to classic rock. "When I first brought up the Who, nobody got it, I fought everyone on this," Hurwitz says. "The people at Virgin wanted to skew this thing young, and I am looking to bring in the kids who have never seen the Who but really want to."

Hurwitz says that as the talent budget, which was more than $2 million, became glitzier, the ticket price began to inch up. "It started at $75, and then we realized if we can book the Who and raise the price $10, isn't it better for everyone?" Hurwitz says. "And it kept going up with every great addition we put on there, and at some point we said we don't want to go over $100."

Booking talent is only one part of staging a major festival. We will look at other facets of this complex segment of the business in Chapters 12 and 13.

CASINO BUYERS

As buyers of talent, casinos have become extremely viable alternatives for many touring acts, in many cases providing venues and paydays for acts who have exhausted other opportunities. And while many casinos historically used talent as a loss-leader perk for high-rollers, more and more casinos now look to talent and ticket sales as a profit center. While Las Vegas and Atlantic City, New Jersey once cornered the market on the casino entertainment experience, today casinos are found throughout the United States. This is a development that booking agents have greeted with enthusiasm.

The entertainment these venues offer is as varied as the communities in which they're located. These newer casinos are frequently far from major cities, thanks to federal laws that have allowed their development on Native American tribal lands. Examples of these would be the Seminole Hard Rock Hotel & Casino near Hollywood, Florida, and the Menominee Casino in Kenosha, Wisconsin.

Casino and resort talent buyers have become some of the most savvy buyers in the business, cognizant of economic and demographic drivers that mainstream promoters do not even have to consider. Once the bastion of talent appealing to an older demographic, casino concerts have now become as diverse as concerts in the mainstream world.

In broad terms, the well-heeled baby boomer demographic, which has discretionary money to spend on gambling, has long been a primary target for casinos. And given that yesterday's headbanger is today's forty- to fifty-something fan, rock music is now frequently found in casino venues. In fact, the casino market has enabled a lot of acts to stay on the road and continue touring that might not be able to if they were dependent strictly on hard ticket dates and the fairs and festivals.

In terms of casino talent, the genre menu is fairly broad. What the act can sell is obviously very important to most casinos, but the demographic of the act's fan base is also key. That's where agents like Howie Silverman come in. His Paradise Artists Agency books such acts as Chubby Checker, John Kay & Steppenwolf, Foghat, the Turtles, Paul Revere and the Raiders, and Don McLean. "Casinos are one of our most lucrative and growing markets," says Silverman. "They're looking for anything that's drawing the gambling demo, and that demo right now is baby boomers." Silverman says casinos pay well, his acts love to play them, and their fans like to see them there.

But increasingly, casino talent buyers also are focusing on bringing in acts that appeal to a more youthful demo. So while country, adult contemporary, and comedy remain popular for bookings, R&B, modern rock and hip-hop acts are on the upswing at gaming establishments. For example, Jim Koplik, president of Live Nation Connecticut and buyer for the Mohegan Sun in Uncasville, Connecticut, enjoyed sellouts in 2006 from acts including Kid Rock, Godsmack, and Stain'd.

"As the markets evolve so does the selection of talent playing the venues," says Terry Jenkins, director of entertainment for Boyd Gaming Corporation. "I think it's important to give your guest base a broad range of entertainers to choose from, [including] comedy, country, R&B and middle-of-the-road." He adds that there is no rule of thumb as to which acts work best in casinos. "I wish I had one!"

And, as is now more often the case in casino bookings, acts are expected to carry the bulk of their own weight in ticket sales, often with only the high-rollers "comped," or admitted for free. In fact, Jenkins says the perception that casinos strictly buy talent to spur the "drop," or gambling revenues, is a "total myth." The percentage of talent gaming institutions buy that is intended as a stand-alone hard ticket revenue producer "really depends on the venue," Jenkins says. "Some of them market heavily to known players, others expect the acts to pay for themselves and [comp] only top-tier players."

Jenkins adds that for the most part the stigma that casino entertainment is cheesy has disappeared, though not completely. "I think it's management's perception of their acts playing casinos," he says. "The money's good but some managers don't think it looks good when their clients play the casinos."

PRIVATE DATE BUYERS

Private and/or corporate bookings are one of the fastest growing segments of the live industry. Buyers in this market range from Fortune 500 companies to Mom and Pop businesses to birthday party planners for the well-heeled. Acts that have played private events include Elton John, the Eagles, the Rolling Stones, Sheryl Crow, Jimmy Buffett, and Black Eyed Peas.

"I can tell you that the private/corporate business is definitely a growing trend," says Greg Janese, an agent at Monterey Peninsula Artists/Paradigm that specializes in the private/corporate business. The Convention Industry Council Economic Impact Study of 2005 indicated that in 2004, the meeting, convention, exhibition, and incentive travel industry generated $122.3 billion in direct spending in the United States. Of this, corporate meetings and events account for $40.3 billion. "That means that companies nationwide are spending $40 billion a year on corporate meetings, and talent would very much be within that budget."

Private engagements are purchased in a variety of ways according to Janese. "I can be contacted by a corporate production company that is producing the meeting for the corporation," he says. "I can be contacted sometimes directly by the CEO's office, if it's a private party.

In the latter scenario it is wise to insist that a professional producer is involved in the date. "Too many times these guys will contact me as the agent and they'll be clueless as to what's involved in putting a show on," says Janese. "Even though it might be in their backyard for a hundred people, you still have to have all the stuff you would need for a regular venue. So I insist there is a producer involved, and oftentimes I'll help them find a producer."

The agent also lets it be known in the business planning meeting which of his or her acts are available for these type dates. "We'll go through my roster and I'll get a feel for what kind of audience it is, what's the purpose of the event, have they had entertainment before, if they have what worked well for them," Janese says. "I get some demographics, then I will suggest acts that I feel would be appropriate for that particular situation."

Acts can usually command a higher guarantee for a private date than they would a public performance because other revenue streams, including merchandising and percentages of ticket sales, are not available. Plus, since these dates are generally one-offs, the buyer usually picks up all travel and production expenses. "In many ways it's really no different from a public date," says Janese. "You need a good promoter to take care of the details and make sure everything comes off flawlessly at a public concert, and you need the exact same thing at a private date."

National acts traditionally have been reticent to let information on their private bookings be made public, but the stigma of corporate sellout and blue-haired audiences seems to be abating. "There was a point of view where an artist didn't want people knowing about [these bookings] because it wasn't considered cool," Janese says. "There is just a wider range of acceptance today than there was ten years ago."

The revenue available from this market has helped make it more palatable to artists, Janese adds. "And the audiences are changing, they're not so stuffy any more. Pharmaceutical companies, for example, book name talent all the time for product launches and sales meetings, and their audience is twenty-something guys."

CHAPTER 10

Getting Paid

Entertainers want to be paid for their services. Talent buyers want reward for their risk. The basics of how these two objectives are reconciled is the focus of this chapter.

Before any formal agreements can be signed, the talent buyer and the act's booking agent must first agree on the *fee structure*, the method for paying the act. The fee structures, commonly called "deals," run the touring-industry gamut from the uncomplicated flat guarantee to the more complicated backend deal, including the straight percentage deal, the per-ticket deal, the versus deal, and the plus deal. In addition to the basic fee structure, talent buyers sometimes may also offer a *bonus*, a larger percentage or higher guarantee, to the act.

Talent buyers may obtain the act for a fee that is lower than the act's going rate. They do this by offering the act value in the form of favorable routing, multiple shows, and several bookings in the region. The talent buyer may also use a *middle agent*, a third party with experience as a booking agent or concert promoter, to negotiate the best deal possible.

The fee structure negotiated for a deal is based on the bargaining power of the act. The booking agency for an emerging act playing small venues is typically not able to negotiate a sophisticated backend deal and must settle for a modest flat guarantee or a straight percentage deal. The agency representing a superstar act touring arenas or stadiums has the clout to land a profitable backend deal with a guaranteed minimum payment.

An important goal for each side of the negotiations—the agent and the talent buyer—is removing as much risk as possible using the fee structure. The act hopes for some assurance that they will earn enough income each week to cover tour expenses and show a profit. Therefore, the booking agency tries to avoid deals that may pay the act less money, or nothing, when ticket sales are lower than expected. Similarly, the talent buyer tries to structure the deal so that he or she can recoup most expenses for the show before paying the act, even when ticket sales are low.

THE FLAT GUARANTEE

The *flat guarantee* fee structure pays the act a specific amount of money—usually paid by the talent buyer just prior to the show, at intermission, or soon after the show—regardless of ticket sales. When the act is promised a flat guarantee and the show sells only 40 percent of available tickets, the act still receives the guaranteed payment. However, when the show is a sellout, the act still gets only the agreed on flat guarantee, often less than a backend deal would have paid.

When the act is paid the flat guarantee, a fee structure more predictable than one based on a percentage of ticket sales, the act and their team can more easily create the tour budget. Knowing the income side of the budget in advance helps the act and their team better determine what expenses are logical for the tour. This removes the risk of launching the tour based on a "crystal ball" estimate of income.

Because the talent buyer must pay the act's flat guarantee regardless of ticket sales, the talent buyer assumes substantial risk in this fee structure. The talent buyer must pay the guarantee as well as other expenses—advertising, venue rental, security—regardless of the income from ticket sales. When there is an ice storm on the night of the show causing ticket sales to be low, the promoter's expenses would likely exceed income. And the show's promoter does not have the option of renegotiating the guarantee when ticket sales are lower than expected. However, some agents who have longtime relationships with certain promoters will offer a *fee reduction*—basically a break on the guarantee—when ticket sales are low. Agents do not like offering reductions, but sometimes will in order to keep the promoter from getting financially hurt too badly.

The flat fee is not only used for ticketed events. "The flat guarantee is used when the show is a soft ticket event, one with no admission charge or one where the admission fee admits the ticket buyer to a fair, festival, or theme park," says Charles Dorris, an agent and vice president with the William Morris Agency. Dorris explains that the flat guarantee fee structure is used instead of paying the act a percentage of ticket sales because, "the soft ticket show generates little or no ticket revenues." Steve Lassiter, an agent and partner with Agency for the Performing Arts (APA) says, "The flat guarantee is used when the event includes several [headline] acts. And an act performing a casino show with no admission fee would normally get paid a guarantee."

In addition to soft ticket shows, the flat guarantee is commonly used for club acts. When the act has shown that they can draw an adequate audience, they are able to negotiate a flat guarantee. However, when a club act has strong bargaining power, their agent tries to negotiate a more profitable backend deal.

THE BACKEND DEAL

When the agent negotiates a backend deal, one that determines the act's payment only after ticket sales revenues have been computed, depends on the negotiated percentage of box office revenues that the act receives. The backend deal is used when the show is a hard ticket show. "A *hard ticket* show is one that charges the real going rate for a ticket to see the act," according to Dorris. The agent and talent buyer have several different backend deals from which to choose, including the straight percentage, the per-ticket, the guarantee versus a percentage, and the guarantee plus a percentage.

Because attendance and ticket sales are not known when the booking agency and the talent buyer negotiate the backend deal, final payment is determined at *box office settlement* (settlement), a meeting normally held during or immediately after the show when representatives for the talent buyer pay the act. The tour manager or the tour accountant typically represents the act at settlement to review sales figures and examine receipts for any agreed-upon expenses. Discussions—sometimes arguments—during settlement usually concern the accuracy of accounting for ticket sales or *cover charges*, admission fees for non-ticketed shows, reported by the promoter. When the negotiated backend deal permits the talent buyer to deduct documented expenses, the tour manager or tour accountant reviews each expense at settlement to ensure that the promoter has not *padded*—inflated—any expense.

When reviewing the offer of the backend deal from the talent buyer, the agent must first know the venue's *total capacity*, the number of sellable seats or realistic capacity, as well as ticket price or prices, the rate of any local tax on tickets, and proposed deductible expenses. With this information, the agent calculates the gross potential, the tax on ticket sales, and the potential income after deductions. Using the projected income and deductible tax and expenses, the agent computes the *potential walkout* (walkout), the act's payment when the show is a sellout. When the walkout and the fee structure appear acceptable, the agent presents the offer to the artist's responsible agent who in turn presents it to the act's manager. (We discuss the written offer, including an example, in Chapter 11.)

DETERMINING GROSS POTENTIAL

Because backend deals vary according to the ticket sales, the agent must know the *gross potential* (GP), the total income from the ticket sales when the show is a sellout. The GP is hypothetical, because it is computed in advance of the show and is based on selling 100 percent of available tickets. It indicates the largest pool of money the show may generate from ticket sales, also called the *door* or *box office receipts*.

To calculate GP, the agent and talent buyer agree on the accurate number of tickets—based on the venue's capacity or the total number of seats—that can be sold for the show. When the agent is not familiar with the venue, he or she may call the venue manager to confirm the number of sellable tickets. The agent may also research *priors*, previous shows in the venue, to determine how many tickets similar acts sold. The agent must be certain that the talent buyer has not inflated the realistic number of tickets that can be sold, as ticket sales affect the act's earnings in the backend deal. Two variables that can impact the capacity of a given show are production elements and staging, because the sound consoles and the stage set may consume space otherwise available for ticket buyers.

The talent buyer also discusses the proposed ticket price or prices with the agent. The talent buyer is aware of ticket prices other acts have charged for the venue and suggests a price or prices. When the event is *general admission*, each ticket buyer pays the same amount but ticket holders are not guaranteed a specific seat; when tickets are *scaled*, ticket prices vary by the location of the seat in the venue and each ticket buyer is guaranteed a specific seat. When the agent wants more assurance that the ticket price is not too high or too low for the venue and market, he or she will once again research priors, both for the venue and similar venues in the same market. In addition, the agent informs the talent buyer when the act has set an upper limit on their ticket prices because they believe that higher prices would discourage their core fans from attending. Other acts, especially superstars touring stadiums, may have predetermined ticket prices that are nonnegotiable.

When the agent and talent buyer agree on the potential number of sellable tickets and the ticket price or prices, they compute the GP. For shows with general admission tickets, they multiply the number of sellable tickets by the ticket price to arrive at the GP. When the tickets are scaled, they multiply the number of tickets at each price level and total the results. Because the gross potential is based on a sellout show, the agent may use other ticket sales scenarios—60 percent or 70 percent—to determine a safer projection of box office receipts. The following example calculates the GP for a show with tickets scaled at $34, $50, and $65.

12,000 seats at $34 = $408,000

8,000 seats at $50 = $400,000

2,000 seats at $65 = $130,000

GP = $408,000 + $400,000 + $130,000

GP = $938,000

COMPUTING TAX ON TICKET SALES

Because many state and local governments impose an amusement or entertainment tax on concert tickets, a charge similar to a sales tax on tangible goods, the gross potential includes the tax and the ticket value. Therefore, when tax must be deducted from the gross ticket sales, the agent and the talent buyer calculate *net potential*, total income from ticket sales before tax. Although agents typically allow the talent buyer to deduct the amusement tax before calculating the act's percentage, the agent may insist on using the pretax gross to compute the backend. *Net potential* is the income the talent buyer earned from ticket sales after tax; GP minus net potential is the amount of tax paid to the government.

Calculating the net potential and the entertainment tax is not as simple as it may appear. The most common mistake is multiplying the GP by the tax rate to arrive at the amount of tax owed. Because GP is the face value of all potential tickets, it includes the value of each ticket *plus* its tax. Therefore, multiplying the GP by the tax rate results in taxing the existing tax in the GP, thereby overestimating the total amount of entertainment tax and underestimating the net potential.

The formula for determining net potential is: Net Potential = Gross Potential / (1 + tax rate). The following example demonstrates the correct method for calculating net potential when X is the Net Potential and the tax rate is 7 percent (.07 when converted to decimal form).

X (Tax Rate) + X = Gross Potential

X (.07) + X = Gross Potential

1.07 X = Gross Potential

1.07 X / 1.07 = Gross Potential / 1.07

X = Gross Potential / 1.07

Net Potential = Gross Potential / 1.07

DEDUCTING EXPENSES

In addition to the entertainment tax, the talent buyer may request that other expenses be deducted from the ticket sales. When the proposed deal is one that permits the talent buyer to deduct expenses before computing the act's percentage, the agent requests an *expense projection* sheet, a budget sheet that presents all deductions proposed by the talent buyer.

"The expense projection sheet gives us the financial equation to properly compute and project the act's breakeven and walkout potential," says Dorris. "The expense projection also lets us know that the promoter has done the necessary research. We don't want 'guestimates' of what expenses are when we consider the deal." The expense estimate is attached to the performance agreement and is an important document at settlement because it affects the act's percentage or potential percentage of backend earnings. "The expense projection sheet is critical to the backend deal and we don't leave it to chance."

The *variable expenses*, usually called *variables*, are expenses affected by ticket sales. Variables include the cost of renting the venue when the rental fee is a percentage of ticket sales. Box office fees typically include a 3 percent box office fee and a 3 percent charge for each credit card transaction, variables that cannot be determined until the box office has closed.

The talent buyer typically requests that the venue surcharges, also variables, be deducted from the ticket sales. Steve Lassiter explains, "A historic theater may assess a *restoration surcharge*, for example $2 per ticket, to help maintain the original character of the venue. Amphitheaters may use a *parking surcharge*, an additional fee added to the regular ticket price." The parking surcharge aids in preventing traffic jams outside the venue, because it eliminates the need for each car to stop and pay for parking at the show. It is worth noting that these add-on fees, including *service fees* from ticketing companies, are being met with increasing consternation by fans.

The *fixed expenses*, those not impacted by ticket sales, are easier to estimate than variable expenses because they will not vary, or will vary only slightly, after the agent and the talent buyer strike the deal. Common fixed expenses include the cost of advertising the show, payments to the local stagehands, and the venue charges for the ticket takers, the ushers, and the other venue staff.

THE STRAIGHT PERCENTAGE DEAL

A *straight percentage* deal pays the act a percentage of income from cover charges or ticket sales. Although it may be used for a show in any sized venue, the straight percentage deal, commonly called a *door deal* or *playing for the door*, is a common fee structure used to pay an emerging act playing in a small or medium-sized club. The agent for a major act is more likely to negotiate a "versus deal" or a "plus deal," both of which are discussed later in this chapter, than a straight percentage deal.

When the act has a door deal, settlement is held after the venue stops selling tickets or discontinues collecting the cover charge. At settlement, the talent buyer multiplies the door receipts by the agreed-upon percentage to determine the act's payment. Like other backend deals, the straight percentage deal depends on accurate accounting of ticket sales.

Door deals at small clubs are more vulnerable to inaccurate accounting when the talent buyer uses an employee to collect the cover charge—cash—at the door and does not use prenumbered tickets or a third-party ticket company. As a result, the act and their team may suspect that the talent buyer has underpaid them when their percentage of the door is lower than anticipated. The act may suspect that the employee responsible for collecting the cover charge has allowed friends into the club for free. And the act may be concerned that the club's employee at the door has *skimmed*, taking some of the cash from the door, when the settlement amount is lower than expected. Acts have several options that may help ensure a more accurate accounting of the door.

When the club collects a cash cover charge at the door, the act can diplomatically place a member of the act's team near the door to count each person who pays to enter. At the end of the night, the headcount multiplied by the cover charge should match the door presented at settlement. The presence of the act's representative at the door also discourages the employee from allowing friends to enter without paying. When the act keeps the *guest list*, the list of persons the act allows to enter without paying, to a minimum, the door more closely reflects the attendance.

When the club cooperates by selling printed tickets for the *presell*, or advance ticket sales, and *walkup*, those sold at the door the night of the show, the act has some evidence to review at settlement. As the ticket buyer enters the club, a venue employee tears the ticket, gives one half back to the ticket buyer, and places the *drop stub*, the remaining half, in a box or apron pocket. At settlement, the door receipts should equal the *drop*, the total number of drop stubs, multiplied by the ticket price. And *deadwood*, unsold tickets, plus the drop should equal *manifested tickets*, the total number of tickets that were either printed or in the box office computer. When the venue uses tickets, the box office representative presents a *settlement sheet*, a spreadsheet that includes the total number of tickets sold and the deadwood that remains, another aid to auditing ticket sales.

When considering the straight percentage deal, the agent may allow the talent buyer to deduct documented expenses before calculating the act's percentage. The agreement for this type of deal includes the expense projection sheet and may include fixed deductions, variables, or both. The straight percentage deal that allows deductions shifts much of the risk for the show from the talent buyer to the act, because the act is the last "expense" to be paid. When the talent buyer's deductible expenses exceed ticket sales, the act is paid nothing. Therefore, this fee structure is better for the talent buyer than a percentage deal without deductions. However, the act's agent would not present this deal to the act without strong assurance that the show will be profitable. It is more likely that the agent would negotiate one of the versus deals explained later in this chapter.

THE PER-TICKET DEAL

Although the support act is generally paid a guarantee, the agent for a strong support act may negotiate a *per-ticket* fee structure, a specific amount of money per ticket sold at each concert. This fee structure is not a common backend deal, but it has advantages for the headliner and the support act.

A good per-ticket deal usually gives the support act the potential to earn more money than a flat guarantee, especially when the headliner is a major act. Another attractive feature of this fee structure is it is easier for the support act's tour manager or tour accountant to calculate their payment at settlement. To determine the backend payment, the act's representative simply multiplies the number of tickets sold by the negotiated per-ticket fee, without the need for computing deductions or percentages. The headliner may use this fee structure to attract a strong support act, one with a large fan base, something that will help sell tickets.

However, when ticket sales are low, the support act may earn less using the per-ticket deal than they would have with a guarantee. Therefore, when the support act has strong bargaining power, their agent negotiates a per-ticket deal that includes a minimum guarantee in case ticket sales are low.

THE GUARANTEE VERSUS PERCENTAGE DEAL

The *guarantee versus percentage* deal, most often called a *versus deal*, offers the act the security of the guarantee as well as the potential to earn more than the guarantee from the backend percentage. In the versus deal, the act earns the guarantee or the percentage, whichever is *largest*. When ticket sales are lower than projected, the act is paid the guarantee; when sales meet expectations, the act receives the backend percentage of the box office receipts.

The guarantee portion of the versus deal is the same as a flat guarantee: a negotiated amount of money. The percentage side of the versus deal resembles a straight percentage deal. The two versus deals are the guarantee versus a percentage without deductions, and the guarantee versus a percentage with deductions. The deductions may include fixed expenses, variables, or both.

The Guarantee Versus Percentage Deal without Deductions. When considering the versus deal without deductions, the agent multiplies the net potential by the backend percentage to determine the walkout. Although it is easy to calculate walkout for this deal, the agent must be assured there is a significant difference between the guarantee and the walkout. When there is little difference, the deal is likely to be no better than a flat guarantee and the agent bargains for a higher percentage or larger guarantee.

The act's payment at settlement for this fee structure is determined by multiplying net ticket sales by the agreed-upon percentage. When the percentage is greater than the guarantee, the act is paid that amount. When it is less, the act is paid the guarantee.

The Guarantee Versus Percentage Deal with Deductions. The *versus deal with deductions* permits the talent buyer to deduct agreed-upon expenses before calculating the act's backend percentage. As with other fee structures that permit deductions, this fee structure requires the talent buyer to submit an expense projection sheet before the agreement is finalized. The talent buyer must also present documentation for deductions—receipts and invoices—at settlement.

When discussing this backend deal, the agent calculates the *breakeven* for the show, the percentage of tickets that must be sold to pay "all expenses, including the act's guarantee," according to Lassiter. When the act has a versus deal with deductions, they receive their backend percentage only after ticket sales surpass the breakeven. When the breakeven is high—80 percent or higher—the act is less likely to earn the backend percentage than if the breakeven percentage were lower. Therefore, unless the show has a high probability of success, when the breakeven is high the agent examines the requested expenses and negotiates to lower them.

THE GUARANTEE PLUS PERCENTAGE DEAL

The *guarantee plus percentage* deal, usually called simply a *plus deal*, is the most complicated backend deal, but it is quite common for major acts touring large venues. The plus deal has three primary components: the guarantee, the deductible expenses, and the backend percentage. Unlike the versus deal, the act is paid the guarantee before expenses are deducted. At settlement, the talent buyer deducts the documented fixed and variable expenses from the ticket revenues minus the guarantee. Breakeven for this fee structure includes the act's guarantee and the documented expenses. A variable expense the agent may permit in the plus deal is the *promoter profit*, normally 15 percent of the total fixed and variable expenses. The act's percentage is paid when the ticket sales surpass the *split point*, the figure computed by adding the breakeven and promoter profit. "The split point," Lassiter explains, "is the point after which each dollar grossed is split between the act and the talent buyer."

When computing the walkout for the plus deal with promoter profit, the agent first calculates net potential. The act receives the guarantee regardless of the backend; therefore it is treated as a fixed expense. Adding the guarantee to the other fixed and variable expenses, the agent arrives at the breakeven. The agent then calculates the promoter profit by multiplying the total expenses by the promoter profit percentage. Adding the promoter profit to the other expenses produces the split-point. The agent then subtracts the split-point from the net potential to arrive at the backend potential. Finally the agent multiplies the backend potential by the act's percentage. This backend amount plus the guarantee is the act's potential walkout.

Because the goal of the agent is to negotiate a plus deal that pays the act their backend income as well as the guarantee, the agent looks closely at the percentage of tickets that must be sold to reach the split-point. When the split-point approaches near-sellout sales, the deal is not prudent for the act and the agent negotiates to lower expenses or to increase the guarantee, or to do both. When the split-point is at a reasonable percentage of sales for the type of concert and the market, gaining payment from the backend is more likely.

The expense projection sheet for a guarantee plus percentage fee structure reveals the financial information necessary for the agent to evaluate the talent buyer's offer. (An example of an offer form with an expense projection sheet is presented in Chapter 11.) The expense projection includes the breakeven, the split-point, and the potential walkout, information that helps the agent evaluate the proposed deal. It demonstrates the vast amount of research the talent buyer must do when preparing an offer for a sophisticated backend deal that includes fixed expenses, variables, and the 15 percent promoter profit.

THE BONUS

The talent buyer expects the act and their team, including their label, fan club, and publicist, to help promote the show. To motivate the act and their team to provide aggressive promotional support for the concert, the talent buyer may offer a bonus that takes effect when the number of tickets sold for the show exceeds a specified level. The bonus may be used in combination with the backend deal or the flat guarantee.

Charles Dorris notes, "The agent may negotiate a guarantee of $7,500 plus a bonus of $2,500 when ticket sales reach or exceed 1,000. Although rarely used, the bonus structure may include an increase in the act's guarantee or backend percentage when their public profile increases after the performance agreement is signed. The bonus may apply when the act appears on a national television talk show, has a hit record, or wins an award. When something legitimately increases the act's reputation, they will sell more tickets."

NEGOTIATING FEE REDUCTIONS

The talent buyer may negotiate a fee reduction and pay the act less than the agent's *pitch price*, the initial asking price, when the talent buyer is able to offer the act favorable conditions, including good routing and multiple shows. A fee reduction may offer the talent buyer who would not ordinarily be able to afford the act's going rate the opportunity to book the act. When the talent buyer is not a working professional in the touring industry, he or she may employ a middle agent to negotiate on their behalf.

Taking Advantage of the En-Route Reduction

The act's agency and manager try to route the tour with the shortest distance between each show. When a tour requires the act and the crew to travel a long distance, expenses, including fuel for buses and trucks and overtime pay for drivers, increase. A long trip also forces the act and the crew to spend more time on the bus and less time settling into the hotel and enjoying some free time in the next city. As a result, when the agent has the opportunity to route the tour with short travel time between dates, something that keeps the act, the crew, and the act's team happy, he or she is eager to negotiate an *en-route reduction*, a fee structure that is typically less profitable for the act than a deal the agent would normally accept.

The talent buyer understands the importance of good tour routing and uses it as a bargaining tool whenever possible. The talent buyer frequently researches itineraries published in online publications including *Celebrity Access*, *Billboard.Com Tour Finder*, and *Pollstar Online* in search of tours that are developing. The talent buyer searches the itineraries of the acts he or she may want to promote, looking for shows already booked in the region. When there are open days between the shows already booked in the region, the talent buyer is in a good bargaining position to obtain an en-route reduction.

The agent is less likely to offer the en-route reduction when the tour is selling well and there are other talent buyers in the region interested in the act. However, when the agent is anxious to finish booking the tour, he or she may contact a talent buyer in the market that offers good routing and begin the conversation by offering an en-route reduction.

Capitalizing on Multiple Shows

When the talent buyer offers to book the act for *multiple shows*, or *multiples*, with the act playing two or more consecutive shows in the same venue, the agent is likely to accept a lower fee than he or she would for a *one-off*, a single show. Multiples offer several benefits: the act and crew enjoy more time and less work between shows; the agent earns multiple commissions; the act's team is pleased to see lower travel expenses; and the talent buyer may earn a substantial profit. For multiples to be successful, the act's fan base in the market must be large enough to fill the hall more than once.

Benefiting from Co-operative Buying

Co-operative buying (Co-op buying), when several talent buyers in a region book the same act, offers the act good routing as well as multiple bookings. When capitalizing on a co-op buying discount, each of the independent talent buyers agrees to promote the act on a different date, and all co-op dates fall within a short period of time, ideally seven or fewer days. The shows booked for a co-op buying deal are typically in non-competitive locations—markets or venues—yet they provide good routing for the tour.

Most colleges and universities have a student committee that promotes concerts on their campus. In an effort to help student talent buyers gain better bargaining power by using co-op buying, a group of university representatives formed the National Association of Campus Activities (NACA) in the 1960s. NACA has succeeded in attracting hundreds of campus talent buyers to their national conference and their seven regional conferences held each year, events at which acts may showcase, agents are available to discuss deals, and campus representatives "shop" for acts to book. The Association for the Promotion of Campus Activities (APCA), an organization formed in 1994, encourages campus representatives to take advantage of co-op buying through its annual conference and seven regional conferences as well.

Talent buyers from campuses in close proximity to one another attend an NACA or APCA conference and discuss acts of mutual interest. When several schools in an area are interested in booking the same act in the same time frame, they negotiate a co-op buying deal, usually before leaving the conference. To help campus talent buyers understand the benefits of co-op buying, agents are asked by each organization to disclose the act's fee for an *isolated date*, a single show, and the fee for a co-op date. When the act requires the talent buyer to pay travel expenses in addition to their fee, the co-op buyer pays less for the act's mileage than those who book isolated dates.

BARGAINING THROUGH THE MIDDLE AGENT

When the buyer is inexperienced in negotiating sophisticated fee structures and requires assistance booking the act, he or she may hire a middle agent to act as his or her consultant. The volunteers for local music festivals and the members of college concert committees often use the middle agent, someone with extensive experience in the concert industry, to contact the act's agent, negotiate the deal, and advise the talent buyer until the show is completed.

The act's agent typically prefers working with the middle agent because the middle agent understands standard industry practice and does not consume as much of the agent's time as would the novice talent buyer who needs many terms and procedures explained. When the middle agent books acts for several different festivals, the agent may negotiate several bookings through the same middle agent. And because the middle agent is ordinarily a better negotiator than the talent buyer, the act's fee may be substantially less than the pitch price, something beneficial to the talent buyer.

The talent buyer pays the middle agent a *procurement fee*, compensation for their work. The procurement fee may be a percentage of the act's total fee or the festival's entertainment budget. An alternative payment method is a flat fee for all work performed by the middle agent.

Knowing the assortment of artist fee arrangements arms the agent and the talent buyer with the vocabulary to bargain for an advantageous deal. Like a customer and the auto salesperson haggling price, the talent buyer discusses options with the agent. Steve Lassiter expresses the sentiment of most agents and talent buyers: "It isn't just about money; it's the game that excites me." When initial discussions appear to signal a potential deal, both parties begin to negotiate a binding deal. In the following chapter we discuss the process of negotiating and creating a contractual agreement to stage the show.

CHAPTER 11

Performance Agreements

Note: The reader is cautioned that contract law is a complex legal area. When creating the performance agreement, the reader is encouraged to seek the advice of an entertainment attorney familiar with the concert and touring industry.

At the heart of the concert is the deal the act strikes with the talent buyer. When the agent is satisfied with the talent buyer's fundamental offer, the agent typically cements the deal with the *performance agreement*, the written legal document that describes the terms and conditions of the deal. The performance agreement for a major tour typically contains three general sections: the essential terms of the agreement, the additional terms, and the *riders*, attachments to the basic contractual agreement that describe additional requirements the talent buyer must provide to assist the act with their technical, hospitality, security, and merchandising needs.

Although the act and the talent buyer may form a verbal (unwritten) performance agreement, enforcing it is difficult. When one party disagrees with the other's recollection of the stated promises, it is unlikely that valid evidence exists to help resolve the disagreement. Because performance agreements, even simple ones, contain many mutual promises, the written agreement is always better than the verbal agreement.

NEGOTIATING THE BASIC TERMS OF THE PERFORMANCE AGREEMENT

The basic terms of the performance agreement are negotiated between the agent, representing the act, and the talent buyer, representing the concert promoter. They begin negotiating the deal through a series of telephone calls or e-mails in which they discuss the basic deal points—venue, date, fee structure—of the proposed concert or concerts. When their discussions regarding the basic deal points draw to a close, the talent buyer and agent move to the next stage: establishing the deal in writing.

The negotiation of the key issues of the performance agreement progresses toward the written agreement when the agent suggests that the talent buyer submit an *offer*, usually a brief document referred to as an *offer form*, which contains the basic deal points, including the fee structure. Although the offer form includes information that may be included in the performance agreement, it is itself not the contractual agreement; it is an indication from the talent buyer that he or she is willing to receive the legal performance agreement from the agent that includes the basic deal points articulated in the talent buyer's offer as well as the standard terms and riders. After receiving the offer form, the agent presents it to the *responsible agent* (we described the responsible agent, or RA, in Chapter 1) for the act who, in turn, contacts the act's manager for final approval of the offer. In order to ensure that all necessary information is contained in the offer form, the agency for which the agent works may create a standard offer form. Some agencies have an online offer form to standardize and expedite the offer process.

PERFORMANCE OFFER FORM INCLUDING EXPENSE PROJECTION

Act:	Touring Band
Promoter:	Indie Promotions
Show Date(s):	August 1, 2007
Venue:	Anytown Arena
Ticket Price(s):	2,000 @ $120
	3,000 @ $85
	10,000 @ $32
Average Price:	$54.33
Capacity:	15,000
Gross Potential:	$815,000
Tax Rate:	9%
Taxes:	$67,294
Venue Surcharge:	$2 per ticket
Surcharge:	$30,000
Net Potential:	$717,706
Act Offer:	$100,000 plus *80%

*after expenses and 15 percent promoter profit

continued

Fixed Expenses	
Advertising	$40,000
PRO Licenses	$1,500
Hospitality	$4,000
Local Crew	$2,000
Ticket Takers	$3,000
Ushers	$3,000
Insurance	$20,000
Uniform Police	$3,000
Venue Security	$3,000
Towels	$100
EMT (2)	$500
Spotlights (4)	$150
Risers/Platforms	$400
Act Guarantee	$100,000
Fixed Subtotal:	**$180,650**
Variables	
Rent Guarantee	$25,000
Rent Percentage	8%
Ticket Commissions	3%
Credit Card Rate	3%
Total Variables:	**14%**
Estimates	
Breakeven	$210,058
Breakeven Tickets	3,866
Breakeven Percent	25.7
Deal Calculations	
Promoter Profit Rate	15%
Promoter Profit	$31,509
Split Point	$246,696
Split Point percentage	34.37% of total tickets
Act Rate (After Split Point)	80%
Walkout Potential	$476,808
Walkout Potential	66.44% of net potential

When the offer is accepted, the agent prepares and sends two or more copies of the performance agreement to the talent buyer. The talent buyer makes a photocopy of the agreement to use as the markup copy. He or she may solicit input from the venue's operations staff and the talent buyer's production coordinator and legal counsel as to the proposed terms of the agreement. After reviewing the agreement and writing comments on the markup copy, the talent buyer calls the agent to discuss any points of concern. When the promoter hiring the act is a fair or festival that provides the stage set, sound, and lights for the show, the talent buyer may include a *universal rider*, an addendum to the performance agreement that describes all sound, lights, and staging that will be provided for the act at the concert site. The universal rider is necessary because each act performing at the fair or festival must use these same basic production elements. The talent buyer may request that an *in-house rider*, additional terms that the talent buyer hopes to include in the agreement, also be attached to the agreement.

The talent buyer strikes the text when necessary, inserts new text when needed, and initials the modification when the agent approves the change. This process is followed for each change made to the agreement. After adding the approved modifications to each copy of the agreement, the talent buyer signs and dates each copy of the agreement and returns all copies to the agent. When the agent agrees to a substantive modification or a large number of changes, he or she may prefer to create and send a revised agreement.

When the agent receives the signed copies of the agreement, he or she sends them to the agency's contract department. The contract department will alert the agent to any questionable modification and ask the agent to discuss it with the talent buyer before signing the agreement. When the agreement contains substantive changes, the contract department may send the copies to the business affairs department for review or, in rare instances, forward them to the agency's legal counsel.

When the agency is satisfied with all changes, the agent initials each modification, counter-signs each copy, and returns one copy to the talent buyer. The performance agreement is legally enforceable in the civil courts when it contains a legal offer; contains promises to exchange *consideration*, something of value to each party entering into the agreement, typically the fee paid to the act and the performance that the talent buyer receives; and has been accepted by the representatives with legal authority to sign on behalf of the act and the talent buyer. When the agreement contains the necessary legal elements and is signed and dated by both parties, it is an *executed contract*, a legally binding document that holds each party responsible for each promise contained in the agreement.

After the performance agreement is fully executed, it may be modified with an *addendum*, the written attachment that adds new conditions to the original agreement, or an *amendment*, language that changes the agreement. The addendum includes signatures of the agent and the talent buyer to demonstrate that both accept the changes.

DRAFTING THE ESSENTIAL TERMS OF THE PERFORMANCE AGREEMENT

The first section of the performance agreement, typically contained on one page, contains the essential terms of the agreement for the concert or concerts. Sometimes referred to simply as "the contract," it serves as the primary understanding to which the additional terms and the riders are attached to form the comprehensive performance agreement.

When the act is affiliated with the American Federation of Musicians (AFofM) and the show is in the United States, the agent uses the standard AFofM union contract. The agency, working with the act's attorney, attaches *additional terms*, standard contract terms and conditions, to the contract. The agency sends the copy of the executed agreement to the union after all parties have signed it. The union sends an invoice to the act for *dues*, fees the act pays the union to perform each AFofM sanctioned concert.

The three fundamental elements of a legally binding contractual agreement—the offer, the consideration, and the acceptance—are revealed in this section of the performance agreement. Although the agent prepares and presents the performance agreement, the act is bound to the terms of the agreement; the agent merely represents the act. Therefore, the *offeror*, the legal party presenting the offer to enter into the agreement, is typically the act or the company formed by the act. The *offeree*, the party who receives the offer, is typically the talent buyer. The talent buyer may accept the offer as it is presented in the original agreement or negotiate to modify it. Although the talent buyer may legally decline to accept the offer contained in the performance agreement, he or she generally would not have sent the offer form were the deal not attractive. And when the talent buyer does not negotiate further or accept the offer, the agent may hesitate to work with the talent buyer in the future.

To be considered a legally binding agreement, the offer must be presented without fraud, coercion, or deception. Any misrepresentation of the act by the agent may cause the offer to be considered fraudulent and the agreement to be nullified in court. For example, when the lead singer for the act has left the band, and the agent fails to reveal this change to the talent buyer, the talent buyer may rightfully claim that there was deceit in the offer and seek to have the agreement invalidated.

Acceptance, another necessary element of the legally binding agreement, is demonstrated by the signatures of both parties and the date when signed by each party. By accepting the offer, the talent buyer indicates that he or she understands the terms and conditions contained in the agreement, including those presented in the additional terms and the riders. Furthermore, by accepting the offer, the talent buyer agrees to fulfill each promise described in the agreement.

To enter into the performance agreement, the talent buyer must have the legal capacity to evaluate and accept the offer. When the offeree is a minor, he or she typically has limited capacity to enter into the legal contractual agreement unless he or she has undergone the legal process to be judged able to sign agreements themselves. Individuals under the influence of alcohol or drugs may have limited capacity to evaluate and accept an offer, but the person who willingly drank alcohol or consumed "recreational drugs" generally does not have as strong a defense as someone who was tricked into drinking alcohol or was on prescription medication, two rare circumstances. Members of the military and citizens of other countries generally have limited capacity to enter into contracts in the United States.

The performance agreement customarily includes mutual promises of consideration: the talent buyer offers payment of money and the act promises the performance. When the show is a charitable event and the act agrees to perform for free, the services of the act are considered a "gift." Because it lacks consideration, the agreement to perform for free may not be considered a legal contract.

STATING THE DATE OF THE OFFER

The first paragraph of the agreement includes the date—day, month, and year—that the offer is made. The date of the offer is important when the initial agreement is later modified with an addendum. The typical statement is, "This agreement is made this _____ day of _____ (month), in the year _____."

ESTABLISHING WHO IS ENTERING THE AGREEMENT

The performance agreement, like other business contracts, begins by defining the parties who are entering the agreement. The talent buyer typically enters the agreement as a company and is represented by the executive responsible for booking the act. The act may enter the agreement one of several ways. The band may enter the agreement *severally*, as individual band members, causing each band member to assume total personal financial liability when the act is directed to pay a *judgment*, a financial payment ordered by the court, for illegal actions including failing to fulfill promises made in the performance agreement. When the band enters the agreement *jointly*, with members joined to form one company, the business entity may shield the individual members from personal liability. Consequently, when the act enters the agreement jointly, the type of company formed by the band is crucial. The act may also enter the agreement *jointly and severally*, causing the company and each individual band member to be liable for any judgment, something the act's team may discourage. When the act is jointly and severally liable, the talent buyer has more options for collecting the judgment, because the assets of each individual as well as the assets of the act's company are potentially at risk.

When the act is a solo artist, the agreement may include the act's *stage name*, the fictitious name by which he or she is commonly known in the music industry (e.g., Sting), or the act's legal name (e.g., Gordon Matthew Thomas Sumner). When the act is a duo or band, the agreement may include the act's stage name as it is commonly known in the music industry (e.g., Beastie Boys) or the legal names of each band member (Michael Diamond, Adam Horovitz, and Adam Yauch).

The band is considered a *general partnership*, more than one person doing business as a company, unless they form another legal business entity. However, each member of the general partnership is liable for expenses incurred by the company. The solo artist is generally viewed as a *sole proprietorship*, a business formation that is controlled by one individual or a married couple, unless he or she has created a different legal form of business. However, when the act's company is a sole proprietorship, the individual is personally liable for all expenses incurred by the sole proprietorship.

Because touring acts are susceptible to many types of lawsuits, the act may form a legal business entity to serve as the legal offeror (e.g., Beastie Boys Touring, Inc.). When the act forms a *corporation* or a *limited liability company* (LLC), the business entity is a *legal fiction*, a business formation with the legal rights of a real person. Because the corporation or LLC acts as a separate "person" in the eyes of the law, it may enter into agreements with other businesses or individuals, and it may sue or be sued by other companies or individuals. Therefore, the individual members of the band typically cannot be held personally liable for contractual promises of their corporation or limited liability company, only for the assets they have invested in the company. When the offeror is the act's corporation or LLC, the company promises to "present the services of" the act. When the act has little bargaining power, the talent buyer may, as a precaution, insist that the act enter the agreement severally.

When the parties to the agreement have been identified, the agreement typically creates a *descriptor*, a unique term for each party. The descriptor is written in capital letters to help readers recognize references to each party, something that continues consistently throughout the agreement. The talent buyer may be called "PURCHASER," "CLUB," or other logical term. However, the talent buyer typically avoids any implied employer/employee relationship, because the traditional employer is obligated to withhold income tax and social security for employees, something that is both time consuming and expensive for the talent buyer. As a result, the identifier "EMPLOYER" should *not* be used in the performance agreement. When the talent buyer is identified as PURCHASER, he or she is less likely to be considered a traditional employer by a branch of government. PURCHASER has thus emerged as the most common identifier for the talent buyer. The act has traditionally been referred to as "ARTIST" in performance agreements, a term that may be singular or plural and male or female.

DESCRIBING THE LOCATION OF THE SHOW

The location of the show includes the venue's name and its street address. When the show is part of an outdoor festival that has no street address, the description of the location, city, and state is necessary. Inclusion of the street address of the venue, especially when the show is at a club, reduces the likelihood of the act getting lost while trying to find the venue.

PRESENTING THE DETAILS OF THE SHOW

The details of the show include all pertinent information necessary to establish the obligations of the act. They typically include:

- The day of the week, date, and time of the show or shows
- The minimum length of the concert
- The time of the load-in
- The time of the sound check
- The billing: Headline, Co-Bill, Support Act, or Opening Act

DESCRIBING THE PAYMENT

The description of the consideration—the payment—includes those items that affect the act's income related to the show. This section includes:

- The total guarantee amount and/or the backend fee structure
- The amount of the deposit and deadline for the arrival of the deposit
- The description of any travel and accommodation expenses the talent buyer must pay
- The merchandising rate (the percentage of merchandise income the act pays the venue)
- The form of payment (Cash, Certified Check, or Cashier's Check)
- The currency of settlement (U.S. Dollars, Euros, or other Currency)
- The form of payment for earned percentages, bonuses, or overages, when applicable (e.g., "cash at settlement")
- The requirement that all of the ticket revenues above the estimated gross potential be paid to act in cash at settlement

BINDING THE ADDITIONAL TERMS AND RIDERS TO THE AGREEMENT

Because the signature of each party appears at the end of the simple one-page agreement and before the attachments, the additional terms and riders must be referred to and made a part of the comprehensive performance agreement. To do this, the basic agreement includes the statement, *Any terms presented on the reverse side of this contract as well as any addenda, including additional terms and riders, attached hereto are incorporated into this agreement with the full weight and force.* This statement makes all additional terms and riders that appear after the signature lines of the basic agreement a part of the comprehensive agreement with the full legal force of the basic agreement.

INCLUDING TIME LIMITS

To insure that the talent buyer signs and returns the performance agreement quickly, the agent may place a time limit on the offer. The *Cinderella clause*, as it is sometimes referred to, permits the act to withdraw the offer when the deadline for acceptance passes. This is a necessary clause, because the agent may refuse bids from other talent buyers while waiting for the agreement to be signed and returned by the talent buyer. The Cinderella clause included in the performance agreement often is, *If this contract is not signed and returned within ten days, ARTIST has the right to terminate this agreement without liability.*

ACCEPTING THE OFFER

Acceptance of the agreement is the final step in establishing the legally binding contract. The statement, *In witness whereof, the parties hereto, have hereunder signed their names to this agreement on the day and year last above written* appears above the signature lines. In addition to signatures of each party and the date when signed, the acceptance of the terms of the agreement by each party may include:

- The typed or printed name of the person signing on behalf of each party
- The legal entity—act or company—for which each party is signing
- The title of the offeror and the offeree
- The legal capacity of the individual—president, CEO—signing the agreement when representing an LLC or corporation

ADDITIONAL TERMS

Additional terms, sometimes referred to as "boilerplate" because attorneys often select and use these contract clauses as needed, are clauses commonly attached to the basic performance agreement that carry the same legal importance as the deal points stated in the basic agreement. The agency's contract department works closely with the act's insurance company, business manager, attorney, and management firm to create the additional terms, clauses that are unique to each act and each tour. The agency may have standard clauses that are included in the agreements of each act on the agency's roster. As previously mentioned, the page or pages that contain the basic deal points should include the statement that binds the additional terms, as well as the riders, to the performance agreement.

The following additional terms, or ones similar to these, are often included in the additional terms of the major act's comprehensive performance agreement. Each of these terms is followed by the language typically used in a performance agreement.

FORCE MAJEURE

The additional terms of the major act's agreement usually include the *force majeure* clause, language that allows the act to cancel the concert appearance, without legal liability, when certain stated conditions prevent them from performing. Force majeure, the French term for "act of God," commonly includes a lengthy list of circumstance that may occur and prevent the act from performing.

ARTIST's obligation to perform is subject to the detention or prevention by sickness, inability to perform, accident, means of transportation, act of God, riots, strikes, labor difficulties, epidemics, and any act or order of any public authority or any cause, similar or dissimilar, beyond ARTIST's control.

INCLEMENT WEATHER

When the act has included the force majeure escape clause in the contract, they may also include an additional clause stating that they, not the talent buyer, will determine when the performance is delayed or cancelled due to weather conditions. The act may also insist that they are paid when the event is cancelled due to weather conditions.

Notwithstanding anything contained herein, inclement weather shall not be deemed to be a force majeure occurrence and the PURCHASER shall remain liable for payment of the full contract price even when the performance(s) called for herein are prevented by such weather conditions. ARTIST shall have the sole right to determine in good faith whether any such weather conditions shall render the performance(s) impossible, hazardous, or unsafe.

ARTIST CANCELLATION

Acts are called upon, often with little advance notice, to appear on television talk shows or other events that are essential for their career development. Because these activities are vitally important to them, the act often adds a clause that reserves the right to cancel the concert with little advance notice.

Unless otherwise stipulated in writing, ARTIST may cancel the engagement without liability by giving PURCHASER notice at least thirty (30) days prior to the performance date.

ANTICIPATORY BREACH

The act enters the agreement because the talent buyer has established a good reputation in the industry and has maintained sound financial standing. Therefore, the act expects the talent buyer to maintain the same good reputation and dependable financial stability from the time the agreement is executed until the act is paid in full. When the act learns that the talent buyer has failed to pay another act, they may accuse the talent buyer of *anticipatory breach of contract*, the assumption that the talent buyer may neglect to fulfill promises presented in their performance agreement. To allow themselves the opportunity to legally cancel the agreement in the event that the talent buyer is in anticipatory breach of contract, the act may include an escape clause that allows the act to terminate the agreement and keep deposits and/or forthcoming fees when the talent buyer's good reputation changes.

This agreement is made in reliance upon PURCHASER's good reputation for the prompt discharge of all obligations. Notwithstanding any other provision contained herein, if, on or before the date of any scheduled performance hereunder, the financial standing or credit of PURCHASER has been impaired or is unsatisfactory, and as a result thereof, PURCHASER's ability to fully perform hereunder is uncertain or impaired, then ARTIST shall have the right to demand security, satisfactory to ARTIST, to ensure PURCHASER's promised compensation anticipated hereunder. When the requested security does not arrive by the date indicated, ARTIST may cancel the engagement without liability.

DEFAULT BY TALENT BUYER

The talent buyer makes many promises that should be carried out before, during, and after the performance. The act typically includes a clause that gives them the right to terminate the agreement when the talent buyer fails to fulfill one or more of the promises, including payment of the deposit and providing rider requirements, prior to settlement. In rare instances, the act may refuse to perform the concert and demand payment in full when the talent buyer neglects the performance agreement requirements.

If PURCHASER refuses or neglects to comply with its material obligations hereunder or to provide any of the items required of PURCHASER hereunder or fails or refuses to proceed with the engagements which are the subject of this agreement and/or to make any of the payments referred to herein, then in any of such events, (i) ARTIST, in ARTIST's sole discretion, may thereupon terminate this agreement without liability of any kind to PURCHASER, (ii) ARTIST shall have no further obligation to perform this agreement, (iii) ARTIST shall retain all amounts theretofore paid to ARTIST by PURCHASER, (iv) PURCHASER shall remain liable to ARTIST for any additional reimbursement amount and promised compensation herein provided, and (v) ARTIST shall be entitled to exercise all remedies then available to ARTIST at law or in equity. Without limiting the foregoing, PURCHASER shall indemnify ARTIST and hold them harmless from and against any loss, damage, or liability (including reasonable attorneys' fees) resulting from any breach or failure on the part of the PURCHASER to perform any of its warranties, covenants, or obligations hereunder.

BILLING

When the act is the headliner, they typically add a clause stipulating that the names of any support or opening acts appear less prominently in billing than the headliner.

ARTIST shall receive 100 percent sole star billing in any and all publicity releases and paid advertisements, including but not limited to programs, fliers, signs, lobby boards, and marquees. No other name or photograph shall appear in type with respect to size, thickness, boldness, and prominence of the type accorded the ARTIST. No other name or photograph shall appear on the same line or above the name of the ARTIST.

ADVERTISING MATERIALS

To ensure the quality of the advertising materials used to promote their shows, the act often creates and maintains an inventory of posters, flyers, and other printed materials for use by the talent buyers. The act may hire an outside production company to create advertising materials for radio and television. Major acts may include a clause that stipulates that only advertising material that has been provided by or approved by the act may be used by the talent buyer.

ARTIST shall provide to PURCHASER the only approved ad mats for use in connection with this performance and any and all broadcast advertising or promotion must be purchased from and coordinated with [insert name of advertising production company for act and/or tour]. No other advertising, either print or broadcast, shall be used without the explicit written consent of the ARTIST.

PUBLICITY

To control communication with broadcast and print journalists, a major act typically employs a publicist or publicity firm to coordinate tour press and to communicate with promotion and publicity departments of the artist's label as well as the talent buyer. The act generally insists that the talent buyer get their permission, through the tour publicist or publicity firm, for interviews and publicity materials. The act typically includes a clause that prevents the talent buyer from arranging photo opportunities, press receptions, VIP receptions, or other appearances without prior approval of the act's publicist.

PURCHASER agrees to cooperate with the publicist in charge of tour press for ARTIST before, during, and after the scheduled performance. Any and all requests for publicity (interviews, video magnification or taping, press coverage, pictures, and so forth) must be submitted in writing to ARTIST by mail or fax to [insert name and address of the tour publicist]. Phone or e-mail requests are not acceptable. It is further understood that PURCHASER will in no way obligate the ARTIST to participate in any photo session of any kind at any point in relation to this performance or any other event unless authorized and approved by ARTIST's publicist.

CONCERT PHOTOGRAPHS, RECORDINGS, AND BROADCASTING

Although some acts permit fans to use flash cameras and recording devices during their shows, major acts typically expect the talent buyer to control the taking of photos and recording of music during the concert. The act may demand that no flash cameras or recording devices be allowed in the concert venue. The act may also be concerned that the still photographers and the videographers might stand near the stage and block the views of some fans, especially those in the first few rows. Therefore, media photographers generally must obtain a *shooter pass*, the satin or laminated security pass that identifies him or her as an approved member of the media.

Both audio and video recording of concerts present potential copyright law violations and are typically not permitted unless authorized by the publicist. The act generally includes a clause in the agreement to prevent unauthorized broadcasting of the act's rehearsal or concert by any medium. Acts that permit their fans to make live recordings of shows customarily restrict the use of the recordings to personal or noncommercial use and prohibit sales of the recordings.

PURCHASER will deny entrance to any persons carrying cameras or video recording devices. Without limiting in any way the generality of the foregoing prohibition, it is understood to include members of the audience, press, and PURCHASER's staff. PURCHASER will prevent unauthorized photography, video recordings, and audio recordings during the performance. Members of the media who are authorized to photograph or create audio or video recordings of the ARTIST must do so under the direction of the ARTIST's designee. PURCHASER agrees to prevent the broadcasting, or reproduction by radio, television, or any other device of ARTIST's performance, or any part thereof. No portion of the performance or rehearsal rendered hereunder may be broadcast, photographed, recorded, filmed, taped, reproduced, or embodied in any form without ARTIST's prior written consent.

CONTROL OF PRODUCTION

The act's production personnel know best how to set up and operate all equipment and materials necessary to present the act. Therefore, the act typically includes a clause that requires the local stagehands, the venue's employees, and the talent buyer's staff, to take their direction from the act's production manager and appropriate department heads.

ARTIST shall have the sole and exclusive control over the production, presentation, and performance of concert event herein agreed upon. It is specifically understood and agreed that the representative of the ARTIST shall have sole and absolute authority in directing personnel operating all lighting and sound equipment during rehearsal, sound check, and each performance scheduled herein.

CONTROL OF PERFORMANCE

To prevent the local talent buyer from adding an opening act, a master of ceremony or a non-approved event to the show, the act customarily adds a clause to the agreement that insists on its total control of the performance.

ARTIST reserves the approval right of any other persons to appear in conjunction with this performance and the right to determine the length and nature of their performance(s). PURCHASER agrees that there will be no master of ceremonies, no welcoming speeches, no introductions, and no ceremonies at intermission except as ARTIST may approve and direct.

PERMITS AND RESTRICTIONS

The act's production manager must know in advance of the act's arrival when there are any laws, rules, or regulations that may affect production of the show. Permits may include a local pyrotechnics permit, licenses to use copyrighted music during the concert, state and local health permits, special events license, and amplified noise permit. (Permits and licenses are discussed in Chapter 12.)

PURCHASER must inform ARTIST's production manager or other responsible ARTIST representative of any legal or facility restrictions, limitations, or ordinances that may prevent any of the ARTIST's production requirements from being carried out.

INDEPENDENT CONTRACTOR

The act's contract often includes a clause that clearly indicates that the act is not an employee or employer to avoid previously mentioned governmental requirements. Furthermore, the language typically reminds the talent buyer that the performance agreement does not establish a partnership or other ongoing business relationship.

ARTIST signs this agreement as an independent contractor. This agreement shall not, in any way, be construed so as to create a partnership or any other joint undertaking or venture between the parties hereto, and neither party shall become liable for any representation, act, or omission of the other.

FOLLOW THE LAW AND RULES

Because the performance agreement must be based on promises to do lawful acts, it often addresses any potential illegal acts—requests for alcohol in a restricted venue or use of pyrotechnics when prohibited by local ordinances—that may be included the agreement. The agreement often includes a clause that protects the remainder of the agreement when one or more provisions are in violation of laws, rules, or regulations, including provisions included in local labor union agreements. In this way, laws, rules, and regulations supersede any illegal acts inadvertently included in the agreement.

If there is any conflict between any provision of this agreement and any law, rule, or regulation, such law, rule, or regulation shall prevail and this agreement shall be curtailed, modified, or limited only to the extent necessary to eliminate such conflict. Nothing in this agreement shall require the commission of any act contrary to laws, rules, or regulations of any union, guild, or similar body having jurisdiction over services or personnel furnished by PURCHASER.

Recognize Regulations and Requirements of Unions

In addition to the reference to union rules in the previous clause, the act may require the talent buyer to comply with *all* regulations of collective bargaining agents (unions) having jurisdiction over local personnel. To avoid responsibility for union sanctions related to the concert, the act may include a clause that transfers to the talent buyer all responsibility for following union regulations and requirements.

PURCHASER agrees to comply with all regulations and requirements of any union(s) that may have jurisdiction over any of the said materials, facilities, and personnel to be furnished by PURCHASER.

Favorable Conditions

Because the act's performance agreement may be an updated version of previous tour's agreement, it may include a clause that should have been removed but was overlooked. In anticipation of this occurrence, the act may include language that serves as a safeguard. This clause also ensures that addenda or riders added by the talent buyer do not reduce the effectiveness of the act's terms and conditions.

In the event of any inconsistency between the provisions of this contract and the provisions of any riders, addenda, exhibits, or any other attachments hereto, the parties agree that the provisions most favorable to the ARTIST shall control.

Liability for Talent Buyer Promises

The act frequently includes a clause requiring that the signature on the contract for the offeree be valid. This statement causes the individual who signs the agreement for the offeree to be personally responsible for the promises made in the agreement.

The person executing this agreement on PURCHASER's behalf warrants his or her authority to do so and hereby personally assumes liability for the payment of said price in full.

INSURANCE

Any event attended by a large number of people has the potential for someone to be injured. For this reason, the act customarily includes a clause that the talent buyer secure personal liability insurance to cover the audience, the local personnel, the act, and the act's crew in the event of an injury. The act typically requires the talent buyer to have insurance that includes coverage for damage to the venue and damage to, or theft of, music instruments. The act typically requires the talent buyer to provide proof of insurance for a minimum of one million dollars. Because the cost of liability settlements continues to increase, the venue may require the talent buyer to show proof of insurance that exceeds one million dollars.

PURCHASER agrees to provide comprehensive general liability insurance (including, without limitation, coverage to protect against any and all injury to person or property as the consequence of the operation of the equipment and instruments provided by ARTIST and/or ARTIST's employees, contractors, and agents). Such liability insurance shall be in the amount required by the venue, but in no event shall have a limit of less than $1,000,000 combined single limit for bodily injury and property damage. Such insurance shall be in full force and effect at all times that ARTIST or any of the ARTIST's agents or independent contractors are in the venue. ARTIST and ARTIST's booking agent shall be listed as additionally named insured under such insurance and purchaser also agrees to provide a policy of workman's compensation covering all of ARTIST's employees or third-party contractors. PURCHASER further agrees to provide full all-risks insurance coverage for all equipment and instruments provided by ARTIST and/or its employees, contractors, and agents against fire, vandalism, theft, riot, or any other type of act or event causing harm or damage to, or loss of, the instruments and equipment so provided. Certificates of insurance relating to the coverage listed above shall be furnished by PURCHASER to ARTIST at least fourteen days prior to the performance. The PURCHASER warrants that he or she has complete and adequate public liability insurance.

INDEMNIFICATION

The additional terms of the performance agreement also typically include a clause that requires the talent buyer to *indemnify*—hold the act legally harmless—in the event that the talent buyer does not obtain the proper level of insurance. Indemnification prevents a third party, including an injured fan, from holding the act legally responsible when the talent buyer has not purchased the appropriate insurance policies and is unable to pay costs associated with a judgment or out-of-court settlement. Unless the artist demonstrated negligence that causes the injury, the talent buyer accepts all legal and financial liability.

PURCHASER hereby indemnifies and holds ARTIST, as well as their respective agents, representatives, principals, employees, officers, and directors, harmless from and against any loss, damage, or expense, including reasonable attorney's fees, incurred or suffered by or threatened against ARTIST or any of the foregoing in connection with or as the result of any claim for personal injury or property damage or otherwise brought by or on behalf of any third party person, firm, or corporation as the result of or in connection with the engagement, which claim does not result from the active negligence of the ARTIST.

THE AGENT IS NOT RESPONSIBLE

The booking agent does not control the actions of the act for which he or she procures performance agreements. For this reason, the agent usually insists on the inclusion of a clause that causes both the talent buyer and the artist to recognize that the agent is not responsible for act's actions.

Agency is not responsible for the actions of ARTIST and merely acts as agent. Neither ARTIST nor PURCHASER will name agency in civil action or other lawsuit related to ARTIST's actions.

DO NOT TRANSFER THE AGREEMENT

When the talent buyer enters into the performance agreement with the act for one or more concerts, he or she may want to sell one or more dates to another talent buyer. When the talent buyer uses this business maneuver, called a *buy and sell deal*, he or she negotiates a fee for each concert, and later "sells" one or more of the shows to another talent buyer for a higher price. The difference in price—the "markup"—may result in a substantial profit for the original talent buyer. Because the act has no assurance that the new talent buyer has the expertise to promote the show in a professional manner, they often include a *nontransfer clause* in the performance agreement.

This agreement cannot be assigned or transferred without the written consent of ARTIST.

MODIFICATIONS TO THE AGREEMENT

Both parties to the agreement may discuss and agree to changes after signing the agreement. To prevent misunderstandings regarding changes agreed to verbally, the performance agreement includes a clause that requires all modifications to be in writing and signed by both parties.

This agreement contains the complete understanding of all parties and cannot be amended, supplemented, varied, or discharged except by an instrument in writing signed by both parties.

THE LEGAL VENUE

The legal venue is the location—county and state and city or county—of the court that the lawsuit would be tried in the event of a breach of contract dispute. The act typically includes a clause that requires the legal venue to be the city in which the act's attorney or the booking agency's legal counsel does business.

The validity, construction, and effect of this contract shall be governed by the laws of the County of [insert preferred county] in the State of [insert name of preferred state], regardless of the place of the concert performance.

THE TERM DESCRIBING THE ACT

Because *ARTIST* may refer to one or more band members, *PURCHASER* may indicate an individual, company, or group of persons, and the pronoun *he* has historically been used to mean male or female in contract clauses, a clause may be added to the agreement that clarifies the terms.

The terms ARTIST and PURCHASER used herein shall include and apply to the singular, the plural, and to the male or the female gender.

Copyright Licenses

Federal copyright laws require a *performance rights license*, the permission to perform the song in public, for copyright protected music. The act typically includes a clause that requires the talent buyer to secure the license or licenses from ASCAP, BMI, and/or SESAC (formerly The Society of European Stage Authors and Composers), the largest performing rights organizations in the United States.

PURCHASER will secure all necessary copyright licenses and permissions including, but not limited to, performance rights licenses, necessary to present this event.

Proper Performance Venue

The act typically includes a clause that requires proof that the talent buyer has obtained a bona fide rental agreement for the days and times of the show or shows and to pay all venue rental fees. The act commonly includes a clause that requires the talent buyer to provide a venue that is a safe and proper place for the show.

PURCHASER represents that he or she has a lease covering the performance(s) which will be shown to the ARTIST or their representative, at their request. PURCHASER agrees, at his or her own expense, to furnish the aforementioned venue on the dates and times agreed upon in this performance agreement, including rehearsal and sound check. PURCHASER promises that all facilities provided, including dressing rooms near the stage, will be well heated, adequately lighted, clean, and in good order with all necessary personnel including police, ushers, ticket sellers, and ticket takers.

Nondiscrimination

The act has a moral and legal interest in preventing discrimination of any sort regarding potential ticket buyers. While the act typically intends for a nondiscrimination clause to indicate their objection to discrimination, their legal counsel includes the clause to transfer to the talent buyer all criminal and civil liability for legal charges of discrimination.

PURCHASER agrees that admission to, and seating in, the venue will be without regard to race, color, religion, or national origin.

Sponsorship Rights

Corporate sponsorship of concerts and tours has increased dramatically since 1980. Tour sponsors are typically guaranteed exclusivity for their product or service. To prevent competitive sponsors at the local level, the act commonly includes a clause to prevent the talent buyer and the venue from securing a sponsorship deal without the act's permission.

All forms of sponsorship, whether part of an ongoing series or specifically for ARTIST's show, must be authorized by ARTIST. ARTIST shall have, at their sole discretion, the authority to deny any potential sponsor requested by PURCHASER.

COMPLIMENTARY TICKETS

The act may include a clause in the performance agreement that limits the number of complimentary tickets offered by the talent buyer to journalists and the general public. The act often requires the talent buyer to make complimentary tickets easily recognizable to help prevent complimentary tickets from being sold.

PURCHASER agrees to distribute no more than one percent of the available seats or tickets as complimentary tickets relative to this performance. Further, PURCHASER must supply the representative of ARTIST a statement detailing to whom each complimentary ticket was given. Each complimentary ticket will be issued only as a fully punched, or in some other distinguishable way, complimentary ticket. PURCHASER agrees to supply radio, television, and print media personnel with complimentary tickets from the above-mentioned allotment.

TAXES

A clause may be added to the agreement by the act that requires the talent buyer to pay all taxes related to the show. The talent buyer may negotiate to modify the statement to indicate that the amusement or sales taxes for the tickets is deducted from the gross box office revenues before any percentages are paid to the act. The talent buyer may ask that *work dues*, fees assessed by the AFofM for each touring musician, be the act's responsibility.

PURCHASER shall pay and hold ARTIST harmless of and from any and all taxes, fees, dues and the like relating to the engagement hereunder and the sums payable to ARTIST shall be free of such taxes, fees, dues, and the like.

TALENT BUYER ADDITIONS AND MODIFICATIONS

Because the performance agreement is usually created by the act's team, the clauses contained in it are to the act's benefit. After reviewing the performance agreement, the talent buyer may ask to modify some clauses or add others. The clauses that follow are among those that may be added at the talent buyer's behest.

DEFAULT BY THE ACT

The talent buyer protects himself or herself from losses that are the result of the act's failure to appear and perform by including a clause that transfers financial liability to the act when the show is cancelled without cause. This is an addition to the performance agreement that the act's team often resists.

ARTIST shall indemnify and hold PURCHASER harmless from any loss, damage, or liability (including reasonable attorneys' fees) resulting from any breach or failure on the part of ARTIST to perform any of its warranties, covenants, or obligations hereunder.

THE RADIUS CLAUSE

The talent buyer can prevent the act from performing in the same market in the same general time period with the inclusion of a *radius clause*, the requirement that the act not perform for the stated period of time before and after the event within the specific geographical area.

ARTIST agrees that during the period commencing on the date hereof and ending 30 days following the date hereof, ARTIST shall not furnish ARTIST's performing services within a 90-mile radius of the venue stated in this agreement without PURCHASER's written permission.

REVIEW OF RIDERS

When the riders are not available when the offer is presented, the talent buyer may ask to insert a Cinderella clause. The clause permits the talent buyer to terminate the agreement after reviewing all rider requirements. The Cinderella clause created to protect the talent buyer is: *"Purchaser must receive all of the complete and accurate riders by _____ (date and time) and the riders must be mutually agreed upon by PURCHASER and ARTIST or this agreement is null and void."*

RIDERS

As defined on page one, a rider is an attachment to the basic agreement that describes additional requirements the talent buyer must provide to assist the act, including their technical, hospitality, security, and merchandising needs. Because many of the rider requests proposed for inclusion by a major touring act are related to and under the supervision of the production manager, these provisions may be included in one comprehensive document known as a *production rider*. As previously mentioned, each condition presented in the riders, regardless of how insignificant it may seem to the talent buyer, is a legal part of the agreement. When the talent buyer ignores an obligation contained in the rider, the act may consider the buyer in breach of contract, demand full payment, and refuse to perform. However, the act is unlikely to enter into a legal fray with the talent buyer unless the cause of the breach is a major omission, including failure to obtain liability insurance, required licenses and permits, and failure to provide adequate stage set, sound systems, and lighting.

The act's team creates the riders that are unique to the act and the tour. The act typically has a rider for *one-off* or *fly dates*, shows that are not part of a structured tour and for which the act carries only their instruments, and *backline shows*, concerts for which the talent buyer provides all technical support except the act's backline gear and their instruments, as well as a *tour rider*, for an organized tour for which the act carries all production equipment as well as their instruments, backline, entourage, and production crew. The size of the anticipated venues is the major consideration when creating the language for the riders. Riders for stadium tours are much more extensive than are those of arena tours, and those for theater and club performances are less complicated than arena show riders.

As the production elements of concerts have grown in size and sophistication, the riders have increased in length. The technical rider and performance agreement for the Beatles' 1964 U.S. tour was six pages long. A major stadium tour launched today may have riders that total more than one hundred pages.

THE CONTACT INFORMATION

The rider for a major tour typically contains the key contacts for the act. This allows the talent buyer's staff and the venue's employees to communicate with the appropriate representatives for the act. The contacts may include the booking agency, the manager or management firm, the tour manager, the production manager, the tour merchandising company, the company responsible for creating tour advertising materials, and the tour press coordinator. The list may also include record label contacts for the publicity, the artist development, and the tour promotion departments.

THE TABLE OF CONTENTS

The table of contents lists the page number for the topics included in the riders, allowing the readers to locate specific information without the need to browse the entire rider or riders.

THE TECHNICAL RIDER

The *technical rider*, often called simply the *tech rider*, provides information regarding the physical areas, the local personnel, the electrical power, and the equipment that the act requires when they arrive at the venue. When the act is touring without sound and lights, their technical rider provides a detailed description of the sound and lighting systems which the local talent buyer must provide. The technical rider may include the following:

- The location of the house console and monitor console in the venue

- The dimensions—height, length, and width—of the stage risers

- The *stage plot*, the diagram of instrument, amplifier, microphone, and direct input box locations on the stage. When the act does not tour with production equipment and personnel necessary to assemble their stage set and gear at each venue, the talent buyer depends on the stage plot to illustrate how the stage must be arranged before the act arrives to assemble their backline equipment (Figure 11.1).

- The *input list*, often included in the stage plot, is the description of the microphone or direct input signal feeding each channel of the sound console, including the preferred brand of microphone and the desired signal processing effects for each channel (Figure 11.1).

- The *lighting plot*, the detailed diagram that indicates the types of lighting instruments, their locations, and the color of each instrument. The lighting plot is essential when the act does not tour with lighting equipment and personnel and requires the talent buyer to provide lighting equipment as illustrated in the lighting plot (Figure 11.2).

- The *rigging plot*, the diagram of all rigging points and the maximum weight that each rigging point must hold (Figure 11.3).

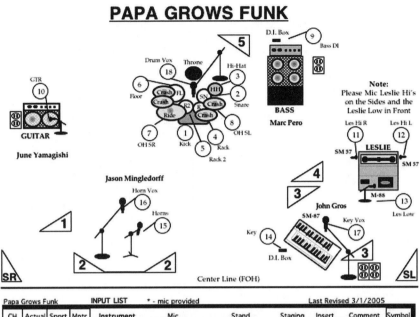

PAPA GROWS FUNK

CH	Actual	Spprt	Mntr	Instrument	Mic	Stand	Staging	Insert	Comment	Symbol
1			1	Kick	M88 or Beta 52	Small Boom	U.S.C	COMP 1	Not a D 112	K
2			2	Snare	Shure 57	Small Boom	U.S.C			SN
3			3	Hi Hat	AKG 451 (cond)	Small Boom	U.S.C			HH
4				Rack Tom	Seinheiser 604	Claw or Boom	U.S.C	GATE 1		R
5				Rack Tom 2	Seinheiser 604	Claw or Boom	U.S.C	GATE 2		R2
6				Floor Tom	Seinheiser 604	Claw or Boom	U.S.C	GATE 3		FL
7				Over Head SL	ATM 33R	Boom	U.S.C			OH ->
8				Over Head SR	ATM 33R	Boom	U.S.C		over ride	OH <-
9			4	Bass	Active D.I.	DI Box	U.S.L	COMP 2	Needed	Bass
10			5	Guitar	Shure 57	Small Boom	U.S.R			GTR
11			6	Leslie Hi L	Shure 57*	Claw or Boom	D.S.L	COMP 3		Les Hi
12			7	Leslie Hi R	Shure 57*	Claw or Boom	D.S.L	COMP 4		Les Hi
13			8	Leslie Low	M88 or Beta 52	Small Boom	D.S.L	COMP 5	Mic Side	Les Lo
14			9	Keys	Passive D.I.	DI Box	D.S.L		Needed	Key
15			10	Tenor Sax	Seinheiser 421	Small Boom	D.S.C	COMP 6		Horn
16			11	Tenor Vocal	Beta - 58	Boom w/ Round Base	D.S.C	COMP 7		Jason
17			12	Key Vocal	Beta - 87 *	Boom w/ Round Base	D.S.L	COMP 8	phantom	John
18			13	Drum Vocal	Shure 58	Boom w/ Round Base	U.S.C			

Papa Grows Funk   INPUT LIST   * - mic provided   Last Revised 3/1/2005

Monitors: Mix 1 - GTR, K, Sn1, Sn2, Hh, Hh 2   Mix 2 - Horn, Horn Vox   Mix 3 - Les Hi's, Les Lo, Key, Key Vox
Mix 4 - Bass   Mix 5 - K, Sn1, Bass, Key, Key Vox, Drum Vox
Side Fills - K, Sn, Sn2, Horn (little bit), Key Vox (little bit)

FIG. 11.1. THE STAGE PLOT CREATED BY: *E!* (DUDEONTOUR@HOTMAIL.COM) FOR THE BAND PAPA GROWS FUNK (WWW.PAPAGROWSFUNK.COM).

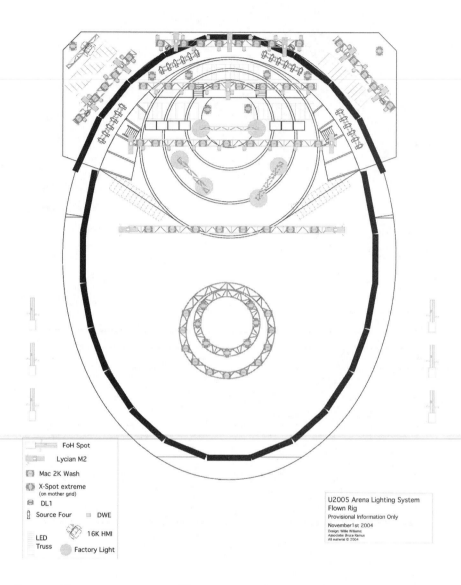

FoH Spot
Lycian M2
Mac 2K Wash
X-Spot extreme
(on mother grid)
DL1
Source Four   DWE
LED
Truss   16K HMI
Factory Light

U2005 Arena Lighting System
Flown Rig
Provisional Information Only
November1st 2004
Design: Willie Williams
Associate: Bruce Ramus
All material © 2004

FIG. 11.2. THE LIGHTING PLOT FOR U2 CREATED IN NOVEMBER 2004 BY WILLIE WILLIAMS, DESIGNER, AND BRUCE RAMUS, ASSOCIATE.

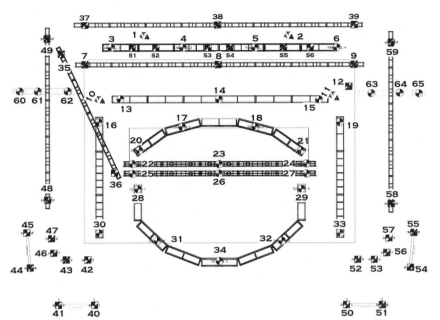

SHAKIRA ARENA TOUR 2006

AUDIO LOAD TOTAL: 25492LBS / 11563KGS

LIGHTING LOAD TOTAL: 35777LBS / 16228KGS

VIDEO LOAD TOTAL: 7000 LBS / 2631KGS

TOTAL SHOW LOAD: 68269LBS / 30422KGS

| Project SHAKIRA 2006 |
| Title RIGGING PLOT ARENA |
| Scale 1:140 | Date 080806 | drawn by JERRY RITTER |
| Version | REV 6 |

FIG. 11.3. THE RIGGING PLOT, INCLUDING THE MEASUREMENT AND WEIGHT SPREADSHEET, CREATED BY JERRY RITTER FOR THE SHAKIRA ARENA TOUR 2006.

Point#	Point Description	US& - DS=Y	Left& - Right=X	Lbs	Kg	Hook Height		Motor Type
	Lighting Points							
1	FA 1	45'	-16'	0	NA	NA		NA
2	FA 2	45'	16'	0	NA	NA		NA
3	Par wall 1	42' 6"	-24'	975	442	75'	22.7 M	1 ton
4	Par wall 2	42' 6"	-8'	1225	556	75'	22.7 M	1 ton
5	Par wall 3	42' 6"	8'	1225	556	75'	22.7 M	1 ton
6	Par wall 4	42' 6"	24'	975	442	75'	22.7 M	1 ton
7	Gauze 1	39'	-30'	450	204	70'	21 M	1/2 ton
8	Gauze 2	39'	0	600	272	70'	21 M	1/2 ton
9	Gauze 3	39'	30'	400	181	70'	21 M	1/2 ton
10	FA 3	31'6"	-25'	0	NA	NA		NA
11	FA 4	31'6"	25'	0	NA	NA		NA
12	SL lighting C/P	36'	32'	750	340	70'	21 M	1/2 ton
13	SR spot truss	30'6"	-22'	1100	499	70'	21 M	1 ton
14	Ctr spot truss	30'6"	0	1598	725	70'	21 M	1 ton
15	SL spot truss	30'6"	22'	1100	499	70'	21 M	1 ton
16	SR trapeze	24'	-27'	1460	662	70'	21 M	1 ton
17	US ellipse 2	25'	-8'	1362	618	70'	21 M	1 ton

continued

Point#	Point Description	US& - DS=Y	Left& - Right=X	Lbs	Kg	Hook Height	Motor Type
	Lighting Points						
18	US ellipse 3	25'	8'	1362	618	70'	1 ton
19	SL trapeze	24'	27'	1460	662	70'	1 ton
20	US ellipse 1	20'6"	-18'6"	900	408	70'	1 ton
21	US ellipse 4	20'6"	18'6"	850	386	70'	1 ton
22	Austrian US 1	17'	-20'	950	431	70'	1 ton
23	Austrian US 2	17'	0	1125	510	70'	1 ton
24	Austrian US 3	17'	20'	925	420	70'	1 ton
25	Austrian DS 1	15'	-20'	950	431	70'	1 ton
26	Austrian DS 2	15'	0	1125	510	70'	1 ton
27	Austrian DS 3	15'	20'	925	420	70'	1 ton
28	DS ellipse 1	11'	-18'6"	940	426	70'	1 ton
29	DS ellipse 5	11'	18'6"	775	352	70'	1 ton
30	SR trapeze	1'	-27	1460	662	70'	1 ton
31	DS ellipse 2			1160	NA	70'	1 ton
32	DS ellipse 4			1130	513	70'	1 ton
33	SL trapeze	1'	27'	1460	662	70'	1 ton
34	DS ellipse 3	-6'	0	1860	844	70'	1 ton
35	SR cable truss (LTS)	39'	-34'	900	408	75'	22.7 M	1/2 ton

continued

Point#	Point Description	US& - DS=Y	Left& - Right=X	Lbs	Kg	Hook Height	Motor Type
	Lighting Points						
36	SR cable truss (LTS)	15'6"	-24'	650	295	75'	22.7 M	1/2 ton
37	US curtain truss	47'	-28'	500	227	75'	22.7 M	1/2 ton
38	US curtain truss	47'	0	650	295	75'	22.7 M	1/2 ton
39	US curtain truss	47'	28'	500	227	75'	22.7 M	1/2 ton
	Stage right audio points						
40	SR PA 1	-14'	-28'	3239	1469	75'	22.7 M	2 ton
41	SR PA 2	-14'	-36'	2312	1049	75'	22.7 M	2 ton
42	SR PA 3	-4'	-30'9"	600	272	75'	22.7 M	1/2 ton
43	SR PA 4	-4'	-33'3"	600	272	75'	22.7 M	1/2 ton
44	SR side PA 5	-2'	-40'6"	2213	1004	75'	22.7 M	1 ton
45	SR side PA 6	6'	-39'6"	1582	718	75'	22.7 M	1 ton
46	SR side PA 7	9"	-36'	500	227	75'	22.7 M	1/2 ton
47	SR side PA 8	3'3"	-35'	500	227	75'	22.7 M	1/2 ton
48	SR audio cable truss	6'	-40'	450	204	75'	22.7 M	1/2 ton
49	SR audio cable truss	34'	-40'	750	340	75'	22.7 M	1/2 ton
	Stage left audio points						
50	SL PA 1	-14'	28'	3239	1469	75'	22.7 M	2 ton
51	SL PA 2	-14'	36'	2312	1049	75'	22.7 M	2 ton

continued

Point#	Point Description	US& - DS=Y	Left& - Right=X	Lbs	Kg	Hook Height		Motor Type
	Lighting Points							
52	SL PA 3	-4'	30'9"	600	272	75'	22.7 M	1/2 ton
53	SL PA 4	-4'	33'3"	600	272	75'	22.7 M	1/2 ton
54	SL side PA 5	-2'	40'6"	2213	1004	75'	22.7 M	1 ton
55	SL side PA 6	6'	39'6"	1582	718	75'	22.7 M	1 ton
56	SL side PA 7	9"	36'	500	227	75'	22.7 M	1/2 ton
57	SL side PA 8	3'3"	35'	500	227	75'	22.7 M	1/2 ton
58	SL audio cable truss	6'	40'	450	204	75'	22.7 M	1/2 ton
59	SL audio cable truss	34'	40'	750	340	75'	22.7 M	1/2 ton
			Stage right video points					
60	SR video	32'	-33'8"	900	408	70'	21 M	1 ton
61	SR video	32'	-40'	1300	590	70'	21 M	1 ton
62	SR video	32'	-44'4"	1300	590	70'	21 M	1 ton
			Stage left video points					
63	SL video	32'	33'8"	1300	590	70'	21 M	1 ton
64	SL video	32'	40'	1300	590	70'	21 M	1 ton
65	SL video	32'	-44'4"	900	408	70'	21 M	1 ton

*** Array offloads to pullbacks when in place

continued

	LBS	KGS
Audio load total	25492	11563
Lighting load total	35777	16228
Video load total	7000	3175
Total show load	**68269**	**30967**

- The request for a forklift when it is needed to move production equipment
- The *crew call*, the number of local stagehands for load-in, running crew, and load-out of the show. The crew call includes the number and qualifications, including truck unloaders, truck loaders, follow-spotlight operators, and local riggers
- The *runners*, the local employees who know the city, have a valid driver's license, and have a safe driving record, to run errands for the production crew
- The production office assistants
- The electrical power requirements, including amperage, phase, and grounding, for the sound and lighting systems
- The list of offices needed for the production staff and the tour management and staff, and the number of telephone lines, high-speed Internet connections, electrical power outlets, and photocopiers
- The description of the parking and electrical power needed for the tour's trucks and buses
- The requirement that a washing machine and a clothes dryer be provided in the backstage area
- The request for a local physician to be available in case a member of the tour needs medical attention, because the tour's schedule does not allow time for the act and crew to make an appointment to see a physician

THE HOSPITALITY RIDER

Although there is the common misconception that hospitality riders are simply lists of ridiculous requests for backstage comforts (see the Web site *thesmokinggun.com* for examples of humorous hospitality rider requests), the overwhelming majority of requests in the hospitality rider of a major act are reasonable and necessary. Nourishing food, including fresh fruit and vegetables, may seem like a nuisance to the talent buyer, but it is a valid request for the act and their crew, who often spend more than twelve hours in the venue. The hospitality rider often includes the following requests:

- A local hospitality assistant or assistants when the act has a touring caterer
- The type of ground transportation needed, often a passenger van or a limousine, to carry the act from the airport to the hotel, from the hotel to the venue, from the venue to the hotel, and from the hotel to the airplane or jet—when the act travels by commercial airline or private jet
- A description of the kind of hotel accommodations desired when the tour does not use a travel agency to book hotels
- The number of dressing rooms needed and a description of the dressing room accommodations, including the number of towels, the temperature, the lighting necessary to put on makeup, and the number of restrooms with a shower

- Food and beverage requirements for the touring crew, including breakfast, lunch, dinner, and after-show refreshments
- Food and beverage requests for the act and their entourage, including dinner, dressing room snacks, and after-show refreshments
- A rooming list when the talent buyer is responsible for securing hotel rooms for the act, the entourage, and the crew

THE SECURITY RIDER

The security rider explains to the talent buyer, venue security director, the local security company for the show, and the local police the needs and conditions requested to protect the act, their crew, and their equipment. When the act has a tour security coordinator, the rider identifies him or her and requests that the local talent buyer provide a copy of the security rider, or the security requirements, to the venue security director. The security rider for a major act may include the following requests:

- A condition that the talent buyer warrants and guarantees proper security for the act, the act's personnel, the guests of the act, and the act's equipment, including their instruments
- A request for the name and telephone numbers—mobile and office—of the venue security officer; the names and telephone numbers of the key venue administrators; the location and telephone number of the local police precinct nearest the venue; and the contact information for the appropriate federal and state law enforcement officials
- A stipulation that all contact information be in the hands of the tour security coordinator no less than fifteen days prior to the act's arrival
- A request that the talent buyer send copies of the security plan, including the *method statement*, a general description of how the local security staff will protect the act; the *risk assessment*, an estimate of the dangers that the act may encounter; and the *emergency evacuation plan*, the exit locations and means of transportation when there is an emergency, including a bomb threat, a fire, or a tornado
- A promise that the talent buyer provide the tour's security director the venue security staff rosters, the police and medical staff rosters, the posted security positions, the check-in times for security staff, and the cost estimate for the event security, all of which to arrive one day prior to the performance
- The directive to schedule a security meeting that includes the tour security coordinator, the venue security director, the representative of the local security firm that provides security personnel for the venue, the police department's representative, and the fire department's representative, before noon of the day of performance
- The request for a *security briefing*, a second security staff meeting, usually scheduled ninety minutes before the doors open to paid ticket holders, to discuss the positions of the local security staff and the police officers

- A requirement that the talent buyer provide a copy of each *incident report*, the description of any injury or arrest, to the tour's security coordinator at the *security debriefing*, a post-concert security meeting
- A description of the *stage barrier*, the portable structure placed between the audience and the stage, and the number and the type of security personnel to be positioned near the stage barrier
- A requirement that the talent buyer prohibit unauthorized persons from entering the backstage area and the description of the procedures for issuing security passes, often referred to as backstage passes
- A condition that only the authorized venue employees and the local stage crew be in the venue during sound check
- The mandate that no beverage may be sold in a glass or metal container when the show is an arena, stadium, or outdoor festival concert

THE MERCHANDISING RIDER

As discussed earlier in the book, merchandise sold at the concert venue is a major source of income for the act. The right to sell merchandise that includes the act's name or image is under the control of the act, and they typically hire a tour merchandising company to manage and market their tour merchandise. The merchandising company and the act's team create a rider that defines the terms and conditions that the local venue must follow in exchange for a percentage of merchandise sales. (When the talent buyer is an independent concert promoter who rents the venue, he or she typically does not receive a percentage of merchandise sales.) The merchandise rider may include the following clauses:

- A *most favored nations clause*, which requires that the talent buyer negotiate the lowest *merchandising rate*, the percentage of merchandise income that the act pays the venue, that any other act received
- The stipulation that the merchandising rate be submitted to the act in writing
- Language indicating that the act's merchandising company, or other representative of the act, has sole and exclusive rights to sell non-food and nonbeverage items, including audio and video recordings, photographs, T-shirts, and program books that embody the name, image, or likeness of the act
- A clause that specifies that it is the talent buyer's obligation to prevent, to the best of his or her ability, the sale or distribution of merchandise, especially counterfeit merchandise, by anyone other than the act's representative inside or outside the venue
- A statement that the talent buyer will provide the space, the stands, and the tables to sell the act's merchandise before, during, and after the show
- Language reminding the talent buyer that he or she does not receive a percentage of merchandise sales

BREACH OF CONTRACT

When the talent buyer or the act fails to fulfill the promises detailed in the performance agreement, they are in *breach of contract* and the other party may seek compensation for damages, typically foregone income and all *out-of-pocket expenses*, expenditures related to the concert that cannot be cancelled or will not be returned. The methods for obtaining compensation include negotiating a buyout of the concert, filing a lawsuit in the civil courts, and using mediation or arbitration.

When ticket sales for the concert are weak, the talent buyer may offer the act a *buyout*, a financial settlement in exchange for the right to cancel the show. The touring act is rarely eager to agree to the cancellation, though, because, according to William Morris agent Charles Dorris, "the act has substantial tour expenses and depends on income from each show." Dorris points out that "the tour typically cannot be rerouted to adjust for the cancellation." Therefore, the act is more likely to ask for the full guarantee or to demand that the show be presented as scheduled. Although the talent buyer would suffer a substantial loss by paying the act their fee and canceling the show, he or she would avoid paying some concert expenses, including the venue services and the local crew salaries.

Regardless of the financial settlement for canceling the show, the act tries to avert the negative publicity that inevitably follows a poorly attended concert. "When the concert is cancelled for any reason, the act typically controls the information in the press release to avoid any perception that the act was responsible for low ticket sales," says Dorris. "Low ticket sales may be due to factors unrelated to the act, including too many shows in the market during the same time period."

The party who alleges breach of contract is referred to as the *injured party*. To collect *damages*, financial compensation for losses caused by the breach of contract, the attorney or law firm representing the injured party may file a lawsuit. *Compensatory damages*, the amount of money that the injured party would have earned had the contractual promises been fulfilled, are the most commonly awarded damages. When the talent buyer is found to be in breach of contract, the act is awarded compensatory damages that equal the amount of money the court believes the act would have earned from the concert, including the guarantee, the estimated percentage of ticket sales, and the projected merchandise income. When the act is in breach of contract, the talent buyer may be awarded an amount equal to the projected net profit he or she would have earned from the concert.

Punitive damages, those intended to punish the person who is in breach of contract and to discourage similar behavior in the future, are much less common than compensatory damages. When state statutes permit punitive damages for breach of contract, the judge or jury may award them if it is determined that fraud was present in the offer or acceptance, or if the talent buyer falsely stated that he or she had secured the rental agreement for the venue.

Liquidated damages, a specified amount of money that must be paid by the party in breach of contract, may be included in the agreement to avoid potential litigation. Because concert attendance and expenses are difficult to estimate when the show is cancelled, the act may prefer liquidated damages to compensatory damages. Talent buyers often dislike liquidated damages because they may be less money than out-of-pocket expenses at the time of cancellation by the act. In addition, liquidated damages rarely compensate the talent buyer for potential profits from ticket sales.

Although it is necessary to employ the services of an attorney when filing the lawsuit for breach of contract, mediation and arbitration are two forms of *alternative dispute resolution* that may help resolve the disagreement without the need for an attorney. *Mediation* is a form of alternative dispute resolution that includes an impartial third party. In mediation, the mediator, the third party, meets with the talent buyer and the act. After considering all the facts of the dispute, the mediator recommends a non-binding settlement of the disagreement. *Arbitration*, the more formal type of alternative dispute resolution, is binding—each party must accept the recommendation. The court may direct the parties of litigation to seek mediation or arbitration before the trial to encourage the parties to settle their disagreement without the need for a trial. The arbitration clause may state that any dispute or disagreement resulting from the performance agreement be settled by the American Arbitration Association, a not-for-profit organization formed in 1926 to provide impartial experts to assist in resolving a dispute. Arbitration may be a time-consuming process and it often requires each party to travel to the arbitrator's city.

PART III

ORGANIZING THE SHOW:
WHAT TO EXPECT FROM A CONCERT PROMOTER

CHAPTER 12

Insurance, Licenses, and Permits

Performance agreements and venue rental agreements require the talent buyer to assume legal responsibility for mishaps including personal injuries that may occur as a result of the concert, damage to the act's instruments and equipment, and damage to the venue. The talent buyer also agrees to secure all licenses and permits necessary to stage the show. In addition, the talent buyer must be prepared for the financial losses that may result from the cancellation of the show due to the act's inability to perform, inclement weather, or other circumstances beyond the talent buyer's control. When the talent buyer neglects to secure the necessary insurance policies, the proper licenses, and the compulsory permits, the show may not go on. And when the show does not go on, the legal and financial repercussions can sink the talent buyer's business and end his or her career.

INSURANCE

The talent buyer must be able to provide a valid *certificate of insurance* to show the act that is being secured for a concert and the venue where the concert is to be held that the buyer has purchased the appropriate insurance. This certificate details the type of insurance purchased and level of coverage, as well as the amount of the premium. When the talent buyer has not secured the necessary insurance policies at the required minimum amounts of coverage, the venue and the act are reluctant to proceed with the show. Bob Williams, president of Atlanta's Philips Arena, warns, "If they can't produce a good certificate of insurance, we don't open the doors."

James Chippendale, President/CEO of CSI Entertainment Insurance, a company that has placed insurance policies for more than 3,000 events, including concerts of Bob Dylan, LL Cool J, Ludacris, the Rolling Stones, and Coldplay, has had to do last-minute damage control for promoters who neglected to secure the proper insurance. "I've had a promoter call me and say, 'I have trucks sitting outside of the venue waiting to load in, and I don't have proof of insurance to show the venue, and we cannot load in without it."

"The act wants to see it, the proof of insurance, at the time they're signing the contract," Chippendale explains. Phil Casey, Vice President and head of the Los Angeles office for International Creative Management (ICM), agency for hip-hop artists including DMX and Nas, says, "We would not book a date knowing it was not insured. That would be too great a liability for the client [the act] but for the agency as well."

But agencies book thousands of engagements, and an occasional oversight occurs. "When it does slip through the cracks [of the performance agreement], the act's booking agent calls a day or two before the show and asks for the proof of insurance that the promoter may not have," Chippendale says. "That means the artist isn't going to perform until the insurance is in place." This last-minute panic creates anxiety for the promoter, the act, and the venue. When the venue padlocks the loading dock doors and the act refuses to play the concert, the concert promoter must pay all of the expenses, including the act's fee, the venue rental fee, and all the out-of-pocket expenses, including advertising.

The need for insurance cannot be overstated. A liability claim for an injured concert attendee escalates considerably when the injured fan retains a law firm with expertise in personal injury lawsuits. Generally, the concert promoter is responsible for securing liability insurance for a concert, but the venue and the tour are wise to make sure they are covered as well. "The rudest awakening of all could be for the venue that thinks the promoter has coverage, and then there's an incident and a claim and the venue finds out the promoter has no coverage," says Chippendale. The venue is likely to be held liable for personal injuries or deaths when the concert promoter has no insurance.

When a lawsuit erupts, trial lawyers tend to name any and all parties involved in the event. Peter Tempkins, Executive Vice President and National Practice Leader for the Film, Music, and Touring Division of Dewitt Stern Group insurance company, has placed insurance for concerts including the H.O.R.D.E. tour, the Lilith Fair, the Warped tour, Taste of Chaos, and the Amnesty International tour. "When a patron slips during the concert because of a spilled soft drink, the law firm representing the injured person sues everyone, including the venue management company, the security company, the concert promoter, the band, the concessions company, and even the soft drink manufacturer. I call it the 'shotgun approach' because they sue everyone and know that someone will pay." Tempkins adds, "The attorneys for the individuals and companies being sued usually negotiate a settlement to avoid legal fees that may exceed the settlement amount." Attorneys for injured clients have even sued the radio station that was the media sponsor, the tour sponsor, and the act's manager. And settlements, especially in the cases when several patrons have been injured, quickly add up to millions.

OBTAINING CONCERT INSURANCE

To purchase insurance for a concert, the promoter typically works with an *insurance broker*, an insurance professional who specializes in entertainment insurance. The insurance coverage that these brokers advise promoters to purchase include policies for general liability, event cancellation, artist non-appearance, weather, and pyrotechnics. The broker represents the promoter and places the insurance policy with an *insurance carrier*, the company that issues the policy and assumes the risk. Unlike insurance agents that represent one carrier, entertainment insurance brokers have several carriers from whom to choose and the broker may "shop" for the most appropriate carrier. Chippendale advises promoters to work with a broker who specializes in the live entertainment field. "Find a broker who knows the business," Tempkins adds. "There are only about a half dozen brokers who understand concert industry insurance. They know the carriers with whom they can place concert policies and there are only a few carriers that are active in writing these policies."

To advise the promoter, the insurance broker reviews the performance agreement and the venue rental agreement before the promoter signs each of the contracts. "I try to review the act's rider for the promoter before the promoter signs it. Sometimes I must review it after it is signed," says Tempkins. Chippendale agrees: "It's imperative that the insurance broker gets involved at the time [the promoter] negotiates each contractual agreement. It can be the contract with a supplier, the contract with the venue, or the contract with the artist. They'll all have an insurance clause and those insurance clauses need to be reviewed by your insurance advisor." "The contractual obligations that the promoter is getting into are a big, big, big, big piece of the puzzle," he adds.

"The insurance broker tries to protect the concert promoter by assessing the risk of the event and by recommending insurance options," says Chippendale. "The promoter hires us and we go out and place the insurance [with a carrier] for them on their behalf. I watch the back of the promoter. I say, 'You go do what you do best: find the venue, find the artist, and promote the concert.' I will make sure that we have your butt protected.'"

The broker makes recommendations, but does not do a "sales job" on the promoter. "I stay pretty neutral. I say, 'Here are the options out there,' and then I let the promoter make the final decision," Chippendale says. "When I'm working on a huge event and it's going to be a new 75,000-person summer music festival, the promoter calls me and says, 'Here's what we've got,' and we'll sit down and chat about the event itself. Then the promoter says, 'How do we protect ourselves?' I then start going through the different areas of protection and the costs of those different areas." "I never try to sell people on anything. I just steer the promoter in the right direction, and then place the coverage on the promoter's behalf."

When the promoter signs the performance agreement or venue rental agreement before the insurance broker has reviewed them, the situation can be disastrous. "There can be clauses in there that say 'You are going to have $15 million dollars in insurance for this show.' When you sign that contract, you are promising that you're going to get $15 million, but you may not be able to afford to get that amount, or it [the agreed-upon amount of insurance for your show] may not be available. So then you have to back peddle and renegotiate the contract, which can be very difficult sometimes," Chippendale explains. The promoter should not procrastinate when it comes to securing concert insurance; it should never be assumed that the insurance broker will be able to find a carrier to offer the policies.

The job of the insurance broker has become more difficult, because major insurance carriers have had to make large *payouts*, or settlements, in the last two decades. Many insurance carriers are "gun shy" after reading highly publicized reports of fans injured in mosh pits, crushed to death in crowd stampedes, burned in the flames of fires at clubs, and injured or killed in post-concert gang fights. Jeffrey Insler, North American CEO of Robertson Taylor International Insurance Brokers, a firm that has placed insurance for the mega-festival Bonnaroo and other major events, acknowledges that the job of the broker has gotten more difficult. "The insurance market has been tough since [September 11, 2001]. There's no question about that," says Insler. "The insurers have pulled their horns in. They are much more selective, and there are fewer insurers" writing concert insurance.

COMMON TYPES OF CONCERT INSURANCE

Although there are myriad insurance policies available to the concert promoter, the promoter and the broker analyze the risks related to the show and determine the types of insurance that are essential and those that are affordable. Together, the broker and the promoter create a list of incidents that may result in an economic loss to the promoter and develop strategies for reducing those risks.

Although insurance may reduce the promoter's risk for many uncontrollable occurrences, it cannot protect the promoter from all potential catastrophes. "Our job is to help protect the promoter from risk as a result of the concert," Chippendale explains, "but we can't protect the promoter from everything." Income from low ticket sales is the concert promoter's biggest nightmare, but it is one of the few financial disasters that insurance cannot alleviate. Chippendale explains, "I can't help the promoter if he or she goes belly up because nobody showed up to the show. But what I can do is protect the promoter from going belly up if the artist doesn't show up at the show and the promoter has to return all the money."

General Liability Policy. The touring act and the concert venue routinely require the promoter to provide *general liability insurance*, coverage for losses that come as a result of personal injury or property damage from a concert. The general liability insurance policy, sometimes referred to as *spectator liability insurance*, may offer the promoter financial protection in the event that a member of the audience, the act, the touring crew, the venue staff, or the local stage crew is injured. Chippendale describes general liability insurance as "the absolute necessity coverage." Venues often require the promoter to have a general liability policy of at least one million dollars. However, the minimum amount of liability coverage may be larger depending on the venue, the act, and the number of attendees.

The performance agreement and the venue rental agreement typically require the *named insured*, the concert promoter, to include the act and the venue as *additional insured*, individuals and businesses that are not affiliated with the concert promoter but are protected under the insurance policy. Other businesses that fear lawsuits from a concert, including the event sponsor and the tour sponsor, may ask to be named as additional insured as well.

Event Cancellation Policy. When the show is cancelled, the promoter loses ticket revenues, must pay the ticket service company a fee to administer ticket refunds, and has to return any income paid by local sponsors. The money the promoter has spent on advertising is *sunk costs*, expenditures that are not retrievable. Therefore, the concert promoter often obtains *event cancellation insurance*, a policy that reimburses the promoter for the net loss caused by the event being cancelled, postponed, or rescheduled.

The event cancellation policy typically reimburses the promoter for major losses when the event is cancelled due to an occurrence listed in the policy. Causes for cancellation normally covered include floods, hurricanes, and other catastrophic weather conditions that prevent the majority of the audience from traveling to the venue; delays in transportation; delays in delivery of equipment essential for the show; and some national disasters. When a condition named in the insurance policy disrupts the concert, the insurance carrier compensates the promoter for financial losses that may include foregone income from tickets sales; *out-of-pocket expenses*, money already spent; and revenues that must be returned to the sponsors.

The event cancellation policy describes events and conditions that are not covered under the basic policy. These exclusions may include the cancellation of the event due to: poor ticket sales; war or riots; nonappearance of the act; and fraud, misrepresentation, or concealment. Excluded causes for cancellation, including an act of terrorism and a declared war, may be negotiated, however, and, for an additional cost, be included in the policy.

Artist Nonappearance Option. A performance agreement routinely includes an *escape clause*, a statement that permits the act to cancel the show when one of the conditions listed in the performance agreement occurs. As explained in Chapter 11, the act may cancel the show without liability when they are unable to perform due to unforeseen circumstances, including an illness or injury to the singer or other key band member; the breakdown of a bus or truck preventing the arrival of the act, the crew, or the equipment in time for the show; or when the act is invited to appear on a nationally televised talk show or awards ceremony. When the act is unable to perform, the concert promoter must cancel, postpone, or reschedule the event and suffer the financial losses. Because nonappearance of the act is commonly excluded from the basic event cancellation policy, the promoter may purchase an *artist nonappearance option*, an addendum to the insurance policy that provides reimbursement to the promoter in the event that the act does not appear. The artist nonappearance option is frequently added to the policy, because there is a strong probability that every act will cancel an event at some point in their career.

Some acts have been known to feign illness as a justification to cancel the show, so insurance carriers may include exclusions to the nonappearance option that discourages bogus excuses. Reasons for the act's nonappearance that are often excluded from the policy include injuries caused to the act by hazardous activities (hang gliding or mountain climbing); a preexisting medical condition (often including AIDS); poor voice quality that is not due to illness; and contractual disputes.

Weather Insurance. Weather is the least controllable cause of lost revenue for the concert promoter or festival organizer. Although weather insurance has customarily been included in policies for outdoor concerts and festivals, promoters of indoor events may also purchase weather insurance, because high winds, rain, snow, and lightning can affect the revenues of indoor shows as well.

Adverse weather conditions can cause ticket sales, especially walk-up sales on the day of the show, to be lower than projected. Festivals and shows produced by venues earn a substantial amount of income from food, beverage, and merchandise sales. Because weather may greatly reduce these and other sources of income, weather insurance is a valuable "safety net" for concert promoters and festival organizers.

Pyrotechnics Insurance. The use of pyrotechnics (pyro) as a part of a concert presents a danger to the audience, the act, and the crew, because fireworks are ignited in close proximity to the stage and seating areas. When the liability insurance policy excludes injuries caused by pyro, the promoter must ensure that the event has insurance to adequately protect him or her from lawsuits due to pyro related injuries or deaths. Chippendale explains that the promoter's insurance broker contacts the act to ensure that the act's pyro company is adequately insured. "[The promoter] must get proof of insurance from the pyrotechnics company naming the promoter as an additional insured." Because many cities have enacted local ordinances that prohibit the use of pyro in small venues, pyro is most often used in large venue concerts but not in club shows. Promoters may choose to include pyro insurance in the concert insurance policy as a precaution. "We can add it. It's not really that major of a deal anymore. We just don't see it much," adds Chippendale.

DETERMINING THE COST OF INSURANCE

Insurance carriers are somewhat like Las Vegas odds makers: they underwrite insurance policies based on the probability that something may or may not happen. Variables that may influence the *insurance premium*, the amount of money the concert promoter pays for the policy, include the history of insurance claims for the genre of music, the act or acts, and the venue. The total number of patrons attending the event and the location of the show—city, county, and state—typically affects the cost of concert insurance as well.

The most influential factor considered by the insurance companies when calculating the cost of general liability insurance is the genre of music. The carrier and broker develop a *multiplier*, the cost of insurance per attendee (alternatively referred to as *per capita* or *per head*), after determining the perceived risk of the genre of music. The rate per attendee varies greatly. "Classical music may be fifteen cents per attendee," says Chippendale. "Rock can be up to fifty cents, heavy metal, rap, and hip-hop may be a dollar or more. That's why when I [wrote the insurance policy for] George Strait, I was taking the genre of his music into consideration. Country can be anywhere from twenty cents up to thirty cents per attendee."

Rap concerts have long been a tough sell for insurers, in large part because of a reputation for its fans—deserved or not—for violence. When asked if the reluctance of insurance carriers' to write policies for rap concerts is an obstacle, Phil Casey at ICM, agency for hip-hop artists including DMX and Nas, replies, "Hell yes, it's a problem. It's forcing some in the hip-hop business to possibly do shows without insurance," a risky proposition. Casey confirms that when it comes to rap shows, "If you're trying to buy a new policy, it's damn near impossible." And while he says concert insurance is not the booking agency's responsibility, Casey explains, "We would not book a date knowing it was not insured. That would be too great a liability, not only for the client but for the agency, as well."

Rap is not the only genre that is put under the magnifying glass by brokers and carriers. Carriers have millions of dollars at stake, so they evaluate the risk of any genre that has a history of claims. "They absolutely do their homework on all the youth-oriented, harder stuff, including heavy metal and harder alternative music," says Chippendale.

When an act has had an unusually high number of insurance claims during previous tours and shows, insurance brokers have a difficult time placing the liability policy with a carrier. The carriers "search the Internet and databases for occurrences or even police responses at a concert," Chippendale says. "It's amazing how information they can find on the Internet." A band that performs a genre of music that routinely permits dangerous audience behavior, including moshing and stage diving, may be considered an *uninsurable risk*, an act that the carrier considers too risky to insure.

The cost of an event cancellation policy is determined by the total budget for the show, because the insurance carrier is obligated to reimburse the promoter for the previously mentioned lost revenues. According to Chippendale, the event cancellation premium is based on a percentage of the event's budget that typically ranges from 0.75 percent to 1.5 percent. When weather insurance is included in the policy, the carrier uses scientific data, including actuarial tables based on variables as precise as the geographic area where the show will be held, and the time of day, the day of the week, and the month of the show to help determine the risk. "If [your concert] is in Florida during hurricane season, the rate is going to be much higher than if the concert were in Arizona in the summertime." When the event cancellation policy includes the artist non-appearance option, the carrier considers the act's history of canceled shows to help calculate the additional cost.

LICENSES AND PERMITS

Both the concert venue and the act require the promoter to obtain all licenses and permits necessary to stage a concert. The promoter of an outdoor concert or festival must navigate the river of government offices and agencies to determine the rules, regulations, and paperwork required by the city, the county, and the state in which the event is held.

PERFORMANCE RIGHTS LICENSES

The United States, like other developed nations, recognizes the need to protect the rights of songwriters who create music and the publishers who administer income from songs on the behalf of the songwriters. Federal copyright law grants several exclusive rights to the owners of copyrighted songs, one of which is the right to perform the work in public.

Venue rental agreements as well as performance agreements stipulate that the concert promoter must purchase the necessary *performance rights licenses*, agreements that permit the act to perform copyright protected music during the show.

It would not be cost effective for the songwriter or the publisher to issue a performance rights license for each public performance of the song. Therefore, several performance rights organizations (PROs), the largest of which are the American Society of Composers, Authors, and Publishers (ASCAP), Broadcast Music, Inc. (BMI), and SESAC (originally the acronym that stood for the Society of European Stage Authors and Composers, but now known simply as SESAC) operate in the United States to issue performance rights licenses, often called simply *PRO licenses*, collect the fees for the licenses, and distribute a portion of the fees to songwriters and publishers on their roster.

Each PRO has a Web site that offers a wealth of information about its licensing procedures. The promoter may obtain the concert license online or contact the general licensing department of the organization. The license application varies by the issuing organization, but the cost of each is based on the gross ticket revenues generated by the concert—the number of tickets sold multiplied by the ticket price or prices.

Jerry Bailey, Director of Media Relations for BMI, describes his organization's licensing process as simple and user friendly, as is the process for ASCAP and SESAC licenses. "When a concert promoter calls our licensing department, we immediately fax them the application that includes the terms of the agreement and a simple fee schedule. Schedule A, the rates for ticketed concerts, has two levels. Venues with less than 10,000 seats are charged 0.30 percent of the gross ticket revenues per show. Concerts in venues with 10,000 or more seats have a rate of 0.15 percent of box office receipts." BMI offers a Schedule B, licensing rates for benefit concerts or attractions with no admission charge. "This rate schedule is based solely on seating capacity," says Bailey. The Schedule B rate for a show in a venue of 250 seats or less is $15.00; the license for a concert in a venue with 40,001 or more seats costs $480.00." In addition to the calculated license fee per event, BMI charges an annual fee of $150. The annual fee is the same for promoters who present one show a year as for those who promote many concerts each year.

The PRO license allows the concert promoter to use any song in the organization's catalog. Bill Lee, head of licensing for SESAC, explains, "The license allows [the act] to play one song from our catalog or they can play a thousand songs. It's the same license fee." When the concert or festival includes multiple acts, the show typically includes songs from more than one of the PRO catalogs, and the promoter must secure a license from each organization. Bailey says that the promoter may only need to procure the license from one PRO. "The act may be a solo artist who is an ASCAP writer and does not play songs from the BMI or SESAC catalog. In these rare instances, the promoter would not pay for a BMI or SESAC license."

Although PRO licenses for concerts are relatively inexpensive and easy to secure, some promoters do not buy them. Lee believes that novice promoters are most susceptible to overlook the obligation to purchase the PRO licenses. "Honestly, the concert industry is not that difficult for us. It's usually just ignorance of the copyright laws when you're dealing with a small promoter, because they may not be familiar with their obligations. Major promoters are not a problem; they know that PRO fees are a budget line item and they take it off the top."

Because promoters who produce and present many concerts have the burden of securing PRO licenses for each show, the North American Concert Promoters Association (NACPA), an international trade association of the largest talent buyers in North America, created a centralized program to simplify the licensing process for its members. "NACPA administers the PRO agreements for each member of the organization and they compile all the [concert attendance] reports that the members submit to NACPA," says Lee. "NACPA sends one report with one payment for its members. In exchange for making the job of PRO licensing departments easier, the NACPA members get a reduced rate," he adds.

PYROTECHNICS LICENSE

The act, the venue, and the promoter demand proof that a tour's pyro company has insurance to cover touring pyro technicians and the devices that they ignite during the show. To obtain the necessary insurance, the tour's pyro company must provide proof that each of the tour's pyro techs is licensed. However, the branch of government with jurisdiction over the venue requires a local license as well.

Marie Kun, General Manager of Long Island-based Zenith Pyrotechnology, says, "It would be impractical and almost impossible for a tour to have a pyro license for every place that needs one. Therefore, most pyro companies hire a local pyro operator. The local operator helps the promoter and the tour pyro company obtain the appropriate local license. It depends on the requirements of each particular city. The local pyro operator generally does not fire the show, some local operators do the paperwork, but in some cities we do the paperwork and the local operator just shows up and gets a check." The local fire marshal may conduct a site inspection and review the pyro plans before allowing the technicians to fire the show.

OTHER CITY, COUNTY, AND STATE REQUIREMENTS

Each city, county, and state may have laws and regulations that govern concerts. Indoor shows generally have fewer government-imposed requirements than do outdoor shows, but failure to obtain the necessary permits and licenses can allow the insurance carrier to avoid paying claims for injuries related to the concert or revenues lost due to the event's cancellation. And promoters often feel an ethical obligation to follow government regulations, because each requirement is intended to ensure the safety of concert attendees and workers. The following permits and licenses vary by city, county, and state, but they include those that are often required of concert promoters, especially those producing outdoor concerts and festivals.

- Special Event License
- Street Use Permit
- Sidewalk Closure Permit
- Special Event Vendors License for Merchandise Sales
- Temporary Restaurant or Food Vending Permit
- Temporary Liquor License
- Outdoor Fireworks Permit
- Permit for Erecting Tents on Public or Private Property
- State Health Department Permit
- Amplified Sound or Excessive Noise Permit
- Permit Demonstrating Police and Emergency Medical Staff Safety Plan Approval
- Permit Demonstrating Fire Department Special Events Safety Plan Approval
- Public Works Permit for Electrical Power, Staging, Fencing, Bleachers, and Chairs
- Sanitation Permit for Plumbing, Restrooms, and Portable Toilets
- Solid Waste Department Permit for Refuse Removal

Obtaining the necessary insurance, licenses, and permits can be a confusing and complicated endeavor complete with frustrating paperwork and bureaucratic nightmares. However, the personal safety of everyone involved with the event and the financial security of the promoter, the venue, and the act outweighs the hassles.

CHAPTER 13

Budgeting the Show

Creating a financial plan is most often the least interesting aspect of concert promotion. Nevertheless, when a talent buyer loses money on a show—whether it is a concert or a festival—poor budgeting is typically the cause.

The act creates their tour budget; the talent buyer creates a detailed budget for the show. But, unlike the act, the buyer—the concert promoter or the festival producer—has no guarantee to fall back on if the show loses money. When the artist fee includes a guarantee versus a percentage, the deal shifts most of the risk to the talent buyer. While the promoter has a limit on what he or she can earn from the show, there is virtually no ceiling on how much he or she may lose. Although the buyer may purchase event insurance, policies that often add substantial costs to the show's budget, the insurance carrier does not compensate the buyer when the show loses money due to poor financial planning.

Longtime Phoenix promoter Danny Zelisko, currently with Live Nation, believes neither consumers nor acts truly understand how much risk a talent buyer assumes when the buyer puts his or her money on the line for a show. "If the consumers were aware that there is more to this business than a concert producer magically putting a show on sale with a wave of his hand, perhaps the attractions themselves would feel some of the burden that we promoters now carry by ourselves."

The most common reasons for a show losing money include under-estimating expenses or over-estimating potential income. The talent buyer must therefore develop a precise list of cost estimates for the show's expenses and create realistic projections of income based on solid research. After generating the financial data necessary to create the budget, the buyer decides to make an offer to promote the show or to pass on it. When the buyer makes the offer and signs the performance agreement, he or she hopes that the gods of live entertainment smile on the show, because the budget is based on "educated guesses" rather than absolute certainty.

IDENTIFYING AND ESTIMATING EXPENSES

The talent buyer typically begins to budget a concert by calculating the major expenses involved, including the act's fee, the venue rental fee, and the cost of advertising the event. The promoter then estimates other fees, including box office charges, local staffing, production, and permits and licensing. Ashley Capps, president of A.C. Entertainment, co-producer of Bonnaroo Music & Arts Festival, notes that major festival producers begin with the macro-concept, and then move to more detailed cost analyses. "It's very important to flesh out your full concept: desired line-up, number of stages, proposed ticket prices, other potential income streams, and the various production and staffing expenses that you need to support that concept."

The budget should not be done too quickly and it should not depend on "ballpark" estimates. "The important thing is to be realistic, not optimistic," says Capps. When asked what he learned about budgets between the first year [of producing an annual event] and the second year, he warns, "Exactly how wrong you can be!"

Because each show includes different variables, including the act, the venue, and the cost of media in the region, every budget will be different. Each production provides a learning experience for the talent buyer, and a show's financial success or failure can provide valuable—and sometimes painful—feedback. Comparing "estimated cost" to "actual cost" for each budget line helps the buyer develop better projections for the next event. Although the buyer rarely "hits the bull's eye" on each expense estimate, he or she usually learns to create more accurate estimates over time. "It definitely gets easier to manage your budgets as you get experience with the event," Capps notes. "But it doesn't necessarily get less expensive. And staying on top of your budget is a never-ending task."

BUDGETS RELATIVE TO THE VENUE

Club shows typically are less expensive to promote than large venue shows or outdoor festivals and concerts. However, even club shows may range from low-cost to high-cost productions. Ed Stack, general manager of the 9:30 Club in Washington, D.C., explains, "The cost of producing a club show can be $500 to as much as $10,000." Although the term "club show" is often associated with local startup acts, Stack warns against generalizing about a club act. "What is classified as a club tour these days is ridiculously broad. It can range from some guy showing up driving his own car—singer/songwriter style—to Marilyn Manson rolling in with three semis, eight buses, and all the people to support it."

Clubs work on a tight budget for shows and must keep a close eye on the show's major expenses. "The artist guarantee is always the largest expense on a club show. Advertising would be number two, and miscellaneous venue and show-related expenses would come in third," says Darin Lashinsky, Senior Vice President of Outback Concerts, a company that has promoted a diverse list of acts that include John Mayer, the Red Hot Chili Peppers, String Cheese Incident, Brad Paisley, and the Blue Collar Comedy Tour.

Medium to large indoor venues, including arenas, auditoriums, and performing arts centers (PACs) offer well-staffed facilities with comforts that are rarely available in clubs. But the number of employees necessary to open the doors for the show in a venue of this type is substantial. Because the overhead costs to operate these types of facilities do not offer promoters the luxury of creating "bare bones" budgets as do clubs, the arena, auditorium, or PAC show can be pricey to produce.

Even when the talent buyer requests a skeleton crew for a 10,000-seat arena show, the cost is surprisingly high. And advertising costs increase when the number of seats the buyer must sell increases. Like club shows, the "artist guarantee is the greatest expense in almost all cases," says Lashinsky. "Advertising and venue rent tend to be the other big ticket items on any given [medium to large venue] event."

Mega-events—high-priced stadium shows and festivals—often have expenses that may scare most novice promoters. Capps explains that budgets for festivals and other outdoor shows depend on "many different factors, including type of event, artists, level of production value, camping or no camping, and existing infrastructure." It is possible, though, to produce an outdoor festival or concert with a relatively low budget. "I'm aware of three-day events that cost less than $100,000," says Capps. He has also seen "others that cost more than ten million dollars. It all depends on what you are trying to create."

There are many more *line items*, types of expenses, included in a festival budget than those of smaller, indoor shows. "We basically break down expenses into talent and production, but production includes dozens and dozens of line items," says Capps. The myriad line items include "advertising and marketing, staffing, security, golf carts, staging, sound, lights, travel expenses, hotels, water, ice, catering and hospitality, fencing, electricity, and weather-related expenses." Capps estimates that "talent [for a major festival] is about 25 percent of the budget and the remainder is about 75 percent of the cost for a major camping event like Bonnaroo."

Major Concert Expenses

Each show, regardless of the size, includes three major expenses: talent fees, advertising expenses, and venue rent. Although the show budget includes numerous other expenses that add significantly to the budget, these expenditures are predictably the talent buyer's major concerns when determining whether the expenses are cost effective when compared to the income projection.

Talent Fees. As mentioned in Chapter 10, the act is typically assured a guarantee or guarantee versus a percentage. When the act is an established superstar, the guarantee may be staggering, as much as one million dollars a show. The guarantee can include the cost of the headline act and the support act or acts, transportation for the act and the entourage, and special artist requests including towels, food, beverages, and specific furniture.

Estimating its fee can be complicated when it is based on a percentage of ticket revenues. When the backend deal permits the promoter to deduct agreed-upon variable expenses, the promoter must do the calculations for different ticket sales levels. A small math error in the offer form may come back to haunt the talent buyer at the box office settlement.

Advertising. The major challenge of a small venue show is creating an effective promotional campaign with a limited budget. Large venue shows generate a large amount of revenue from ticket sales and permit the promoter to budget a substantial amount of money for media advertising when necessary. This creates a paradox: Acts that play small venues typically need more advertising because they do not have strong marquee value, but gross ticket sales do not allow for much advertising; acts that play large venues typically have strong marquee value and do not need as much advertising per potential ticket buyer as do club-level acts.

Promoters can use a formula—$4 to $6 per sellable ticket—to establish a starting point for the advertising budget. However, the advertising budget based on this type of formula may be too expensive for the small venue show. And when the promoter uses a formula of this type to create the advertising budget for a major act enjoying strong local radio airplay and substantial national publicity, the projected amount of advertising dollars may be more than necessary.

Lashinsky does not believe a "one size fits all" formula, such as the one described above, is practical. "The formula [that I use] is based on the genre of music and market we are promoting in. An example would be a pop show in a market with two pop stations. We have to consider spending advertising dollars on both stations." In addition to expensive radio buys, the promoter must budget for other media as well. Lashinsky's advertising budget may also include "print ads, network and cable TV, online advertising, posters, flyers, et cetera."

As previously mentioned, crafting a budget is easier for those with experience. "We also base our advertising budget on past experience in a market and the cost of local media," says Lashinsky. When the promoter understands the market, the advertising needs are more obvious. "A $12,000 advertising budget for a country show in Evansville, Indiana, is sufficient; $12,000 in Washington, D.C., might get you [only one] week of advertising on radio, TV, and print."

Venue Rental and Services. Venue rental fees may include a flat charge, a percentage of the gross ticket sales, a fee plus a percentage of ticket revenues, or a guarantee versus a percentage of tickets. These fee schedules, like artist fee structures, generally pass the risk for the event over to the promoter. But, like most deals negotiated in the music industry, fees are not etched in stone. When the venue is eager to strike a deal with an independent promoter, the venue may agree to *cap the rental fee*, place a limit on the maximum cost, when the rent is based on a percentage of ticket sales.

Because the number of venues that desire major shows exceeds the inventory of major touring acts, some have begun to offer attractive fee arrangements to independent concert promoters. An attractive fee structure to promoters is the all-inclusive fee which comprises venue services, including ticket takers, ushers, and in-house security, as well as the basic venue rental fee. As competition for concerts and sports events becomes more heated in the future, venues are likely to work more closely with promoters to develop these and other fee structures to help the talent buyer create budgets more quickly and with more accuracy. Although a concert venue may wish to offer discounted rates to entice promoters, local economic factors may limit the venue's ability to be competitive.

When the venue is in a market with expensive real estate and high labor costs, the venue's rent and services reflect the high cost of living. The following table illustrates a sample of published venue rental fees. The reader is warned that the published rental fee may or may not include the costs of the venue's staff and services.

City	Venue / Capacity	Base Rent	%	Other Fees	Box Office
Los Angeles	Dorothy Chandler Pavilion 3,189	$3,500	vs. 10%	5% facility fee	$2,000
San Diego	Jenny Craig Pavilion 5.000	$4,000			$2,000
San Francisco	Orpheum Theater 2,203	$20,000 +labor/all expenses			5%–7%
Oakland	Paramount Theater 3.040	$1,150	plus 5%		$750 plus night-of-show sellers
Los Angeles	Staples Center 20,000	$75,000			$3,000
New York City	Radio City Music Hall 6,013	$30,000	vs. 17.5%		$2,500 plus $0.25/ticket
Chicago	Arie Crown Ballroom 4,249	$5,000			$1,500
Chicago	United Center 25,000		15%		$1,600
Raleigh, NC	ALLTEL Pavilion 20,000	$47,500			
Nashville	Ryman Auditorium 2,362	$3,500	10%		$0.30/ticket

In addition to the rent, the promoter is responsible for most venue services. These budget items include rental of chairs, risers, and other staging gear; equipment rental, including forklifts; the clean-up crew; the piano tuner; the ticket takers; the ushers; the EMT/Medical staff; the custodians; and the staff services supervisors.

The venue management team knows the needs of their venue better than anyone, so the talent buyer is wise to consult with them to determine the number of workers needed for the show. Heather Story, a veteran of the concert industry, managed a 17,500-seat amphitheater where she supervised more than 600 employees on a typical show day. "We had 95 to 120 in-house security personnel, 15 to 30 uniform police officers, eight to ten EMTs and paramedics, and at least forty ticket takers and ushers," says Story. The staff also included "supervisory staff, box office personnel, merchandise sellers and managers, and concessions crew. It takes a lot of employees, most of whom are seasonal, to work a show."

Additional Expenses. Once the buyer has calculated all major expenses, other potential costs must then be considered. Although the show may not include each of the following, the careful talent buyer must consider every expense category that may affect a show's bottom line, including expenses such as special permits and licenses that are not included in the list below.

- A contingency—usually 5 percent of budgeted expenses—for unexpected costs
- Hospitality to meet the needs of the touring crew, the local crew, the act and entourage, press receptions, and VIP receptions
- Production expenses, including the act's production charge-back and local production company fees
- Local stage crew for load-in, running crew (during the show), and load-out
- Teamsters to park, unload, and load trucks (when venue requires)
- Local runners and vehicles for runners
- Venue electrician(s)
- Local firemen
- Miscellaneous supplies
- T-shirt security
- Venue security
- Uniformed police
- Barricade rental
- Box office staff
- Ticket commissions (charges)
- Fees for tickets purchased with credit cards
- Media advertising
- The local publicist fees and supplies
- Security passes (when act does not provide them)

- Complimentary tickets for the act, the media, and the guests of sponsors
- Insurance
- Performance rights licenses (ASCP, BMI, and SESAC)
- Production and road manager office expenses

PROJECTING THE SHOW'S INCOME

A concert promoter has more control over the expense side of the budget than the income side. When the promoter signs an agreement with a radio station to purchase $3,000 worth of advertising, the figure should not vary unless he or she decides to buy additional spots. However, the talent buyer has no control over the number of tickets that may be sold for the show; there is no "sure thing" in the concert industry, even when the act is a superstar.

The buyer begins to develop an accurate budget by estimating the major source of income for the show: ticket sales. Although festival promoters and in-house venue promoters benefit from ancillary income, including merchandising, food and beverage, parking, and venue "fees," the independent promoter is generally excluded from these sources of income. It is not uncommon for the venue, especially a club, to make more money on ancillary income than from the box office. Like a department store that advertises a *loss leader*, a sale item that loses money for the store, the club often uses the band to attract customers who will generate revenue by spending money on alcohol, food, and merchandise.

When the talent buyer projects income for the event, he or she must be both realistic and accurate; assuming the show will be a sellout is a risky assumption. As we discussed in Chapter 4 and Chapter 10, the agent and the buyer begin by calculating the *gross potential*, the total box office revenues when the show is a sellout. Unless the show is a "slam dunk," a concert that includes an act that predictably sells out shows in venues of the same size, the talent buyer is wise to research the act's *tour history*, a list that chronicles the ticket sales from previous shows, and *venue priors*, sales figures for similar shows in the venue.

Predicting the number of tickets that the show will sell is not a precise science and each talent buyer has a system that serves as his or her "crystal ball." After conducting research regarding the acts recent shows, the venue's recent successes, and the *traffic*, other shows in the market, the promoter often relies on intuition. Darin Lashinsky points out, "Every event is different. We usually base our projection on a gut feeling for how a show will do. We know where our breakeven is based on our projected expenses; the profit projection is merely a guess of how we think an event will perform."

A helpful tool the talent buyer may create when evaluating the show and negotiating with the booking agent is a *sales scenario spreadsheet*. Unlike the projected gross potential, this planning tool takes into consideration the fact that not all shows are sellouts. The simple spreadsheet calculates the gross ticket sales for a range of ticket prices and the potential percentages of the *house*, the total tickets sold.

AN EXAMPLE OF A SALES SCENARIO SPREADSHEET

The following sales scenario spreadsheet illustrates the range of box office revenues based on two variables: the ticket price and the percentage of available seats that may be sold. The goal is to better understand potential gross revenue at different prices and percentages of ticket sales. The concert venue in this example is a club with a total capacity of 1,300. The range of ticket prices for this event considers the highest ticket price of similar acts that have performed in the venue. Prices for tickets lower than those included here are not considered because club show fans are typically not *price sensitive*, overly concerned about the cost of the ticket, below $4 when the act is in popular. This example assumes that the show should not be booked if the talent buyer cannot sell at least 50 percent of the tickets. Although the club may be the in-house promoter of the show, low ticket sales reduce ancillary income, and the club's operating overhead is a major consideration. A poorly attended show may not justify opening the doors. In this illustration, the spreadsheet shows the gross revenues generated by the number of tickets sold and the price of the ticket. In this spreadsheet, the gross ticket sales range from $3,250 to $27,300.

Percent of Tickets Sold	50%	60%	70%	80%	90%	100%
Number of Tickets Sold	650	780	910	1,040	1,170	1,300
Ticket Price						
$5.00	$3,250.00	$3,900.00	$4,550.00	$5,200.00	$5,850.00	$6,500.00
$6.00	$3,900.00	$4,680.00	$5,460.00	$6,240.00	$7,020.00	$7,800.00
$7.00	$4,550.00	$5,460.00	$6,370.00	$7,280.00	$8,190.00	$9,100.00
$8.00	$5,200.00	$6,240.00	$7,280.00	$8,320.00	$9,360.00	$10,400.00

continued

Percent of Tickets Sold	50%	60%	70%	80%	90%	100%
Number of Tickets Sold	650	780	910	1,040	1,170	1,300
Ticket Price						
$9.00	$5,850.00	$7,020.00	$8,190.00	$9,360.00	$10,530.00	$11,700.00
$10.00	$6,500.00	$7,800.00	$9,100.00	$10,400.00	$11,700.00	$13,000.00
$11.00	$7,150.00	$8,580.00	$10,010.00	$11,440.00	$12,870.00	$14,300.00
$12.00	$7,800.00	$9,360.00	$10,920.00	$12,480.00	$14,040.00	$15,600.00
$13.00	$8,450.00	$10,140.00	$11,830.00	$13,520.00	$15,210.00	$16,900.00
$14.00	$9,100.00	$10,920.00	$12,740.00	$14,560.00	$16,380.00	$18,200.00
$15.00	$9,750.00	$11,700.00	$13,650.00	$15,600.00	$17,550.00	$19,500.00
$16.00	$10,400.00	$12,480.00	$14,560.00	$16,640.00	$18,720.00	$20,800.00
$17.00	$11,050.00	$13,260.00	$15,470.00	$17,680.00	$19,890.00	$22,100.00
$18.00	$11,700.00	$14,040.00	$16,380.00	$18,720.00	$21,060.00	$23,400.00
$19.00	$12,350.00	$14,820.00	$17,290.00	$19,760.00	$22,230.00	$24,700.00
$20.00	$13,000.00	$15,600.00	$18,200.00	$20,800.00	$23,400.00	$26,000.00
$21.00	$13,650.00	$16,380.00	$19,110.00	$21,840.00	$24,570.00	$27,300.00

MAKING THE BUDGET-BASED DECISION

After the talent buyer has "crunched the numbers," it is time to decide whether the show is likely to be sufficiently profitable. The budget that reveals a potentially small profit may indicate that the show is not worth the risk or effort to produce. The novice promoter may decide to proceed with the event based on emotions rather than intellect. When the expense side of the budget exceeds the realistic income projection, there is the temptation to trim controllable expenses in hopes of "making the numbers work."

A common, but often fatal, decision made to reduce expenses is to cut the advertising budget. Less advertising generally reduces the probability of selling tickets, though. This strategy is counterproductive and typically results in lower box office receipts. The more logical decision is to negotiate lower artist fees and plead for a better venue rental deal.

Ashley Capps explains that budgeting is a dynamic process; it must be constantly refined and updated. "Coming in significantly over budget can be a big problem if you don't have the ticket sales to cover it. That's why you have to manage the process very carefully and review your budget regularly to see how reality is impacting your plans."

Volunteer community festival committees and novice concert promoters often fail to realize that variable expenses may increase faster than ticket revenues. An event selling more tickets than anticipated does not necessarily translate into greater profits. When the Canadian city of Moncton produced a Rolling Stones concert in 2006, they were confident the show would draw a huge crowd. Although it drew between 75,000 and 85,000 concertgoers, the event cost $1.2 million, $670,000 more than budgeted. The concert organizers acknowledged they had underestimated variable costs, including police, medical services, parking, and cleanup expenses that soared out of control as crowd control issues increased. Focusing solely on the income side of the budget often blinds the promoter to the realities of the expense side of the ledger.

Paying attention to detail, staying on top of ever-changing expenses, and relying on well-researched information wins the budget battle more often than breezing through the budget process. When the talent buyer has done a diligent job of budgeting, life is good.

CHAPTER 14

**Promoting
the Event**

Webster's New World College Dictionary, Fourth Edition defines the word "promote" in part as "to further the popularity, sales, et cetera by publicizing and advertising." This definition most certainly applies to concert promotion. Promoting concerts is a mixture of art and science.

The art in concert promotion is derived from the experience, instinct, knowledge of the event to promote and who it appeals to, innate sense of timing, and flair necessary to capture public awareness. The latter element, flair, is where the best promoters can show their stuff. The Rolling Stones, masters of attracting attention, have announced tours by landing in a hot air balloon and playing live on the back of a flatbed truck in New York City. U2 played a rooftop concert in Hollywood à la the Beatles. Paul McCartney once announced a tour during a Super Bowl halftime interview.

The science in promoting concerts is in determining the most effective means of reaching a target audience, researching past history of similar events, budgeting costs efficiently, and making use of the available tools in a comprehensive manner to maximize impact. Among these tools are customer databases, Internet marketing, media coverage, and outdoor, radio, print, and television advertising.

Aside from the stature of the act, promotion is the most important factor in determining a show's success or failure. An immediate sellout requires little promotion beyond an announcement, and adept promotion can boost stalled sales. Poor promotion, on the other hand, can make a loser out of a potential winner.

THE BASICS OF CONCERT PROMOTION

The foundation of concert promotion is not unlike the five building blocks of journalism: who, what, when, where, how. Who is performing, what type of event is it, when and where will it take place, and how do we get tickets (and how much are they)? This is information that absolutely must be provided, even for a guaranteed sellout. It is one thing for fans to know the Rolling Stones will play their city, but if they don't know what venue on what date, and how to get tickets, the information is useless.

The first mission of concert promotion is to provide information, and then to stimulate interest, both generally accomplished through media buying. There's also the timing of the promotion (from announcement to on-sale to late push), the roles of the various players in conducting a promotion, and how to react to various levels of sales activity, from immediate sellout to long hard slog.

The best promoters try to make each show a must-see event. "We try to produce and book each show uniquely to their fans and pay the bands fairly according to each market, and leave everyone with a memorable experience," says promoter Charles Attal of Charles Attal Presents in Austin, Texas. "Each show is unique and we really have to look at the band and their fans and figure out how to find them to promote. The formula is pretty simple: treat the bands and the fans in such a way that everyone leaves happy and wanting more."

Veteran promoter John Scher of Metropolitan Talent states his concert promotion philosophy simply: "Try to put the right act in the right venue on the right date for the right ticket price and it will be successful."

This seems to be a prevailing theme, and when a tour promotion doesn't begin well, it could be doomed. "I would say my philosophy on promotion basically starts with the launch and the set up of the tour," says Arthur Fogel, chairman of global music for Live Nation. "I'm a 100 percent believer that it is virtually impossible to recover from a weak or bad launch, and therefore it's all about the setup: the announcement of the tour, the initial on-sales. Success has everything to do with the strategy of how you do that."

MEDIA BUYING

While no promoter would under-value the importance of free media coverage, or *publicity*, in promoting a concert (and the best promoters wrangle as much publicity as possible), the reality is that the vast majority of concerts cannot rely on enough publicity to put a show over the top. Promoters must pay for exposure, and they do this through *media buying*. Media buying is the purchase of time on broadcast media, space in print, billboards, or the Internet, or some sort of digital delivery, for the purpose of communicating a message, usually advertising. Media buying is a complex endeavor with entire courses devoted to it in advertising and marketing curriculums. In the concert world, media buying is about getting the word out to the right people as efficiently as possible.

Step one in media buying is determining a budget. Promoters can arrive at a ballpark figure by researching what they and others have spent in promoting similar shows in a particular market. The promotional budget largely depends on how tickets are selling. In a best-case scenario, the show sells out quickly and little money needs to be spent outside of just informing the public about on-sales, date, time, et cetera. In a worst-case scenario, tickets move slowly and the promoter needs to prudently buy advertising in an attempt to add juice to sales. Many promoters set their budget by averaging the best- and worst-case scenarios.

Other promoters play it be ear, adapting as sales progress. "We set budgets and hope for the best," Attal says. "If a show pops (sells quickly), we can save on marketing dollars. If the show needs a boost we have to get more creative to stretch our dollars or throw a little gas on the fire if need be."

Scher says he bases his budgets on a worst-case scenario. "Always worst case, and if your ticket sales are ahead of what you anticipated, you can always cut back," he says.

Attal has a formula that takes into account the artist's guarantees, room capacity, and production expenses to calculate what to spend on advertising. "For example, with a 1,200 capacity room on a $4,000 guarantee, we don't have the budget to spend $5,000 on advertising," he says. "I would set it around $2,000."

Media buying is a much more complicated process than it once was, due to several factors. The market is much more fragmented; where there were once just a handful of music formats, there are now many niches. Similarly, consumers get their information from a wide variety of sources, including multiple broadcast mediums and the wide-open Internet.

"It has become increasingly difficult over the years to stratify the core of an act's audience," Scher says. "There are certainly some pop acts that are across the board. That happens every once in a while and you can sort of spread [advertising] everywhere. But I think there is a lot of misspent money in the marketing of concerts. For example, newspaper ads that essentially do very little other than stroke an act's ego by seeing their ad in *The New York Times* or the *Village Voice*, when their audience, especially that younger rock audience, isn't reading the newspaper anymore."

Alternative newspapers that appeal to music and arts lovers can be effective. "But the scatter approach of being in a lot of places hoping to get the 10 percent of the people who might go to your show that are reading *The New York Times*, for example, is probably not wise money spent," says John Scher.

Back in the 1970s and '80s, rock shows, for instance, were best promoted on rock radio. Today, with multiple rock radio formats, an act's audience is not so easily pinpointed. "First of all you have to identify the audience for your act, and the audience for an act isn't always what the act thinks it is," Scher says. "Often an act and their management will tell you what they hope [their audience] is, but they don't know exactly what it is."

For many artists, the promoter's marketing plans must be approved by the artist's representatives, "so there's some compromise there," he says. "But once you can identify where your audience is and you spend your media money in those places, you have a much better chance to be successful."

Charles Attal says a rule of thumb budget allocates 50 percent on print ads, 25 percent on radio ads, and 25 percent on miscellaneous advertising including, but not limited to, Internet and "street" promotion such as flyers and pamphlets. "TV isn't effective on club shows, it only seems to work at the higher level," Attal says.

The average arena-level show promotional budget can be as much as $25,000 to $30,000. For a large theater concert, promoters can expect to spend in the $10,000 to $15,000 range for promotion. Generally, the smaller the venue, the smaller the budget, based on the number of people that must be reached to fill capacity.

As the Internet becomes a more effective means of advertising, most promoters expect more dollars and effort to be focused online. "But you're still going to have to deal with the ego of the artists, the managers, or the agents as to where they're going to see their name in print, and they won't necessarily be wrong," says Scher.

There is print that makes sense, he says. "If you're going to do adult shows, it certainly pays to be in the daily newspaper. I'm not condemning newspapers for everything, but now it has become a bit of a niche. If you're promoting a Barbra Streisand show or a Michael Bolton Show, or any adult artist, those particular ticket buyers are still reading newspapers," Scher adds.

When promoters are competing for artists, a certain amount of "ego-stroking" media buying may be necessary, but common sense must prevail. "It is part of the business, until it gets financially stupid to where you're not reaching an audience but spending a lot of money," says Scher. "A full-page ad in *The New York Times* is $100,000, the *Los Angeles Times* is close to that. Where do you draw the line? You get to a point where you've got to weigh efficiency from a ticket-selling point of view, and creating general awareness, and where you fit the ego between those two things."

More than ever, digital marketing through targeted e-mail blasts has become the most cost-efficient way to reach potential ticket buyers. "Three to five years ago, you were in a really tough situation: traditional media like newspaper wasn't really getting you to the core audience and the Web sites weren't as mature as they are now," Scher says. "I think we're getting better at [digital marketing], but of course as a business model those that are successful at it are getting more expensive to advertise on."

Digital marketing is evolving as a tool, Scher says. "I think what will happen is as various Web sites get more financially sound and are able to monetize their operations a little better, they will find better and more efficient ways to speak to people that are their constituencies. Some are already very good at it."

"Digital marketing is redefining the way we sell tickets," says Bob Schwartz, VP of marketing for Global Spectrum, the Philadelphia-based facility management firm. "The ease in which we can serve our consumers" is the driving factor of e-marketing, he adds.

Timing the Promotion

Timing is the "single most crucial element of the marketing campaign," says Attal. Key dates in a promotional schedule are the initial announcement of the show or tour, the day tickets go on sale (the on-sale), and any other publicity the act may get like a record release, an awards show, or the start of the tour and the day-of-show.

As Arthur Fogel stated earlier, the initial announcement is critical, and it helps to conduct it with some panache, like the Stones and U2 tours mentioned previously. "I know it's simplistic, but when you're hot you're hot," Fogel says. "And if you're not hot, it's not as easy. That's pretty obvious. But I do think that there are ways to kind of insure that you play to your hand, so to speak. How you launch it and where you launch are two of the most important factors."

The timing between the initial announcement, when tickets go on sale, and the show date must be carefully considered. "We love to have five to seven weeks of on-sale, with an announcement coordinated with the band," Charles Attal says. "Ideally, the announcement is usually three days prior to the on-sale. People buy tickets over time and most shows don't sell out immediately. A strong on-sale generates buzz and triggers a viral form of marketing as early ticket buyers become an important part of your 'sales force'."

Another key consideration in announcing the show or putting it on sale is what else is going on in the market. "The main thing is to see what else is on sale that week," says promoter Seth Hurwitz, president of I.M.P. "People will choose between shows, even if they really wanted to see both, and then stick by that decision. The more shows that are on sale on a given day, the less [business] each one does."

Many promoters decry the trend of putting shows on sale weeks or even months ahead of the show date. "I think we've gotten a little off base over the last few years by putting tickets on sale so far in advance that you lose the sizzle," says Scher. "If you start putting shows on sale four of five months in advance, unless the show sells out instantly it's almost impossible to keep up a marketing plan. You take your first flurry of ads when you go on sale and then very often you'll have to stop advertising and marketing for weeks if not months at a time because you don't have an ad budget to support it."

Fogel thinks the gap between on-sale and show date has varied over the years. "Years ago it was a very short window; it was very common for six weeks (between on-sale and show date)," he says. "And then over time that kind of expanded to maybe six months or longer in some situations. And yes it does make it difficult to sustain for that period of time."

But Fogel stresses that each project is different. "There are some where it really doesn't matter if you're six months out or two months out," he says. "But I also think there are those situations where timing is everything. If you haven't gone at exactly the right moment on the curve, it could impact you negatively, particularly in the pop world."

Promoters should be mindful of what competitive promoters might have in the marketplace, as well as one's own shows. "You've got to pull back when shows go on sale. Create the best, most exciting campaign you can to start the show off, but be in a place where you're able to maintain an advertising campaign right up until the time the show happens or the show sells out," says John Scher.

Some in the concert industry believe there is a nationwide trend toward consumers buying tickets closer to show, a trend which crosses all performing arts genres. "So it's really hard to know how to set your expectations on timing," says Kathleen O'Brien, CEO of the Tennessee Performing Arts Center (TPAC) in Nashville. "We keep daily reports on all shows to track their sales trends, which is helpful when looking at like shows or a repeat."

If a show is not doing well, "We go back to our media sponsors and try to get more out of them—ticket giveaways, e-mail blasts with private offers [for] donors, institutional sponsors, partners, et cetera," says O'Brien. "You have to be careful here so that you don't create a customer service issue for people who have already purchased tickets at a higher price."

If a show is stiffing badly, it can be tough to "promote" it into a winner, short of deep discounting or *papering the house*, giving away tickets. Such a situation should be avoided at all costs. Fogel says it is "virtually impossible" to overcome a disastrous sales pattern. "That is why I've always believed that the most strategic decision you can make is where you're going to play and what you're going to charge."

Can a promotional genius ever rescue a stiff? "I think it's very, very difficult and most of the time impossible," Fogel believes. "And therefore what you see happening are situations where people have to scale down venue size, cancel markets, all those sort of things."

In such a scenario, the "inherent flaw," according to Fogel, is in how the tour was put together. "When you put together a tour, do you put it together based on what an act can do in each market or do you simply put it together so that the production can fit, or whatever the reason is? Because, truly, if you're comfortably along in the record cycle, a record has been released and time has gone by, a few singles, and you truly understand, either by market or by territory or by country, where it fits, where it should be playing, then you book a tour to that," he says. "How many times in our business have we seen an arena tour going on sale and it shouldn't be in arenas? That's the crux of it. If your starting point is strategically put together—the right venues, the right ticket prices, the right package, the right support—and then you book to that, then you will [seldom] end up in that disaster scenario that we've seen seemingly more than we should [have] over the years."

THE ROLES OF THE PLAYERS

While the responsibility to promote the show lies squarely on the promoter, there are other players that can be helpful in getting the word out, including the venue, local media, sponsors, and the act's record label.

One of the promoter's best partners can be the venue where the show is to take place. "The venue is critical," says Charles Attal. "People driving by can see upcoming events, or [venue staff] can give flyers, posters, or other promotional materials to their customers."

"Venues are very helpful, particularly arenas that maintain a pretty comprehensive marketing department and e-mail list," adds John Scher. Additionally, many clubs and smaller venues maintain Web sites that potential concertgoers frequent.

Local media can be another critical partner, whether it is via show reviews, CD reviews, or entertainment recommendations. "Reviews of shows only help promoters in that they may resonate to those potential customers who did not buy tickets for this show but may the next time a band comes through," Attal says.

Scher calls local media relationships "incredibly important" to promoters. "For us, maintaining relationships with local media is an enormous priority," he says. "Program directors and business directors at radio, entertainment editors at newspapers, these relationships still have huge value."

Traditionally, a "radio presents" show, where radio stations come on board as a presenting sponsor to take ownership of a given show in the market, provided a considerable boost to concerts. In the 1970s through most of the 1990s, "WXYZ Presents This Band in Concert" was the norm. When a radio station is on board with a concert in a "presents" scenario, the station has a vested interest in the success of the concert, often providing remote broadcasts from venues that can boost walk-up attendance, and numerous on-air "mentions" in the weeks and days leading up to the concert. While these relationships still exist, the changing business climate that make acts reluctant to align with one station over another station for fear of losing airplay has caused a significant dropoff in the number of "radio presents" shows. The exception is listener appreciation concerts that are often bankrolled by the radio station, with or without the help of a promoter.

As discussed in Chapter 2, sponsors can provide valuable marketing support to tours by promoting their association with the artists. Promoters differ, though, on how much support they believe sponsors bring to a given date. "Sponsors may help keep show costs down and therefore allow us to lower ticket prices, but we don't see much marketing benefit if there is a tour sponsor," says Attal. "The exception is a sponsor who really takes a vested interest in getting the word out about a show rather than one who just wants to be attached with the day-of-show activities."

"I rarely find sponsors to be helpful other than to give the artists money. Not never, but rarely," adds Scher.

Another potential promotional partner is a band's record label, though promoters don't seem to put much faith in the labels helping promote a concert. This is not necessarily a bad thing, as promoters and labels have separate agendas: one sells records, the other sells tickets. But the label can be helpful in buying a number of tickets to the show to offer to VIPs, or by generating publicity primarily geared to sell albums. "The label, unfortunately, seems to be taking a smaller role in helping promote bands, particularly at the club level," Attal says. "Their leverage with local radio seems to be slipping."

Agents and managers do have a vested interest in how well a show does, and can provide valuable marketing support and information. Large agencies like CAA and William Morris have marketing departments that can provide valuable support nationally and locally. And the responsible agent is usually on top—or should be—of how shows are doing on a market-by-market basis.

"Good agents clearly can give you a heads up on what kinds of things are working or not working from a marketing perspective," says Scher. "Every once in a while you'll have a clever promoter in another market that comes up with an interesting idea you never thought of, and if it works in one place it might work in another. The agent giving you that kind of information is terrific."

Making use of the managers is also vital. "Talking to the managers and their staff directly and again finding out what's working in some places and not in others and being able to run ideas by them is very important," says Scher.

But the other players can also bring some negative energy to a campaign if a show is not performing up to par. "I love how agents tell you how the act is so big, they can't understand why it's not selling, you must be doing something wrong," says Seth Hurwitz. "Those, of course, are the very same agents that told you they were handing you a no-brainer gift that anyone could promote."

It does seem that an evolving music business is creating new partnerships that can help sell tickets. In 2006, the band Korn was the center of a groundbreaking deal that connected the band, its label EMI, and promoter Live Nation in a partnership to grow Korn's career. Live Nation reportedly invested about $3 million in exchange for 6 percent of Korn's box office, licensing, publishing, merchandising, and CD sales. Earlier, EMI had invested $25 million upfront for an estimated 30 percent stake in Korn's overall business.

The deal made partners out of those who historically pursued distinctly separate agendas. The joint venture allowed Live Nation to invest in the band's overall career, tapping into revenue streams beyond the box office that were previously unavailable to promoters. Meanwhile, Korn received a piece of revenue that had largely been off limits to bands, namely such ancillaries as concessions at Live Nation-owned venues.

The tour was Korn's most successful in years. Band manager Peter Katsis says all the vested parties—label, promoter, band, management—held up their ends of the bargain. "We had to create a model of working together," he says, adding that EMI "undoubtedly" helped get radio behind the tour.

Live Nation executive VP of amphitheater programming Jason Garner says that since everyone has a stake in Korn's success, "there's not a management agenda versus a label agenda versus a promoter agenda . . . Everyone's working together to make sure we maximize the overall pot for Korn."

But such deals are still a rarity. Hurwitz says he "never, ever" relies on the other players to help him put a show over the top. "If a show isn't strong enough to sell on its own, don't book it," he says. And, as Scher points out, "The onus is on you to promote."

SMALL VENUE PROMOTIONS

Promoting concerts in small venues is a unique process. While there are fewer tickets to sell, smaller venues often host lesser-known acts. In many cases, the promoter is faced with hyping the venue, a concert series, a style of music, or even a night of the week, as opposed to relying on star power. In other cases, the act may be a big name, but the intimacy of the venue makes ticket prices higher.

CLUBS

At the club level, the promoter may or may not be the club owner and/or the buyer of talent. For the purposes of this book, we will discuss promoters who also buy talent, and most will tell you that effective promotion begins with effective buying and putting the right act in the right venue. "I start by trying to determine what I think is the right gig," says Hurwitz, owner of the popular 9:30 Club in Washington, D.C. "If the act agrees, that's great but, if they don't, you have a responsibility to yourself, the public, and even them, to try and convince everybody to do what's best. It won't help you the morning after to say 'but that's where they wanted to play'."

Hurwitz advises promoters not to get sucked into making the wrong decisions. "Stay true to your beliefs," he says. "If someone is pushing you past those limits, get off the phone. You are responsible for your own welfare and happiness. Nobody else has that agenda."

Rick Whetsel, president of Nashville's Great Big Shows, promotes concerts at several clubs, primarily the venerated Exit/In. "I originally started out to bring concerts to town that no one else would, artists like Elliot Smith, the Flaming Lips, Stereolab, and others," says Whetsel. "At the time, no other promoter would do it. Since then, I've expanded into other developing artists and, quite honestly, shows to make money to keep the doors open."

Whetsel says he does not have a "formula" for promoting club shows. "We've tried to develop brand awareness for Great Big Shows, with the idea that consumers will return to us over and over to discover good music and to find out when the artists that they're interested in are coming to our area," he says. "It's strictly a show-by-show basis that determines how we divide up our advertising dollars."

Particularly at the club level, the promoter knows what works in his or her venue and market better than any outside entity. "Do not allow others to tell you how to promote in your own market," Hurwitz warns. An exception would be a "net deal," where the budget is determined by an outside entity. "Then spend it like a wife with a platinum card that just caught her husband with a hooker."

Whetsel agrees that "it's tough to rely on others to help you, but you have to. We work hand-in-hand with labels and tour promotion people in order to secure editorial content at the correct publications. This isn't always easy as everyone seems to have a different opinion on which is most important. We rely pretty heavily on our friends in the media to help us out as well."

THEATERS, BALLROOMS, AND PERFORMING ARTS CENTERS

Smaller venues often mean lesser-known artists, or headlining artists who wish to charge more for an "intimate" experience. Both situations create challenges for promoters. "When dealing with up-and-coming artists, I find it is important to understand who the audience is, why they are coming, and how to reach them most effectively," says Mark Shulman, VP of talent for AEG Live in New York, and programmer for the 2,100-seat Nokia Theatre at Times Square in New York. "It's important to note that different genres and age ranges will react differently. The motivation for a sixteen-year-old punk-pop fan is going to be very different than a thirty-five-year-old married couple."

Shulman says pricing should be at a level that can capture a full spectrum of fans, from the "super fan" willing to pay top dollar, to the casual fan. Initial marketing should be targeted toward the primary consumer, then "the information trickles down from there to more casual fans," he says.

The reputation and quality of the "room" or venue can make a big difference in attracting fans who may not be completely passionate about the artist.

"The 'super fan' will go see the band no matter where it is, and the casual fan will go where their friends are going. There is no doubt that the right space is important for the middle 50 percent of fans, but what that right space is may depend on a host of factors such as age range, cleanliness, friendliness of staff, ease of access from transportation, et cetera," says Shulman. "I personally think that too much is made out of the 'style' of the venue as a deciding factor by fans of whether they will attend or not. If it's the place to be on that night, it is where the fans will go."

Many believe that the industry as a whole is shifting towards smaller and mid-sized venues being the "sweet spot" for touring, given far more acts can sell 6,000 tickets or less than can sell 10,000 or more. "I see 1,500 to 2,500 capacity as the sweet spot right now," says Shulman. "We are seeing a decline in number of shows and attendance in all venues from 3,500 capacity all the way up through stadiums. At the same time, there seems to be a steady market for the 2,000 average capacity shows for all genres. It's hard to predict where the market will go from here, but if the media continue to fragment in the coming years as it has done for the past ten, this will be a continuing trend where there will be more popular artists than ever, but fewer breaking through into mass market popularity."

Performing arts centers (PACs) typically program for a multitude of genres, including musical theatre, opera, ballet, symphony, and comedy, and therefore have the opportunity to tap into audiences of all interests. Tennessee Performing Arts Center's Kathleen O'Brien says most PACs have the databases to support that reach. "And a PAC that does its own programming generally has a strong marketing budget to leverage local buys, create media sponsorships, and partnerships. We work with rental clients who want to 'ride our rates' if we do the buys, and, of course, we get the 15 percent agency commission. Many times, that is still much less than what they can get it for."

LARGE VENUE PROMOTION

Large venues are faced with a simple but difficult challenge: they must sell a lot of tickets. Arenas, stadiums, amphitheaters, and festivals must pull in dedicated fans, but also must entice more casual fans, as well.

ARENAS AND STADIUMS

Arenas are the most commonly used large venue for concerts, far busier with music than much larger stadiums. With competition among venues more fierce than ever, the more marketing muscle an arena can provide, the better. In-house arena marketing teams are no longer the stepchildren of the concert promotion world. In today's tight concert business, the arena's in-house marketing staff often takes the lead due to their local relationships and knowledge of their market and venue. Also, the efficiency and economy of digital marketing are giving arenas—with their already valuable databases—more clout than ever.

THE FAN HUMAN

On an average show (excluding special shows where bigger artists play intimate venues or one time concert events), there are usually about four types of fans, AEG Live talent buyer Mark Shulman believes. "There are 'super fans' who are going to come to the show pretty much no matter what. They will pay double the average price, drive through a snow storm, and miss a family event because there is no way they are not going to be there," he explains. "The next group could be called 'enthusiastic fans,' who are knowledgeable about the music, own a record, and want to see the band live to form their own opinion. They will usually spend slightly more than the average price, but would be willing to wait until the next time around if need be."

The next category is the "familiar fan," who doesn't own a record, has heard some of the music, is mildly interested, thinks the ticket price is about right, and wants to get out and have a good time. Last is the casual fan who may have heard a couple tunes, doesn't own a record, can't name a member of the band, but their friends are going and they want to tag along.

"We target our marketing through e-mails, web pages, micro Web sites, print, radio, and street campaigns to fans in the top two categories because they are the drivers," says Shulman. "They are the rallying point who will then spread the word that their favorite artist is coming around and see who else would be willing to come with them. They may get a couple enthusiastic fans, a familiar fan, and a couple of casual fans [to go with them]."

Trying to target from the casual fan up is a lost cause, according to Shulman. "I have seen this attempted, particularly by radio events, and it often results in less than stellar box office numbers. Each fan that has bought a ticket becomes an advertiser which is why getting the ball rolling from the start is so important." says Shulman. "It's very hard to gain momentum from a dead stop mid-campaign."

Digital marketing is "critical" for the U.S. Airways Center in Phoenix, according to Paige Peterson, president/GM of sports and entertainment services, which oversees the arena, as well as downtown Phoenix venues Chase Field and the Dodge Theatre. Peterson says an average of 35 percent of concert tickets for U.S. Airways Center are sold through their internal marketing program, Downtown Live, which utilizes the synergy of three buildings managed under the same banner. "The percentage sold via the Internet is much greater, but our marketing efforts with Downtown Live have been very successful," he says.

Bob Schwartz, VP of marketing for Global Spectrum, says that often more than half of Global's ticket sales for family shows and concerts come as a result of Internet marketing, with consumers both finding out about and purchasing tickets electronically. For the Global-run Wachovia Center in Philadelphia, a presale e-blast for two Bon Jovi shows sold more than 12,000 tickets, and Paul McCartney's presale e-blast sold 5,000 tickets.

Global event marketers are able to intelligently utilize database marketing, according to Schwartz, for example, sending e-mail blasts about an upcoming country show to those who bought tickets to a previous country show. "That doesn't cost us any money, and it's a minimal effort to get this out to tens of thousands of consumers who are our target audience," says Schwartz.

Agents and promoters are very much taking notice of what the arenas can offer in terms of marketing. "In-house marketing from the arena is a crucial and necessary value-add this day and age," says Ken Fermaglich, agent for 3 Doors Down, adding that some arenas—but not all—are being proactive in offering in-house marketing. "Sometimes, they need to be prodded."

And in a market situation where there are more arenas than there are tours to play them, venues are quick to let promoters and agents know what they have to offer. "When we're pursuing any show, we inform them about what all of our marketing efforts will include," Peterson says. "I think the promoters are more than comfortable and are in fact supportive of our efforts."

In the 1970s through most of the 1990s, stadium shows were commonplace, driven by hugely popular acts like Pink Floyd, the Rolling Stones, and the Grateful Dead. In the new millennium, only Kenny Chesney, Jimmy Buffett, the Rolling Stones, Dave Matthews Band, and a handful of others played stadiums, and then only a few. As of this writing, no act is capable or desirous (stadium shows are very expensive to produce) of booking a coast-to-coast stadium tour.

Needless to say, it's tough to move 50,000 tickets or more. And, unlike their arena counterparts, stadiums often do not have an extensive database of concertgoers to tap into, at least beyond their primary sports tenants. While they can and do make use of their sports-team database—successful Jimmy Buffett shows at Fenway Park in Boston and Wrigley Field in Chicago would be examples—marketing stadium concerts relies primarily on giving the show status as a "major, must-see event."

AMPHITHEATERS

Amphitheaters are unique in many ways. They are outside, they typically have about one third of capacity as reserved seats (with the rest general admission on the lawn), they are usually owned by the promoter (usually Live Nation), and being at the mercy of the weather, they must promote twenty to thirty shows in about a four-month warm-weather window.

Whether promoting a concert in an amphitheater or in an alternate indoor facility, such as an arena or theater, "the one constant is that each marketing plan is uniquely customized to accomplish the mutual goals of the artist and the promoter," says Bob Roux, president of Live Nation's South region. "Perhaps the main difference between promoting shows in amphitheaters and promoting in other venues comes from the deal itself and the related ticket prices. In amphitheaters, we traditionally sell tickets to two separate audiences: (a) those fans that are more inclined to purchase reserved seats, and (b) those fans that are more predisposed to purchasing lawn tickets."

Such a structure usually allows for a wide disparity between the price of the reserved seats and the price of the lawn seats. "With this metric in place, as a promoter you are now able to market the amphitheater shows to a much wider audience from a disposable income standpoint. The core fans of the artist in most cases want the reserved seats and are quite comfortable paying what might be considered market price for those seats, or what they might expect to pay to see the artist in an arena. Then there is the "casual fan" that will strongly consider attending the show, but also considers the value proposition a bit more," Roux explains.

Roux says that because of the large number of lawn seats available for sale in most amphitheaters, typically 10,000 to 12,500, most artists agree to price these lawn seats in the $9 to $25 range to maximize ticket sales. One of the most recent marketing trends takes this pricing dynamic a step further and offers the casual fan an additional incentive to not only attend the event, but to encourage others to attend the show with them as well. This is accomplished by packaging and pricing four lawn tickets (a "four-pack") at a significant discount to the price of four individual lawn tickets.

"Once you have all of the pricing dynamics in place, we tend to stress price much more in our marketing campaigns for the amphitheater shows than we would do for non-amphitheater shows," Roux explains. "Besides the pricing, and how those ticket prices are accentuated and articulated in the marketing plans, most plans differ very little between the amphitheaters and the alternative venues. Each utilizes a wide variety if marketing platforms including the Internet, television, radio, print, and billboards."

The "warm weather window" can actually be a marketing tool. "Because of the fan's affinity for the outdoor concert experience, the environment itself becomes part of the value equation when fans determine whether or not to attend a concert," says Roux. "The hibernation factor also contributes to the advantages of the warm weather window that fans experience with outdoor concerts. In most of the United States, where the majority of amphitheaters are located, people spend a majority of their time indoors during the late fall, early spring, and winter months. Once the weather warms up, people just want to be outside again and this fact is amplified when they can enjoy the weather in combination with their favorite pastimes, such as attending a concert."

Roux discounts critics who say amphitheater shows can get lost in the promotional shuffle. "Each of the amphitheaters in the Live Nation network have determined through years and years of experience what marketing methodology works best for their particular market," he says.

"In some cases, like Nikon Theatre at Jones Beach in New York, they have determined that putting the entire season on sale in the spring, much like is done with professional sports, is the most effective way to maximize ticket sales. This one-day season on-sale is then reenforced by individual marketing plans that in most cases are rolled out chronologically throughout the season to coincide with the timing of the event itself."

Many other amphitheaters simply put each show on sale individually in some type of preordained chronological order. "For some of the venues in the northern climates, whose seasons may run from twelve to sixteen weeks, that also promote thirty to forty events annually, there are some weekends when multiple shows go on sale," Roux says. "In those cases the mix of shows is so musically diverse that the marketing does not overlap between shows and audiences so each show is still allowed to maximize their individual ticket sales."

FESTIVALS

Festival promotion puts promoters in the position of promoting an event with several acts as opposed to a single headliner concert. Often, the message is about the synergy of the total package of acts and environment, as opposed to a single act's or package's drawing power.

Charles Attal, co-producer of Lollapalooza and the Austin City Limits Music Festival, says festival marketing follows a similar formula as concert promotion, but on a much larger scale. "In addition, on the festivals we spend more time marketing the event, the experience, the venue, and the ancillary activities rather than just focus on marketing the individual bands," he says. "At a successful festival the whole is more than the sum of the parts and it is important to convey that message."

With total budgets for major festivals in the millions of dollars, much more money is on the line than a typical concert. "From a financial standpoint, the capital at risk on a festival is significantly larger so the stakes are much higher. You just can't afford to make a mistake marketing a festival," says Attal. "The timeline is also much longer for a festival, so you have to be more creative and continually think of ways to market the event to different patrons without getting stale."

The time between on-sale and show date for a festival can be as long as five or six months. "You have to stretch your marketing dollars over this period and think of ways to generate marketing events that continually get people excited," Attal says. "On our festivals, we rely heavily on Web-based marketing and try to leverage the local and national media coverage."

Some festivals are fortunate enough to not have to buy any traditional media. The first Bonnaroo Music Festival, held in a rural field sixty miles south of Nashville, Tennessee, went on sale as an untested event in 2001, and sold out at 80,000 tickets in eleven days without ever spending a dime on traditional advertising. Bonnaroo was that rare event able to create enough buzz through an online community of music fans that they sought out the event rather than vice versa.

NATIONAL AND INTERNATIONAL PROMOTERS

When a promoter buys an entire tour to promote nationally or internationally, as opposed to local or regional promoters working with concerts in specific markets, the rules change. The promoter must be mindful of a comprehensive budget and national awareness, as opposed to just promoting a show in one or a few markets.

Arthur Fogel, producer of worldwide tours by U2, Madonna, and Sting, and national tours by Crosby, Stills, Nash & Young, says he puts together his budget on a "worst-case scenario." Such a strategy allows the tour to deal with ebbs and flows in ticket sales.

"Say it's 100 markets. You're not dealing with 100 budgets, you're dealing with one budget," Fogel explains. "You have a working budget for the tour and it may be that in 90 of the 100 markets you don't have to spend your whole budget, and in 10 markets you have to spend three times your budget."

The process is not as complex as it sounds, he says. "You basically have a budget for the tour for marketing, advertising, and promotion, and ultimately you have to manage that on a per-market basis. But [a single budget] gives you the advantage of being able to spend what you need to spend on a market that's under-performing."

Fogel has taken several acts around the world since working on the Rolling Stones' "Steel Wheels" tour in 1989, and he admits the game is different in foreign markets. "Outside of North America, it's much more about your media partners and media sponsors and promotional partners than it is in America, where [promotion] is to a larger degree driven by paid advertising. In Europe, it's very common to have radio and/or television partners in each country."

These international media partners know how to get the message across locally. "Europe is a collection of countries, and you basically have to put a marketing program in place in each country. It doesn't work to just sort of try and do something pan-European. You have to have a lot of trust in your partners, and you have to put together deals that make sense and deliver you a lot of high-profile coverage."

As an independent promoter with regional expertise, John Scher believes there is no substitute for local input, even on a national or international tour. "Candidly, the state of the industry right now, the local and regional promoter that really knows their market inside and out is being lost. First of all, I think there are very few people that are buying the talent and buying the advertising and marketing any longer with their own money, and I'd go so far as to say probably the great majority of people who are buying talent and buying media never risk their own money," he points out.

This is the case even if there is a regional person on the ground in the market for this national promoter. "It's corporate money and I think they're not trying hard enough and they're not trained well enough. This isn't the case everywhere; there are still great buyers and great marketing people, and some of them work for big corporations," he says. "But I think fundamentally in order to be successful in the concert business, artists and their managers and their agents need to let regional and local promoters do what they think is right."

Whether it is a national or international tour, promoters should understand that an act might mean one thing in one city or country, and quite a different thing in another. "It's very relevant that there aren't that many acts, in fact there very few, that are at the same level worldwide," Fogel says. "There are very few of those. More often than not, an act is at different levels in different parts of the world."

While cultural factors can impact how a message is best delivered in a given region, the basics of delivering a tour are pretty much the same worldwide, he says. "You can set up a tour as best as possible on a national or international basis in terms of profile, but in terms of setting up an on-sale, you basically have to apply the same principles no matter where it is in the world."

"There are different things that maybe capture the attention of ticket buyers depending on where it is in the world, but I do think that the world has shrunk to the point that it's not that much different no matter where you go. There's no question that the difference from when we first started doing international tours in 1989 and now is dramatic in terms of awareness of what's going on anywhere in the world."

Having watched superstars perform worldwide, Fogel says audiences are pretty consistent. "There tends to be a greater excitement level when someone plays somewhere for the first time, but generally I think that on a worldwide basis people have come to appreciate and expect the same level of show. It's not like you can bring your 'A' show to New York and bring a 'C' show to Buenos Aires. You basically have to deliver the same level of show anywhere in the world today."

CHAPTER 15 Ticketing the Show

In the world of live entertainment, tickets are the keys to the kingdom. Their use by those promoting and producing events to control admission dates back to the traveling shows and circuses of the 1800s and before. But the business of ticketing—how tickets are sold, distributed, authorized, and validated—has undergone tremendous change in the past two decades. The ticketing industry is currently in the midst of a revolution spurred by digital technology, and today more than half of all tickets sold are purchased via the Internet: the *secondary market*, or reselling of tickets, is thriving; and print-at-home tickets and cell phone barcodes are a reality.

While ticketing is simple in principle—promoters sell a ticket that is used by the consumer to gain admission to an event—it is one of the most complex issues facing the concert industry today. In short, it has evolved from simply controlling who attends an event, to being a profit center, and to being one of the concert industry's most valuable marketing tools.

CONCERT TICKETING FROM THE 1970S TO TODAY

Concertgoers in the 1970s went through a far different experience in obtaining their tickets than do their counterparts today. In those days, concert tickets were either picked up at the venue box office, or purchased at record stores or other retail outlets, including pharmacies, supermarkets, or department stores. In a typical scenario, a fan would go to the record store, ask the clerk for tickets to a particular concert, and the clerk would pull out a shoebox with stacks of tickets held together with rubber bands. Sometimes a venue seating chart would be available so the patron could choose his seat from the available tickets, and sometimes not. Either way, the experience was decidedly low-tech.

"You had 'hard tickets' and what you would do is order a set number of tickets for a show, and we would have runners who would run those around to all the local department stores, record stores, et cetera, and allocate tickets to each store," recalls Terry Barnes, chairman and CEO of Ticketmaster, who began his career in the concert promotion business. "Based on prior history, you may give one store 300 tickets, you may give another store only 100 tickets, and so on."

Barnes says that most of the really good seats were generally held at the box office. "And the further you got out of town, the smaller the allocations would be and the worse the seats would be," he explains. "We would have a person in the office who would call every store and get ticket counts. We knew exactly what had been sold and what hadn't, and usually the day before the show or the day of, we would have the runners go out and gather up all the unsold tickets and bring them back to box office to get reorganized for what we hoped would be a good walkup at the door."

The promoter controlled the inventory, working in conjunction with the venue. Any unsold tickets after the show were referred to as *deadwood*. "At the end, you'd gather up all the unsold tickets—'deadwood'—and then go to settlement, because the tour manager would be paid on 'tickets sold.' He would have to see a copy of the manifest and the tickets you printed, then the deadwood, so he would know what was sold and what wasn't," Barnes explains. "If you had sold another couple hundred tickets that you weren't paying them on, then he'd never know it unless you showed them the unsold tickets."

Most promoters and venue managers that were involved in the process agree that settlement was a much more grueling experience in those days. "Settlement took a lot longer," says Barnes. "Today it's much more automated, people walk in with a Ticketmaster audit that accounts for every ticket in the house, sold or unsold. Obviously going to automated ticketing helped speed up the process."

In retrospect, the ticketing aspect of the concert business in the 1970s was somewhat amateurish by today's standards. "It was brutal," says live event industry veteran Peter Luukko, president of Comcast-Spectacor and chairman of Philadelphia-based venue management firm Global Spectrum. "The settlements lasted forever. As a facility, we used to have to get all these hard tickets back, and, lo and behold, somebody in the box office might have forgotten to get some guy who owned a pharmacy's tickets, we would have a concert going on, and we'd be running over to the outlets trying to get tickets. Because the band would want a charge-off if you didn't have the deadwood."

"Obviously, computerizing ticketing revolutionized our business," Luukko adds.

COMPUTERIZED TICKETING AND THE RISE OF TICKETMASTER

The automation of the ticketing business was largely spurred in the 1970s by a company known as Ticketron, a computer software and hardware company owned by Control Data of Minneapolis. Ticketron's primary concern was the lottery business, with live event ticketing being a small division. According to Barnes, Ticketron had two different ticketing systems, one for season ticketing, and one for single ticket sales. While Ticketron's business was computerized and automated, the fact that the two systems were not integrated meant that all ticket buyers were not pulling from the same inventory pool.

Meanwhile, three guys in Tempe, Arizona, built a software system at Arizona State University they called Ticketmaster. Albert Leffler (who is still with the company) was a staff member of ASU's Gammage Auditorium, working as a paid intern in Arts Administration; Peter Gadwa was a graduate assistant specializing in software programming in ASU's Psychology Department; and Gordon Gunn was a Phoenix businessman. The three jointly founded the company, with Leffler writing the specifications and Gadwa writing the software, and they came up with a system where all tickets came off of one inventory control system, fully integrated.

Both Ticketron and Ticketmaster aimed to contract with buildings, promoters and sports teams. But there were two major differences between their modes of operation. "Ticketmaster was the better mousetrap, a totally integrated system," Barnes says. "We thought Ticketron had the model backwards and we turned out to be right. Their model consisted of looking at their client as the consumer and they charged very low service charges because they didn't want to upset the consumer. They would charge a fee to the promoter, the building, et cetera, to sell their ticket for them."

For example, if the client was a team, Ticketron would charge that team 50 cents for every ticket they sold for them. Then they would charge the consumer 50 cents and get their revenue from a total $1 service charge. "We came along and said the consumer is not the client, the client is the person that owns the ticket. The Chicago White Sox are the clients," Barnes explains. "So we went in to the White Sox and (Chicago promoter) Jam Productions and said 'We're not going to charge you 50 cents a ticket to sell your tickets, we'll do it for free. In fact, we'll charge the customer $1.25, because we're going to provide a much better service.'"

Under this system, the Ticketmaster client—the team, building, or promoter—could actually receive a revenue stream from ticketing based on royalties paid by Ticketmaster. "You can turn what used to be a cost center into a profit center," says Barnes.

Barnes explains the royalty or rebate concept as similar to a hot dog vendor at a stadium. "When you go to a ball game and get a hotdog, it costs you $5. You know the hot dog didn't cost $5; the vendor has to pay the venue a royalty: a fee to be in the building selling their hot dogs. The same with ticketing. We pay royalties or commissions back to the buildings on the service charges."

The Ticketmaster model proved extremely effective. "The consumers were happy because we put up outlets all over the place, as many as we could. So the consumer didn't have to drive downtown to the arena, park and go in," says Barnes. "We brought the best available seat right to your neighborhood; you could go to your local record store and get as good a seat as if you went downtown to the arena. You had the next best available seat out of the entire inventory, because it was all on one system."

The public responded as Ticketmaster set up outlets and phone centers across the country. "All of a sudden, the outlets were selling most of the tickets, and if you wanted to call on the phone you got the next best available seat as well, because the outlets, the phones, and the box office (because there was no Internet yet) were all pulling off the same inventory," says Barnes.

This integration represented a huge advancement of the business. "As a promoter, you not only had much better distribution, but if you had Bob Seger come in, for example, and you thought you might do two or three shows, you could sit there in real time and see how ticket sales were going, and roll to another show. All of sudden you were seeing multiple shows where before you might have been a little bit afraid to add a date."

Initially, Ticketmaster would sell hardware, license software, and allow clients to sell tickets in their own buildings, paying royalty and licensing fees. When the company received a major capital investment in the early 1980s, "we flipped it to a service model, where we owned the company and rendered services to the clients, rather than sell hardware and license software," Barnes says. Ticketmaster became aggressive in acquiring new business and regional ticketing companies, while at the same time investing heavily in research and development.

"We had to be bulletproof," says Barnes. "The one thing everybody demanded was a ticketing service that worked. You needed a system that could handle a lot of pressure, especially on Saturday morning when you were putting shows on sale."

In 1991, Ticketmaster acquired Ticketron. By the end of 2006, Ticketmaster had a presence in twenty countries, including China, and it planned to double that in five years. The company moved 119 million tickets in 2005 (the latest year for which figures were available at this writing), generating total fee revenue of about $950 million. Ticketmaster's international business made up about 25 percent of revenue in the second quarter of 2006.

In the past, it was common for fans to camp out at the venue or other outlets in order to ensure their place in line to buy tickets when the on-sale began for large, in-demand concerts like Pink Floyd or the Rolling Stones. These campout events did have their social value and were enjoyed by promoters hoping to hype the show, but the convenience factor was low. Today's version of this is ticket buyers anticipating the on-sale with various parties "camped out" by their phone (pushing redial as often as necessary), on their computer (repeatedly attempting to log on and/or purchase), and/or in line at an outlet. Cell phones for each "team" member make this type of networking efficient.

THE IMPACT OF THE INTERNET ON TICKETING

The first ticket ever sold on Ticketmaster.com was in Seattle in November 1996. "We hadn't even gone public. We just turned it on to get the bugs out and see how it was working and all of sudden we sold one ticket to a Seattle Mariners game, one ticket," says Barnes. "We had our operations person look up the guy and we called him. We said 'We're just live, we haven't advertised, nobody knows about it, and you bought a ticket. You're the first person to buy a ticket on Ticketmaster.com. Can we ask you why you bought a ticket online?' He said 'Yeah, because I don't like talking to people and I don't like talking to you,' and he hung up." People want the control, don't want to be bothered."

By the end of 2006, Ticketmaster sold more than 70 percent of its tickets domestically online. "When we built and set up the superstructure across the country we had seventeen phone rooms for Ticketmaster. Now we're down to three," Barnes says. "New technology offers vast efficiencies through interconnectivity and so much of our business has shifted online. Today our customer care centers not only take care of phone sales but also inquiries about online orders."

The use of the Internet as a ticket-selling medium has also created a hugely effective marketing tool because of the data collection necessary for credit card sales, as well as information voluntarily offered by customers. Additionally, the Internet has fostered a fast-growing secondary market, in many ways legitimizing the practice of *ticket scalping*—the practice of buying tickets with the intention of reselling them at a price much higher than face value. Both of these dynamics are discussed in greater detail later on in this chapter.

What the Internet and new technology have done more than anything is give the ticket buyer options. He or she can search for events online, purchase the ticket online, have it mailed to them or print it out on their home printer if they desire, or even have a bar code text-messaged to their cell phone that can be scanned at the venue.

"The ticketing business is finally changing," says Andy Donkin, co-president of Tickets.com. "Technology is allowing the barriers to entry to come down, which means that innovation goes up, which means there are a lot more choices for artists and venues. The ticketing business is actually an e-commerce business today."

THE BUSINESS OF TICKETING

As ticketing progressed from cost center to profit center to marketing tool, the business of ticketing has become more complex. But the opportunities available through creative ticketing operations exceeds what anyone would have imagined back in the "deadwood" days.

TICKETING COMPANIES

Four primary companies—New Era/Paciolan, Vertical Alliance, Ticketmaster, and Tickets.com—can offer arenas a bid on ticketing services these days. Facilities have a range of options, basically depending on how "hands on" the building management wants to be. "A lot of it depends on the level of control the facility wants," says Luukko, whose company owns and operates New Era/Paciolan software. "You can completely farm your ticketing out or take control of the whole situation in-house."

The option of "farming it out," or *outsourcing*, basically means venue management does not have to handle all the aspects of ticketing, other than managing the box office and its personnel. On the other hand, "by maintaining the control, you get the ability to make changes, control all the data, control all of the service charges," says Luukko. New Era is a subsidiary of Comcast-Spectacor and a sister company to venue management firm Global Comcast. "I think it's absolutely the way to go. I'm biased, though, so it's tough to ask me."

The New Era system is powered by Paciolan software and technology. Founded in 1980, Paciolan bills itself as a "venue-enabler," providing a fully integrated ticketing infrastructure that puts venues in direct control of their ticketing operation. The model is set up where New Era/Paciolan licenses the system to the venue, which in turn executes it to the degree they wish, including determining service fees. "We allow the building to create their own brand," says Fred Maglione, president of New Era. "We run the call centers, set up the Web presence, and set up and manage the outlets, but not under the New Era brand, under the brand the client wants to create. Every touch-point is controlled and managed by the client."

Similarly, the Vertical Alliance system is licensed to venues, including horse tracks, sporting venues, arenas, and universities. The Vertical Alliance model also integrates parking and merchandising into the system, and adds kiosk sales to the online and box office sales mix.

Unlike New Era and Vertical Alliance, the typical Ticketmaster deal is a turnkey operation. "What Ticketmaster does is a lot of heavy lifting, especially for the big buildings and the sports teams," says Barnes. "You're going in, bringing all the equipment they need for each team that's in the building, season ticketing, invoices, renewal notices, all that back room stuff. In return for that we get the right to sell tickets to the public."

Some clients may pay certain fees for certain services, "but by and large we supply a lot of equipment at Ticketmaster's expense as part of the deal to get them up and running," Barnes says. There are varying levels of services, from very minimal to very complex.

Another major competitor in the ticketing business is Tickets.com, which was initially conceived in the mid-1990s as an open online ticket marketplace. Tickets.com acquired several ticketing software companies and went public in 2000. "We had a great time until the market crashed, then we retrenched and created an alternative to Ticketmaster, both in the services business and the licensing business," says Andy Donkin of Tickets.com.

In 2005, Tickets.com was purchased by Major League Baseball Advanced Media, which was created by owners of baseball teams to create a platform for online ticketing and commerce for all thirty MLB teams, and now has more than 1,000 domestic and international clients, including venues, sports teams, and museums. "We actually run two lines of business. We have a services business which is similar to what Ticketmaster does: Internet, retail, phone center, kiosks, and interactive voice response," says Donkin. "Then we have a licensing business where we license the software to the client, we run the online channel and they run all the other channels."

SERVICE CHARGES AND REBATES

As for who controls the ticket pricing for any event, it's not the ticketing company. "A lot of people think we set ticket prices," Barnes explains. "We have nothing to do with ticket prices, zero. It is told to us 'this band is playing in this building and the ticket prices are this, this and this.' We do not own the tickets. We sell the tickets on behalf of the building."

But the ticketing company does set service charges, at least when ticketing is outsourced. Service charges are far and away the primary revenue source for Ticketmaster and Tickets.com, and how these fees are arrived at is generally via negotiations between the ticketing companies and the client. "The higher the ticket price, the higher the service fee, and a lot of that has to do with credit card charges," Barnes says. "The credit card fee on a $100 ticket is a lot higher than on a $10 ticket."

There is no rule of thumb on setting service charges, but rather fees are determined market-by-market, client-by-client. Consumers have long grumbled about service charges, but for ticketing companies they represent a return on investment for millions spent in research and development.

"For us it's a business proposition: what are all the costs and investments that we have to make in the business, what services do we provide, and what can the market support?" Donkin says. "I think the industry together kind of shoots themselves in the foot. When you walk into a grocery store and pick up a tube of toothpaste, does the price say '$2, is the price of the toothpaste, plus 50 cents margin, total $2.50?' In the ticketing business, you basically have the ticketing company having to put their fees out there and of course the consumers are going to be upset because they're not going to understand what [the fees] are. It's a value proposition, like any other business."

Like service charges, rebates or royalties are typically scaled to the ticket price. These rebates have become a significant revenue stream for venues, particularly large, high-volume buildings.

"Every service provider pays some kind of royalty, license fee or rebate back to the building for the privilege of doing the business for them," says Barnes. "This is a relationship business and we know who the client is and we try to take very good care of them. If we don't do our job and do it well, we know there are people out there they can replace us with."

COLLECTING, CONTROLLING, AND USING TICKETING DATA

Ticketmaster revolutionized the live event business by making ticketing a profit resource for venues. Now ticketing has become a marketing tool because of information gathered when consumers by tickets. When consumers purchase a ticket with a credit card, by far the most popular method of payment in ticket buying, ticket sellers know who they are, where they live, and what type of events they like to see right off the bat. Much more information is available if consumers "opt in" to be contacted, or marketed to, by the ticketing company or venue. Demographic and psychographic information—income, likes and dislikes, what is important and not important, the list goes on and on—can be learned about the consumers and used to market future events.

The question of who controls the data collected through ticket sales has in the past been a matter of contention. "If we're doing a show inside one of our arena clients, we take direction from the arena. The arena certainly gets full access to [the data], and they typically are pretty good at sharing it with the act," Barnes says. "They let us have certain use of it as well for certain marketing initiatives that we want to do on behalf of their events."

Ticketmaster and the venues can market extremely effectively by notifying customers about upcoming concerts. The customer must, however, consent to being sent this information when buying a ticket online. Ticketmaster sent out one billion e-mail alerts in 2006 to customers who wanted to know when certain types of events were coming to their market. Through the buying habits of fans, venues, ticketers, promoters, artists, managers, agents, and others know who goes to see what, and how often.

Most concert professionals agree this data is being shared more willingly by all the involved players these days. "If everybody's sharing this database, it's only going to help everyone," Luukko says. "If we can put this data together on various genres of music, it will only help that type of show sell out. If we can get a database of people that attend shows like Metallica, AC/DC, and Mötley Crüe, for example, then the next show like that that comes in we have an incredible presale ability to test our market and determine what that show is worth."

Marketing to the customer does not have to end once the consumer buys a ticket. If the venue knows a customer is coming to a concert, "you send them an offer for a T-shirt, a CD, or something else, and then to take it a step further with the advent of bar coding. We know who's in the house, we can add stored value to [the barcode], we can add food and beverage, money for merchandise, et cetera," Luukko says. "Ticketing has gone from this archaic way of getting into an event to a convenience and a profit center, to now a really fantastic marketing tool."

THE SECONDARY MARKET, DYNAMIC PRICING, AND PRESALES

The concept of ticket brokers or *scalpers*, profiteers who buy tickets at face value with the intention of selling them at a huge markup, has changed dramatically in recent years. While the term "ticket scalper" may conjure a vision of someone standing on the street corner outside the venue selling tickets prior to a concert, the Internet has created a new "street corner" for ticket resellers.

Once viewed as a scourge on the industry (and still viewed that way by some), the reselling of tickets, defined today as the secondary market, has become legitimized to a large degree as regular ticket-buying customers have found an open marketplace on the Internet through which to buy and sell tickets. The secondary market is thriving, and at the same time ticket auctions, often referred to as *dynamic pricing*, have once again changed the way consumers purchase tickets. The secondary market and dynamic pricing are intertwined on the Internet, where consumers can bid in real time. At the same time, promoters, artists, and venues have found value in creating *presales*, opportunities for preferred customers to purchase tickets prior to the general public.

THE SECONDARY MARKET AND DYNAMIC PRICING

The Internet has created a new breed of profiteers who, like the scalpers of yore, purchase tickets with the intent of reselling. Also in this mix are people who now are able to unload tickets they are unable to use. Mass-appeal sites like eBay conditioned consumers to online buying and selling, and it did not take long for ticket sellers to enter this game. After watching Internet entrepreneurs jack up the price of tickets for the past few years, the core concert business has slowly warmed up to ticket auctions and dynamic pricing.

But dynamic pricing initially was met with some resistance from the players in the primary touring business, including artists, venues, promoters and recognized ticketing companies like Ticketmaster. Secondary-market outlets like eBay, StubHub, TicketsNow, and RazorGator, however, originated and profited from the online ticket auction market; and ticket buyers embraced the concept.

"There is a very large and active secondary ticket market out there," Dell Furano, CEO of merchandising firm Signatures Network, says. His in-house research shows that nearly 50 percent of the first fifteen rows of concert seats ends up in the hands of secondary ticket brokers.

"It's very simple: The premium seats, the 15 percent to 20 percent of seats at the best locations are empirically worth more than their face value," Furano says. In this regard, the consumer and the secondary market have shown what the market will bear. "What has happened is the ticket brokers have gone in and rescaled the house, so to speak."

As concert promoters see what consumers are willing to pay for great seats, ticket prices have risen accordingly. Few would doubt that the huge prices consumers pay on the secondary market have contributed to the rise in ticket prices in the primary market.

Clearly the secondary market and these secondary "ticket brokers" would not flourish as they do if there were not demand from the consumers. Some people just do not have time or do not care to be involved in the initial "mad rush" of an on-sale. Others may not hear about a show until it is already sold out. While the "legitimate" business argues that secondary brokers profit without contributing to the show or taking a risk, secondary market proponents maintain they are fulfilling a consumer need.

According to Jeff Fluhr, co-founder of StubHub, "There are over one thousand ticket brokers in the country—businesses that buy and sell tickets for a living. And they're playing an important role in the market, in my opinion, because they're taking inventory off the hands of the promoters."

Others don't see it that way. "We don't like scalpers," Luukko says. "They don't invest in the tour, in the venue. They don't have any of the risk associated and the capital needed to build buildings and put on tours. So I don't know why they deserve to make any money off that ticket."

Fluhr realizes some people will never accept ticket reselling. "There are people who don't like the resale of tickets, but frankly I think those people are living in the past," he says. "This is a different age from the street scalper."

Some view ticket reselling simply as economics. "If you think about it logically, [dynamic pricing] puts the fan on an even playing field with the broker in terms of access to the best seats, where the market, more than greed, dictates the ultimate price of a ticket," Randy Phillips, CEO of international promoter AEG Live, observes. "It is the ultimate example of *laissez-faire* economics at work."

If fans find convenience and value in the secondary market and auctions, bands and the "legitimate" industry are keen to capture some of this revenue for the primary market versus the secondary market. Ticketmaster's own secondary ticketing service, TicketExchange, boasts dozens of team and venue clients. "I think people now get the concept that we're trying to take money that goes to brokers and scalpers and the secondary market, and we're trying to put it in the primary market where the people who put on the shows can actually benefit," says David Goldberg, executive VP of strategy and business development for Ticketmaster.

The secondary market is going to get "very, very interesting," Donkin says. "StubHub, RazorGator, all these guys, what they've done is create a gray area between the primary and secondary market. That's not how consumers think about tickets. They don't say, 'Should I go to the primary market or the secondary market?'—they just want a ticket. Now, the teams and the artists who are creating the content are saying, 'Hey that should be our market and we should control it.'"

Today, auctions in the primary market are also beginning to take hold. In 2006, Coldplay and Bon Jovi, for example, successfully offered portions of their ticket inventory for dynamic pricing. For Bon Jovi's tour, officially auctioned tickets averaged $150 to $175 above face value, an increase in revenue that other artists will surely not ignore.

A Ticketmaster ticket auction differs from other online ticket auctions in that "everybody along the line in the value chain has to be aligned and want to do it," says Goldberg. "The artist, agent, manager, promoter, venue all have to decide before an auction happens that this is something they want to do."

Another difference from other secondary sales from sites like eBay is that if, for instance, fifty pairs of tickets are available, there would be fifty separate, individual auctions with a pair of tickets each. "From a consumer perspective, say I have $100 to spend for a pair and I want best seats I can. I go bid $100 and I may lose. It's possible that $100 would've won on another auction, but you can't monitor fifty auctions at same time, and what happens if you won more than one?" Goldberg explains. "Our auction puts all $50 pairs on one auction, so as you're outbid, you move down in quality of seats. So the top fifty bidders win and all will be assigned seats in rank order according to how much they bid."

The number of auctions Ticketmaster facilitates is growing rapidly. In 2005, total auctions for Ticketmaster clients jumped 237 percent over the prior year. The average number of tickets sold per auction rose from seventeen in 2004 to sixty-one in 2005.

As a whole, the industry seems ready to ramp up dynamic pricing. "There certainly seems to be more discussion among agents, managers, and promoters about the use of auctions as a tool to keep dollars out of the secondary market and in the artist's gross at settlement," says Nederlander Concerts CEO Adam Friedman.

The numbers from auctions on secondary sites are eye-catching, with tickets often going for several times face value in plain view of an increasingly frustrated concert industry. "The transparency of the secondary marketplace has really led a lot of people in our industry to say auctions are a good thing," Goldberg says. "It's found money that now goes into the gross."

Dynamic pricing still deals with some perception issues. Artists in general have been reticent to acknowledge their role in rising ticket prices. "There was certainly a concern among some [artists] that auctions would be viewed as gouging of fans," Goldberg says, "but the way we've been doing a lot of these auctions—starting them at what a typical face price would be—everyone has gotten over the perception we might be gouging fans, because the only reason it would go above face price is because the fans bid it up."

Goldberg says Ticketmaster research indicates that about 15 to 20 percent of seats in a given inventory end up trading on the secondary market anyway. "And that's really the same type of inventory that does best in an auction," he says. "That's not to say for some events you couldn't use more than that, and plenty of artists use a lot less than that, but they at least use that quantity of inventory if they want to drive auction proceeds the highest."

"Market price" does not necessarily mean "higher price." If the highest-priced seats sell quickly, that's where the promoter can receive the bulk of the return on his investment in the artist guarantee. Remaining tickets can then be priced lower. "If the artists capture the premium of the better tickets, it should allow for more rational pricing of the balance of the house," says Nederlander Concerts' Friedman. "The auction premiums on the better seats will cover a greater portion of the talent guarantees, reducing the need to overprice the rest."

Conceivably, inventory that is not moving could be skewed downward in price to jump-start sales. Such a concept should be welcomed by an industry accused of "fire sale" discounts and papering houses excessively in recent years. "While most of my peers are focused on the 'lift'—the difference between face value and the final purchase price of the ticket—I have my Web and ticketing execs working on a business model that uses dynamic pricing to help move unsold inventory," Phillips says. "AEG would rather set the 'lowest price acceptable' at a dollar to spur bidding than completely devalue an artist's ticket by papering a house."

Ticketmaster has developed "declining-price auctions" to address just such a slumping sales scenario, where, for example, tickets may be $20 the first hour, $15 the second and $10 the third.

With so many possible ticketing options, the industry appears to be at risk of creating confusion for consumers. "I don't think we're at that point yet, but we're always cognizant of not introducing things that really make it so confusing that it's going to turn off the buyer," Goldberg says. "You don't want three or four different types of presales, plus an auction, plus maybe a back-of-house declining-price auction—all these things that start to add up and make it more complicated."

PRESALES

Ticket *presales*, when certain segments of ticket buyers are allowed to purchase tickets prior to the general public on-sale, have become for many the most telling barometer of the relative "heat" of a given show—or lack thereof.

When U2 went up with a presale for most dates on its Vertigo tour in 2005 via separate promotions with its fan club and American Express, demand was so high it crashed the system. When the Dixie Chicks went up with a presale for their 2006 "Accidents & Accusations" tour, softer-than-expected demand led to the tour being reconfigured.

The first high-profile national presale came with Bon Jovi's 2003 "Bounce" tour, where album purchasers were provided with a code that allowed access to a Ticketmaster presale. Today, "presales are a meaningful component of almost every major tour," says Sean Moriarty, president/COO of Ticketmaster. "We see it across all categories."

Presales can be set up in a variety of different ways. Variations include a massive promotion with a corporate partner like American Express or Target, where customers of the sponsor are given to purchase tickets prior to the general public; a fan club site where paid membership guarantees a shot at prime seats prior to the general public; an album promotion where a music purchase provides access to tickets prior to the public on-sale; a venue-directed VIP program where priority customers like suite or club seat owners buy in advance; or some combination of all of these elements.

It is no exaggeration to say that presales have permanently changed the ticket-selling business. "There's almost a new vocabulary emanating from all this," says Bob Schwartz, VP of marketing for Global Spectrum, the Philadelphia-based facility management firm. "There was never such an activity as a 'presale' a few years back. Now a presale dictates the momentum of a show."

Particularly in the earliest stages of a tour's launch, presales can serve as a test market of sorts, allowing producers to tinker with ticket prices and promotion on a market-by-market basis.

"It can certainly give you a good indication of what the market's like, what are the proper price points," says Scott Siman, manager of Tim McGraw. The McGraw/Faith Hill tours in 2006/2007 used a variety of presale programs, including both artists' fan clubs, and sponsor-coordinated campaigns. "In this age, you can monitor what goes on and try to adapt, but you also have to be smart because each individual market's different."

In addition to moving some tickets, what presales may do best is to provide information. "You're taking a subset of the total inventory, you're marketing it to a discrete population, and you're able to see some results while you still have inventory left to sell to the general public," Moriarty says. "You learn demand levels, price sensitivity levels, and you can adjust as you go."

And in the concert promotion business, knowledge is power. "Two of the biggest challenges in live entertainment right now are pricing and fan awareness," Moriarty says. "About 50 percent of the inventory in live entertainment is unsold, and probably 10 percent to 20 percent is sold at a small fraction of its market value. To the extent that you can use tools like presales as a barometer to gauge demand and assess pricing levels, we're all a heck of lot better off."

PART IV

STAGING THE SHOW: EVENT PRODUCTION

CHAPTER 16

Venue Operations and Services

Call it the hall, the room, the building, or the space, the venue is where the magic happens. Whether it is a club, a theater, a ballroom, a shed, an arena, or a grassy field, if the venue is not a proper showcase for the artist—production is inadequate, ingress/egress is problematic, the building is too large or too small—the concert experience can be ruined. Most people will remember a terrible parking situation longer than they will a great guitar solo. And most road crews remember if the coffee is cold and the load-in was difficult more than if the show was a financial success.

The important things to keep in mind when considering the venue's role in the show are: who the major players are in venue management (venue personnel); what the venue's basic responsibilities are in terms of staging a concert (venue operations); what services a venue can offer artists and tours in order to gain a competitive edge (going "above and beyond" basic operations); and how venues make money (venue revenue streams).

While venue management is a complex and multi-faceted business, most basic principles regarding how to run an effective and profitable concert venue can be applied to facilities of any size.

A club may derive its concessions revenue from a single bar and an arena from a hundred food and beverage points of sale, but in both cases the revenue stream is crucial and must be managed with care.

VENUE PERSONNEL AND OPERATIONS

The primary responsibility of a concert venue is to supply a safe, aesthetically pleasing, user-friendly site with appropriate acoustics for artists to showcase their songs for fans, and an efficient, professional workplace for behind-the-scenes touring professionals. At the same time, the venue must make money, or it cannot continue operating.

While it is true that many public facilities, including arenas and performing arts centers, are allowed to operate at a loss because they are regarded as investments in the public good, any venue that bleeds too much red ink will eventually close its doors. A "municipal" facility, like Nashville's Municipal Auditorium, is owned by the city government and must answer to taxpayers. Many other venues are owned by city, county, or state governments, or a combination thereof. The Pyramid in Memphis was built, owned and overseen by a combination city/county authority, and when it failed to turn a profit as a live entertainment venue, it hosted its last concert, Bob Seger, on February 3, 2006.

Privately owned venues, be they clubs, arenas, amphitheaters or festival sites, have to eventually operate in the black as well, or they will meet a similar fate. Public or private, it takes experienced professionals skilled in the various facets of facility operations to make a venue viable. The building must not, at the very least, make the touring group's job more difficult than it has to be. And, in the best case scenario, venues can go "above and beyond" the call of duty to become a favorite place to play for acts, road crews, promoters, and agents.

VENUE PERSONNEL

At the club and small venue level, its personnel roster is relatively small. Clubs require a general manager/talent buyer, who in many cases is the owner. In addition, clubs usually have a manager assigned to ensure the crucial concessions part of the business functions properly. National club chains like House of Blues and B. B. King's tend to have an in-house marketing/public relations professional on staff, while also receiving talent buying and marketing support on a national level from a corporate or regional office. Full-time staff at a club generally consists of twenty-five employees or less.

As the venues get larger, their management roster grows. Although official titles vary, a typical hierarchy for venues from the theater to arena size includes a general manager (GM), an assistant GM/event coordinator, an operations manager, and a box office manager. Additional positions may exist for public relations, production, club seat and suite sales, sponsorships, and concessions.

The *general manager* is in charge of the venue. In most cases, it is the GM who is its public face and the person responsible for dealing with municipalities, sports teams and other tenants, and any crucial issues that may arise. The GM signs off on all aspects of venue operations, including which acts are booked into the building, maintenance and operations, crisis management, budgeting, any risk taking or talent buying the venue may undertake, and other financial aspects of running the venue.

The *assistant GM* is the second-in-command, and in many cases also serves as the liaison between the venue and the artists, agents, and promoters. This is a key position, charged with taking on any responsibilities delegated by the GM and running the building during events when the GM is not on-site. "The GM takes care of the 'big picture' stuff," says Brock Jones, senior director of booking at the Gaylord Entertainment Center in Nashville, whose duties place him in the assistant GM role. "The assistant GM handles the day-to-day," Jones says. "Our job is to keep as much stuff off the GM's desk as possible."

The importance of the *marketing director* has grown significantly as the venue business has become more competitive and the prudent use of information and databases is more valuable and effective (as explained in Chapters 14 and 15). Venues are usually the "gatekeepers" of data on ticket buyers, and much is riding on how they use this data regarding the success of current and future events. The marketing director is also assigned with building and maintaining relationships with local media and corporate partners and sponsors. A good marketing director can negotiate favorable advertising rates with local media, and secure and keep corporate ticket buyers and sponsors.

The roles of the *box office manager* and the *operations manager* are self-explanatory. The former oversees the venue box office, which can mean interfacing with the outsourced ticketing company or running a complex in-house ticketing operation. The latter makes sure the physical aspects of the building, including maintenance and production, run smoothly.

Across the board, venue management has become a very specialized career choice, particularly at the arena level. The International Association of Assembly Managers (IAAM), the key professional organization for the venue industry, offers numerous training and certification opportunities, including a Certified Facilities Executive (CFE) designation.

Today, most arenas are under "private" management, though the meaning of this term is broad. Private venue management companies like SMG and Global Spectrum, both based in Philadelphia, manage dozens of arenas and other public assembly facilities, and are able to make use of leverage and economies of scale in booking talent, marketing, concessions, and other areas.

Many arenas, particularly in major markets, are owned by their primary sports tenant, usually a professional basketball or hockey team, or both. The team hires a professional manager to run the building who reports to team ownership, essentially again making it a "private management" situation. The days of an elected official or local businessman running a building without any formal venue management training are essentially past.

"In facilities now you need someone who knows how to partner with the team, and that's one of the issues that municipalities are just not suited to do," says Peter Luukko, president of Comcast-Spectacor and chairman of Global Spectrum. "This is such a business now that I really believe that you have to have private management, really an executive who can work with the team and then have the expertise to attract other events such as concerts, family shows and other sporting events."

Luukko points out that "private" doesn't necessarily mean a corporate private management company that runs dozens of buildings. "Municipalities can set the types of goals they want to see in the community and the type of facility they want to have, then hand it over to a professional to follow up on it," he says.

Longtime venue manager Allen Johnson, executive director of Orlando (Fla.) venues including the Amway Arena, Bob Carr Performing Arts Centre, and the Florida Citrus Bowl, concurs. "People skills are still paramount, but we are beyond the need to be related to the mayor nowadays. An entrepreneurial spirit and creative thinking are now mandatory, because the business model is changing every two years now instead of five to ten years."

As always, venue managers "still need a good business sense and understanding of budgeting, marketing and accounting," he adds. "We are spending a lot of time focusing on the fan experience and ways to enhance that, so today's

GM needs to be out experiencing what others are doing and thinking of ways to stay ahead of their competitors."

On the amphitheater side of the venue business, Live Nation, the world's largest promoter, owns the overwhelming bulk of North American sheds, and manages them both nationally and locally. These Live Nation venues have on-site GMs and in most cases a promoter "on the ground" in each market. But Live Nation also buys tours on a national level to route through its amphitheaters, and cuts national deals for sponsorship, ticketing, merchandising, concessions, and other facets of operations. In sum, Live Nation amphitheaters are both micro- and macro-managed.

VENUE OPERATIONS

When it comes to staging an event, the venue is basically responsible for the box office, security, production assistance, ushers and ticket takers, concessions, crowd control/security, and serving as liaison with the promoter, the band, and the production manager. "The venue should provide assistance to the promoter and the production manager in anything they may need, and we're generally the stagehand liaison," says Luukko.

At the club level, the first thing that should be waiting for a tour when it arrives is ample parking. "That could be anything from a couple of vans to, with some of these club tours these days we'll have to accommodate two or three semis and a half a dozen buses," says Ed Stack, GM of the 9:30 Club in Washington, D.C. Obviously the club provides stagehands, has key personnel on site to make sure everything runs smoothly, and gets catering in place. "Security varies, from just having some guy in front of the door to make sure nobody walks in off the street, to three or four guys out on the street making sure nobody hassles the star buses."

Johnson says the main responsibilities of an arena in hosting a concert are providing a "clean, safe, comfortable environment that is appealing" to patrons; "ease, cooperation, professionalism, and competency" when it comes to load-in/-out and production; "safe, well-planned, trained, customer-friendly, and responsive" crowd control; and concessions at a "fair price and profit, edible, with variety, and a good presentation."

Any new venue today is expected to have state-of-the-art production capabilities. "A flexible seating plan with capacity options is also a plus," says Pam Matthews, GM of the Ryman Auditorium in Nashville. "Ample fly and wing space, plenty of well-appointed dressing rooms with showers, catering facilities, elevators, a loading dock, nice lobby areas, and a private space for meet-and-greets are all important."

Many older, historic buildings, particularly theaters, are challenged with limited space to improve and expand, as well as inadequate funding for capital improvements. If the building holds a nonprofit status, fund-raising opportunities and tax-exemption can assist. In any case, often historic status and aesthetics can outweigh modern amenities in keeping a building well-attended and busy with events.

ABOVE AND BEYOND BASIC OPERATIONS

In today's competitive venue environment, just meeting the venue's primary responsibilities is often not enough. Almost every major market offers booking agents and artists a choice of venues, be it between two arenas, an arena and an amphitheater, or an arena and multiple nights in a smaller venue. When it comes to secondary and tertiary markets, there are dozens of modern, viable venue choices for artists to play. Today's venue managers must be proactive and go "above and beyond" when it comes to attracting events.

The days of waiting for the phone to ring are long over. Simply put, there are more venues out there than there are acts to play them. Most headlining tours rarely exceed sixty or seventy dates, and there are probably 130 to 140 legitimate arena-level plays in North America, according to some estimates. All things being equal, the strength of an arena's staff, particularly its marketing department, can be the tipping point in an agent selecting one venue over another.

Venues must strive to hire employees that are "highly trained, professional, more proactive than reactive, accommodating instead of confrontational," Johnson says. And, as stated in Chapter 15, venues can ingratiate themselves to promoters, agents, and managers in a major way by offering marketing muscle, "Find ways to sell more tickets than your competitors, be creative," says Johnson. "[Marketing] should be results-oriented, not just action-oriented. In other words, it's about getting the job done well, not just talking a good game."

Booking agents are very interested in what the venue can provide in terms of marketing. "Usually, the busier the building, the more staff they have promoting internally, and I think the quality of the in-house promotion team is crucial," says CAA agent John Huie. "On an even playing field, for me that would help sway me toward picking one building over another. And usually the building that is most aggressive about getting a date will be the most aggressive in promoting it."

Venues can also help their case by having a reputation for a crack operations team, and for making the day "easy." Johnson says venues can become a preferred play by "going beyond the expected, [offering] perks for the traveling crew such as good towels, cable television, high speed Internet access, good food, and maybe a place to relax and unwind that is different than other areas."

It can be helpful if the building's operation manager has experience on the road as a touring professional, as is the case with Bob O'Neal, operations manager for the Ryman Auditorium. O'Neal says the most important thing an operations manager can do is "advance" the date effectively. "Make sure that you have your equipment and personnel straight," says O'Neal. "Make sure you have the shortest possible distance to their power source."

O'Neal believes that one of the most important aspects of taking care of road crews is feeding them. "The army travels on its stomach and the food is something that touches everyone's life," O'Neal says. "The buildings that have the most love coming from the touring community are the ones that make sure the food is hot, sufficient, well-prepared, and on time. Lord have mercy on the person that doesn't have the coffee ready when the truckers roll in."

Venues get a reputation for their catering, good or bad. "Being on the road is different than working in your home town," Matthews points out. "Since most folks on the road are stuck in the venue all day and don't have the opportunity to go out, it's very important to make sure they're well-fed. A good meal says you care. I think everything backstage should be as nice as can be. Nice, clean towels are important. Good showers make a big difference in your quality of life."

In short, the act and its crew need to be made to feel welcome. "The act needs to roll in and feel like they're checking into a luxury hotel. We need to make them feel at home, happy to be there, in a good mood, and we need to be ready to do the work for them that we're supposed to do," says Seth Hurwitz, owner of the 9:30 Club in Washington, D.C. "A band needs to feel appreciated and that their show is special, not just one of seven that week."

The mood of the staff can make a difference. "Make sure everybody that works [at the venue] is in a good mood and happy to be here," says Stack. "You cannot under-estimate the value of people's attitude."

One way a venue, particularly an arena, can stay in the loop with agents and promoters is by being willing to take a financial risk on a show by taking the role of a promoter or co-promoter. In these cases, the building will take all or part of the risk involved in paying the act, but also be able to share in the "up-side" if the show is successful. Increasingly, promoters are demanding the building be willing to share the risk. "In order to be successful in today's world, you have to be able to promote or co-promote whenever necessary," says Luukko. "You've got to be a partner, you've got to help make it work. You just don't hand over the keys and walk away."

VENUE REVENUE STREAMS

The primary revenue streams for concert venues are rentals, concessions, parking, sponsorships, ticketing company rebates (see Chapter 15), and *house fees*, which are ticket surcharges, usually in the one- to two-dollar range, that are tacked on to the ticket price. Originally, house fees were designed to defray the cost of the venue's upkeep, particularly with historic buildings. Today, many venues look at house fees as just another revenue stream. As venues are very expensive to maintain, with an annual operating budget in the $5 million range for large arenas, tapping into and maximizing as many revenue sources as possible is paramount.

RENT

Rent and income from hosting events is the primary source of revenue for venues, bringing in one million dollars or more annually at the arena level. Rent is also the area that is most flexible for venues, and this flexibility can provide significant leverage in the venue's ability to attract concerts.

"The rental fee is the most flexible number you have, so let [promoters] focus on that and then make your money on the ancillaries and other premium services such as valet parking, private clubs, and concessions," Johnson advises.

For large clubs and performing arts centers, rent is usually in the $2,000 to $3,500 range per day, versus 10 percent to 20 percent of the box office gross, with caps anywhere from $7,500 to $15,000. For arenas, basic rent runs from $5,000 to $30,000 versus 12 percent to 20 percent of the gross, with caps of $40,000 to $60,000. But venue professionals are quick to point out that the "posted" rent fee is just a starting point.

"Rent is a hard number to pin down. It's very much a floating number," Gaylord Entertainment Center's Jones says. "Everybody's got their basic rent deal, but it changes for every show. For instance, my starting point is $25,000 versus 20 percent of the gross. But we have to take into account things like the ticket price; if it's $25 to $29, you will have a lower gross even with good numbers [in attendance]. We need to give the client an opportunity to make money. If your rent number is 30 percent to 35 percent of the gross, you've just 'rented' yourself out of a deal."

The straight-up rent deal, or a "four-wall rental," where a promoter comes in and takes over the building for a fee, is largely a thing of the past. "It's mostly co-promotes nowadays, with the arena sharing food and beverage, ticketing, parking, facility fees, et cetera," says Johnson.

Most arenas also offer an "all-in" rent deal these days, which includes such expenses as front-of-house production, ushers, ticket-takers, security, box office, and other services. This is opposed to a "line item" situation, where costs are broken out and hashed over at settlement. "The only things we don't roll in [to the rent fee] are things we can't control, like marketing, stagehands, Internet access, catering, and phones," Jones explains.

Jones says most buildings that host a lot of shows have all-in deals these days, adding that it's not wise to 'line-item' the promoter to death." Such a policy can cost an arena a show. "Most people don't know how much input tour accountants and production managers have on where a band plays. Venues have to make the date easy for the act, from the load-in to the settlement and load-out."

ANCILLARIES

The venues consider *ancillary* revenue to be anything generated by an event that is in addition to the primary revenue source from events and ticket sales. Ancillary revenues include food and beverage sales, parking, rebates from the ticketing company (as explained in Chapter 15), and house fees.

Parking can bring in as much as a million dollars or more annually if the building has control of area surface and/or garage parking, and zero revenue if it does not. Venues can also "up-sell" patrons with perks like preferred, VIP, or valet parking.

Concessions are almost always a primary revenue source for venues. At the arena level, food and beverage is usually outsourced to a concessions company, although some venues handle food and beverage in-house.

If concessions are contracted on a *fee account* deal, the building can receive up to 45 percent of gross concessions revenue. On a fee account deal, the building guarantees the concessions company a certain amount of revenue. The venue pays the bills—food, labor, et cetera—and the concessions company gets a management fee, which can total as much as $200,000 or more for large buildings. When sales exceed a certain level, the concessions company receives a small percentage of net profits, usually single digits. Such a system gives the arena control over quality and service.

If food and beverage is handled in-house, the venue's take can go up to about 50 percent of gross revenues. A *commission account*, where the concessions company is paid a certain percentage of gross sales, can increase the arena's share to 50 percent or higher, depending on any capital contributions from the venue toward the concessions operation. The more the venue invests, the more it makes.

Ticket rebates for a busy building with one or more sports tenants can top one million dollars annually. House fees can be as high as a dollar a ticket or more, and given that most large-market venues draw more than 500,000 people annually to concerts, it is easy to see how quickly house fees can add up. It is worth noting, however, that those that don't share in house fee revenues, specifically the promoter, artist, and artist's representatives, are not exactly keen on house fees, as they feel it adds to the price of a ticket without adding to the artist's take. That said, once a revenue stream is added to the mix, it rarely disappears.

"The purpose of getting rebates back from a ticketing company as opposed to just charging more for a ticket is simply to provide a stream of income that you don't have to share with the act," the 9:30 Club's Seth Hurwitz states candidly. "The key to making money in this business is to not share income if you don't have to."

While that philosophy may sound harsh, Hurwitz says that posture is almost as old as the business. "Promoters claim they need to create outside streams of revenues because the acts take too much of the sharing revenue, and the acts claim they wouldn't have to take so much of the sharing revenue if the promoter put everything in the pot. If the money is there to be seen, the promoter's afraid the acts are going to want a piece of it. The acts claim they wouldn't take such a big piece if the promoter showed them everything. Neither side trusts each other; it's been going on for years, and it always will."

SPONSORSHIPS

The days of a major venue carrying the name of a city—Boston Garden, Los Angeles Forum, Philadelphia Spectrum—are pretty much a thing of the past. Given the number of people that attend live events, sponsors have been keen to capture their attention and more than willing to pay for the opportunity. Venues have numerous opportunities to offer sponsors, from signage to videoboards to exclusivity in pouring rights to signs behind urinals. Just about any available space or service has a price.

The king of sponsorship revenue generators is the name-in-title sponsorship, where the sponsor puts its name on the building. That's why the big arenas in Boston, Los Angeles, and Philadelphia, for example, bear the TD Banknorth, Staples, and Wachovia names, respectively. Naming rights deals can be worth as much as $500,000 a year or more, depending on the size of the market. Total sponsorships for an active arena in a major market can be worth several million dollars annually,

Amphitheaters under the direction of Live Nation have also been very effective in capitalizing on naming rights and other sponsorship opportunities. "As traditional media has become more fragmented, corporations continue to look to the experience and value of live entertainment to take to their customers," says Bruce Eskowitz, Live Nation president/CEO of global venues and alliances. And while venues offer a significant amount of traffic, Eskowitz says sponsorships are not necessarily priced or valued by the number of people that pass through the turnstiles.

"[Sponsorship value] has more to do with the quality and quantity of talent that comes through there," Eskowitz says. "It goes up and down. Some years there are more shows, some less. But companies realize whether they want to do something in one market, five, or thirty, this is a unique way to create programs built around live entertainment."

Eskowitz explains that most of these venue sponsorship deals are not just built around the attendance of the show, but the promotion in support of it. "It's not about the 10,000 people at the show. It's about the hundreds of thousands of people that you do a promotion with before the show, the people who are at the show, and how you follow it up."

CHAPTER 17 Day of Show

It's show time. All the planning, preparation, and advance work come to fruition when the trucks and buses roll up to the venue the morning of show day. This is when the reward for careful preparation—or the penalty for the lack thereof—comes into play.

A wide range of players participate in making a concert happen. In this final chapter, we will let those involved explain how their day of show is structured. What is revealed is the importance of preparation or advancing the show in making the day run smoothly. What happens on day of show is the execution, and the right hand always needs to know what the left hand is doing. The days on tour are long, the work is detailed and often tedious, and the margin for error is slim.

THE TOUR MANAGER

On the day of show, Eric Mayers, tour manager for My Morning Jacket and Nickel Creek, has the bus driver wake him thirty miles from the venue. "I get up, make coffee, and sincerely enjoy this rare time when there is no-one else awake. Once the bus is parked, the priority is getting shore power connected and getting my bus driver off the bus and into his hotel for the day."

Even before load-in begins, Mayers likes to get set up in his production office, the hectic "command center" for the production crew. Then it's a quick tour of the venue (if it's new to him) before getting an up-to-date ticket count and audit. "If the runner (venue production assistant) is on, I will have that person also start in on dressing room and directional signage, and getting directions set for the band and crew. While this is going on, I will look over catering and hospitality and make sure all is set for the band."

Thirty minutes before load-in, Mayers checks that the crew is up and ready to work. "I will then enter the venue, interface with the crew chief or steward, and make sure that the crew call has checked in full, and deploy the loaders and hands to the trailer or truck. If I have a stage or production manager on tour, I will leave the stage to them, focus on getting the production office finished, and attend to any office-related work that is needed: receipts, getting laundry going, sending off settlement details from last night's performance, following up with future dates, et cetera."

If the band has press scheduled for the day, Mayers gets them up and ready, as well. "More often than not, it's wake the band up, and get them into the runner vehicle with barely enough time to suck down a coffee and get on air."

Two hours after load-in, Mayers begins to look at crew reductions that can be made before sound check; if he can eliminate some people, the cost of the show is lowered, and prior to sound check is a good time to assess the work force. Then it's lunch, finishing the comp ticket list, and getting house pass requests. "I will also take a walk around the venue and start looking for security issues and any other items that I need to either alert the band to or note during the security meeting. These would be any house staff that might be present during sound check, the best route to the stage from the dressing rooms, et cetera."

When the band is on stage for sound check, Mayers turns in guest lists and pass sheets to the promoter rep, and schedules the security meeting. "After sound check, there is some down time, and this often proves to be a good time to check in with individual crew and band members. I use this as a good time to discuss personal or inter-member issues or stresses. I will also collect set lists from the band, print them, and get the copies to all consoles and crew."

Sometime between sound check and doors, Mayers will eat dinner. "Thirty-minutes before doors, I will make sure the stage is set, with a house wash (house lighting), and that walk-in music is running. The promoter and I will then join for the house security meeting to educate door staff, ticket takers, ushers, and security guards to the band's policies [on] video, audio, photography, after-show, and meet 'n' greets."

Once this is done, and all staff are deployed, Mayers clears the house to open doors. Typically show time is one hour after doors open. When the band is in the wings and ready, he radios crew members to go on stand-by, drop house lights, drop house music, roll intro if needed, and then sends the band on stage. "I will be in the house for the first couple songs, check that security is in place, and then get prepared for settlement. I will also use this time for the caterers to pull all hospitality onto the buses, ice the buses, and strike any 'ambiance' we have placed in the dressing rooms."

Mayers likes to settle the show as early as possible. "Once settlement is done, I will print tomorrow's day sheets, post in the buses, strike the production office, and wait for the show to close."

Thirty minutes before the show ends, Mayers gathers and briefs stagehands and loaders and sends the runner to get food and pick up the drivers at the hotel. "The band comes off, we will meet if needed to go over any production-related issues, and then we get them to the bus or into the runner vehicle to the hotel."

Then it's on to the next town. "Basically, if your advance is strong and detailed, there should be no issue in having a stress- and attitude-free day."

THE VENUE OPERATIONS MANAGER

Bob O'Neal is operations manager for the 2,300-capacity Ryman Auditorium in Nashville, where concert events are usually one- or two-truck productions with two to four buses, including the support act. O'Neal says arranging the parking plan for the tour vehicles is the first order of business when planning for the arrival of a show. "The actual load-in time is set by the technical department. I have to brief my overnight security staff with a specific parking plan that takes into account whether the buses are pulling trailers or have slide-outs that require wider parking spaces. The trucks always go in the same location."

When the tour is "parked," O'Neal meets with the production manager of the tour, takes a walk along the path of the load-in from the trucks to the stage, and stops by the production office to ensure all of the phone lines that have been requested are functioning properly. At this point, the technical department and the backstage services staff begin setting up the show and assigning dressing rooms.

"One of my principal day of show tasks on concert events is the preparation and distribution of a comprehensive document for internal building use called the *event resume*. The information included in the event resume includes the acts on the show; the expected attendance; principal contacts for the artists and promoters; specific information about seating configuration details; event camera policy; whether the event is part of the venue's sponsorship series; whether the bars, concession stands, or gift shop will be open or closed; whether there will be artist merchandise sold at the event and where the merch stand will be located; a show schedule with performance and intermission lengths; and any other pertinent details of the day such as meet 'n' greets, receptions, sound check parties or 'cause' tables for distribution of literature for any particular cause that the artist may support.

"The event resume sets the course for a variety of activities within every department of the building. There is information relevant to administration, security, ushers, box office, retail, concessions, housekeeping, and the technical departments."

The security presence for the event from load-in to load-out, both inside and outside the building, is O'Neal's responsibility. This covers the artists, their tour staff, all production vehicles, and the public attending the show. "The artist's needs, as indicated in the contract rider, are overlaid with the building's specific security coverage requirements to establish a security personnel call sufficient to provide a safe and secure environment for everyone in the building. Usually, after sound check but before the doors open, I will meet with the tour's security spokesperson and receive a security briefing to assure that concerns of the artist are being addressed by the house security and usher staff. We also review the event credentials scheme to be clear on what each particular pass means. This information is then passed along to the security and usher staff. I will also prepare the bill for the event security that gets sent to the show settlement."

From this point, O'Neal says he relies on the "highly capable" Ryman Auditorium staff to take care of business. "Hopefully, I get to step back and watch a great show. As one of several 'managers on duty,' I will be available through the show to respond to almost any imaginable event from patron injuries to technical problems with elevators, heating and cooling systems, or anything that might occur. I will be in the building until the artist departs at the end of the night."

THE SUPPORT ACT

For a supporting act at the arena or amphitheater level, touring can be decidedly unglamorous and monotonous. Drive-By Truckers spent most of the summer of 2006 opening for Black Crowes and Robert Randolph. Patterson Hood, frontman for the band, says his "day of show" as a supporting act begins about 10 or 11 AM as the bus pulls up to the venue. By that time, Hood says, bandmate Mike Cooley would already be awake and on his second cup of coffee as Hood enjoys his first of many. "As I'd start cup two, he would switch to beer."

The DBT road crew is already hard at work. "One of the perks of making it to this level is having a hard-working crew, and I'm thrilled at forty-two to finally be relieved of heavy lifting and general logistics." Hood describes the backstage area of the sheds as "a Wal-Mart parking lot, without the Wal-Mart. The summer and the sun beats relentlessly upon the asphalt until you can fry an egg on it."

Behind the stage is usually either a series of trailers or semi-permanent structures resembling trailers. These structures house a number of rooms for the headlining act, the opening act, and various road managers and handlers. "As we were third on the bill, we frequently didn't have a room of our own, but the headliners usually didn't arrive until much later, so the next quest is finding a semi-clean place for the morning poop." This quest is more of a luxury than those not accustomed to the touring life might understand.

"We toured in vans, hauling our own selves and gear across country for the better part of a decade before getting to move up to riding in a bus with a hard-working crew. It was grueling and often frustrating, but also lots of fun, and I sometimes refer to those days as my Huckleberry Finn adventure. At this point in my life, I'm not foolish or romantically inclined to want to go back or over-glorify it, but that's just how it is."

Traveling by tour bus is much safer, Hood says, "as the driver is usually sober and hopefully well-rested, and Lord knows it's much easier on many levels. [But] the toilets are of the 'no solid' variety, which means that the morning 'constitutional' is often in either a truck stop or a Port-A-John."

After that sort of business is taken care of, the band waits until around 5 PM for a sound check, which may or may not come. Hood says about 40 percent of the time the schedule is too tight to allow the third-billed act a sound check. "Then it's back to waiting until our set time, which on this tour [was] usually at 6:30, just as the doors open and folks start streaming in."

"Show day dinner is usually best when I can eat as early as possible before show time. Three to four hours before the show is best, as I sing lousy when full."

Hood says he prefers a lighter meal before he hits the stage, with Asian cuisine being his preference. "My favorite preshow meal is Vietnamese pho or spicy Thai shrimp soup."

Of course, a support act rarely gets to call the shots as to the menu. "On the tour this summer, we were at the mercy of catering, which often really sucked, was greasy and laid heavy on me. By the end of the tour, I was skipping meals and eating cereal."

The DBT set was about forty minutes, "which means that just as we were getting good and warmed up, it was time for 'thank you, good night' and back onto the bus for more waiting until midnight or so when we would pull out for the next town."

THE TOUR PRODUCER

Kevin Lyman, president of 4fini Productions and producer of the Vans Warped and Taste Of Chaos tours, says he realized early on that he preferred working with many bands over working with one band. "I am not a person who likes routine and I found many of the touring people I came across were the type of people who like structure and routine. They wanted their road cases in the same spot, catering to be quick and accessible, and at the end of the day a shower and a pizza on the bus would make them very happy."

That's not Lyman, and that's not Warped, which moved some 900 people, including about 80 bands, from city to city in 2006. Lyman says his normal Warped day begins about 6 AM when the bus arrives at the venue parking lot. His first move is to turn on his radio (walkie-talkie) to assess the situation.

"If the radio chatter is light, I will take a walk around and ask all my drivers how their evening was. If Kerry Nicholson, our production manager, sounds like he has any issues, I will head over to see if I can help out. When things settle down I will head to the bus around 9 AM to finish up the show schedule for the day. At this point I am listening for anything that might need extra attention or has not been dealt with by the local promoter. If Kerry can keep going and I can fix these few things, the day will go very smooth for us all."

After completing the schedule, Lyman checks in with sponsors, production, and security until about 10:30 AM. "We then get 'doors' at 11:00 AM, and if they have ticket takers and things are smooth, I usually start my daily meetings and calls. I keep a pretty busy schedule of people coming and going by the bus throughout the day. If I hit a low spot, which we all have, I sometimes take a fifteen-minute nap around 3:30. This is if the weather is good and there are no major hang-ups to the day."

Lyman typically has a few conference calls, meetings, and podcasts each day, and then spends some time with various aspects of the touring crew. "Around 5 PM I try to get out and see a few bands and see how the crew in the field is doing. This will take me to about 7 PM, time for a little dinner, and then the show starts to wind down for the day. I have a lot of confidence in my crew, so sometimes I can leave site to eat with some friends or I set up shop under the tent in front of my bus. This is the place anyone can come by and talk about the business or just shoot the bull. There is always an ice chest of beer and soda, and it is my time to meet some of the people I tour with. I then pack up the tents, chairs, and ice chests, and if all is good, get to bed by 1 AM, unless Bus #1 has one of their famous dance parties."

THE CONCERT PROMOTER

Promoter Charles Attal of Charles Attal Presents in Austin says his typical day of show routine is running through the checklist and checking on his entire team. "Hopefully, by this time there are no surprises and everything has been scheduled accordingly. The three main components of any event that are on my checklist are ticketing/contracts/deposits, marketing, and production."

In regard to ticketing, Attal will double check the ticket counts and "make sure we are selling to the appropriate numbers as stated in the offer and contract, and make sure we aren't holding tickets that may need to be released," he says. "Contracts and deposits must all be in the show file and overlooked to prepare for settlement."

As for marketing, Attal makes sure the *ad packs*, a record of tear sheets, invoices, flyers, radio proposals, et cetera, that make up the campaign, are in and reviews what was done to promote the show.

Attal then checks in with the production manager regarding any potential issues that he may need to be aware of or that the production manager may need to be aware of. "For the most part, I stay out of everyone's way and let them set up the show, but I need to be available through the day in case of any emergencies. I usually get to the show an hour before doors and meet the tour manager. At doors, I make sure the lines are running smoothly in order to get everyone inside in a timely manner, and help with any ticketing or customer issues as needed."

Once all the patrons have entered, "I will begin setting up the settlement and will settle either during the headliner's last few songs, or after the show."

THE TOUR CATERER

Sandy Hylton, owner of Sweet Chili Catering (U2), says her show day begins about 9 AM, although this varies from tour to tour. "We are assigned a clean, hygienic space with a sink and power, and we make a kitchen out of that space with the equipment we bring with us. I shop daily and locally with a local runner who takes me to an organic market."

The tour caterer usually provides breakfast, lunch, and dinner, but again it varies from tour to tour. "Meals provided for the band and artists are built around loose guidelines and dietary requirements, likes and dislikes," says Hylton. Local caterers usually prepare separate meals for local crew. "My day finishes when the band leaves the venue, or if we are loading out for another venue, the day finishes about an hour after they leave. It doesn't sound very exciting, but, really, I have the best job in the world."

THE SECURITY STAFF

Scott Nichols has served as security director for tours by U2 and the Rolling Stones, two of the most challenging acts for security. For Nichols, one show day blends seamlessly into the next: he must ensure the safety of the act 24/7, he must keep all instruments and equipment free from theft or vandalism, and he and his staff protect all touring employees.

Because Nichols has sent the security rider to each local promoter and venue and advanced the show several times with the venue security director, he expects no surprises when he arrives at the venue the morning of the show. He and other touring security officers set up their office—a command central of sorts—and go about their respective duties. "The security director for a major tour will hire additional touring security: two for a solo artist, four to eight for a band, and as many as twelve for superstar acts."

Nichols and his staff must ensure that each security team, including the venue security; the *T-shirt security*, the contracted crowd control experts; and the local uniformed police know their respective assignments. "We have a meeting with local police, venue security, and the T-shirt security supervisor on the morning of show day."

As tour security director, Nichols has the stressful job of following and protecting the act before, during, and after the show. "Our biggest challenges are coordinating arrival times, movement to the hotel, movement to the venue, and return to hotel, bus, or jet."

Before the production crew and local stagehands open the trucks, the venue places a security officer at the back door to prevent unauthorized personnel from entering the backstage areas. Nichols explains that he "helps devise and monitor the credentials system [backstage passes] to restrict access to restricted areas.

The local security staff arrives several hours before the show to meet with Nichols, his assistants, and the venue security supervisor. Some uniformed police are posted near the box office or other areas that house money and T-shirt or venue security are positioned in the audience seating area and at each entrance to a restricted area. Throughout the day, the tour security team communicates with one another with in-ear walkie-talkies and cell phones.

Bart Butler is president of Rock Solid Security in Nashville, which provides everything from T-shirt/local security to specialized executive escorts. "My day would normally start with deployments pertaining to conversations with the tour security person and the venue. A meeting time would have been set in advance for last minute changes and to be sure everyone is on the same page.

"There is definitely a meeting with the tour security present so they can disseminate pertinent information about the credentialing and the access given to each credential. Hopefully the rest of the information needed was sent in the security rider, but in most cases this is not what takes place. So, one would receive a lot more info on what to expect and the tours' needs. In some cases a walk through would take place. In most cases this is not done, unless there are very particular security posts that need to be discussed."

Butler concurs that there is normally some type of briefing that will take place in many different departments about the facts of the show. "This is where the supervisors learn all the details and they in turn pass the information along to the staff members. This is where I have a problem, because it seems that only the facts that each supervisor feels are important gets passed along. It is kind of like the old game of 'telephone.' The tour security director passes it to the coordinator and they pass it to the supervisors and then they pass it to the staff. I am sure you can understand how much can get lost. One of the methods I used to combat this problem was to ask that I speak to the entire staff before deployment took place. This may cost the tour a little money, but I have found it to be invaluable."

Any security incidents—detained patrons or injuries—are reported to the security director. After the tour security staff is sure that the act has been safely transported back to their hotel, bus, or jet, the tour security director, the supervisor of the local police, and the venue security director meet for a post-event "debriefing." The tour security staff ensures that all equipment and touring personnel remain protected until the trucks are loaded and, along with the tour buses, leave the venue.

THE PRODUCTION MANAGER

The show day for the production manager and assistants begins early because they are responsible for each production department. And when the show is not set up on schedule, the production manager's head is on the chopping block.

Dale "Opie" Skjerseth is one of the most in-demand production managers in the business, counting the Rolling Stones among his clients. He says he begins his show day by "getting my head around the venue, making sure the stage placement is going to be correct to the seating."

From there, Opie tries to figure out where the trucks will unload, find the dressing rooms, assign production offices, and meet with the local promoter rep, crew boss, and venue personnel. "Then we start planning the [load out] and the rest of the days ahead, making sure everything will be at the next venue."

While the crew is working in the venue, the production manager and his or her assistants, who may hold the title of assistant production manager or production coordinator, set up the production office. The production office typically includes desks, tables, phones, fax machines, walkie-talkies, and other equipment. The production management staff typically distributes security passes and communicates with catering, security, the tour manager, and the tour accountant. A tour with many crew members and elaborate production may have a *production accountant*, an additional accountant assigned to work with the production manager.

Every duty performed throughout the day "has its importance, from the vehicle parking until the last piece gets put on the truck at the end of the night." His day will not end until the last truck is loaded, the truck door is closed, "and I say my thank yous at the end of the evening."

THE STAGE MANAGER

Next to the production manager, the stage manager shoulders much of the responsibility in making sure day of show goes smoothly. Veteran stage manager Rocko Reedy (U2, Journey) says his day begins about an hour before the stagehands start on the clock. "The stage manager's job is more traffic management, setting the pieces up in the correct order, and coordinating local crew with touring crew. It's like a chess game, only you can arrange the pawns ahead of time and always win."

Reedy says a good stage manager calls his production manager on the radio to keep him informed of the progress of events on the floor and any problems that might arise. "A great stage manager works with a production manager that goes to the production office and leaves him to keep things in order by thinking ahead before a problem arises, and dealing with it diplomatically when it does. The stage manager has to maintain control so the production staff doesn't lose control, so a good knowledge of each touring crew person's job is essential. Knowing how to do their job helps me to do mine."

"My day ends when the last piece of gear is on the vehicle taking it to the next load in."

THE STAGE CARPENTERS

Flory Ramirez Turner has toured with many major acts, including U2, the Rolling Stones, Faith Hill and Tim McGraw, Bruce Springsteen, and Madonna. She says she and the other stage carpenters usually gather for breakfast around 7:15 AM and begin load-in at 8 AM. "Our job is to help get the set pieces off of the trucks and put them together to form the stage set. We work with the riggers and even do some rigging ourselves. We also must get the huge video walls assembled because they are a part of the stage set."

If the load-in runs smoothly, the stage carpenters can break for lunch. "But we usually just grab something and get back to work. We generally have dinner around 5 PM and sometimes we are able to go back to the hotel for a little while. Before the show begins, we recheck everything and get ready to do our assigned work for the show."

As soon as the show ends and the act leaves the stage, the carpenter crew begins to load out the show. "When the production is transported by airplanes to the next city or country, we have a tough job—a double load-out. We load the production gear into the trucks, travel to the planes, unload the gear, and load the pallets into the planes."

After load-out, the carpenters travel to the next city and begin the process again.

THE RIGGERS

The tour riggers and the local riggers write symbols on the venue floor indicating the *rigging points*, locations on the overhead beams where equipment will be suspended. The *up riggers* climb to the beams that will support the rigging points; the *down riggers* remain on the venue floor and send rigging gear on ropes to the up riggers. The riggers work quickly because the production equipment that is suspended from rigging points remains on the floor until the appropriate rigging points are completed.

A rigger's day usually starts at 7 AM, according to head rigger Chuck Melton, who has toured with Metallica, U2, and *NSYNC. "The first thing we do is mark the floor where the points need to hang according to the rigging plot. It takes about one hour to mark the floor and call the bridals. A bridal is two pieces of wire rope which connect to the beams in the roof. At the apex of the wire rope we connect a one- or two-ton motor which hoists the lights, sound, and video."

Melton says on average he and his riggers hang 50 to 120 points. "And we usually hang around 75,000 to 140,000 pounds over the artist. This takes about four hours."

Melton supervises twelve to sixteen local riggers hired to help pull the chains to the roof and build the bridals. "It is the head riggers' job to do all the calculations for the bridals. The building engineers tell us where to distribute the weight and we try to distribute the weight evenly. We also supervise the rigging of the lighting trusses and sound points and make sure that they are in safe working order."

THE AUDIO TEAM

Dave Natale has toured as a sound engineer for U2, the Rolling Stones, and Madonna. "At about 8:00 in the morning the audio engineer, the crew chief, and the systems engineer come in and make sure the [rigging] points are in the right place to hang the P.A. When they start putting the points out, there's always a fight for 'real estate' where the points go."

The other department heads may disagree about rigging points for their respective gear. "'You can't have it here, there's a truss here,' you have to work all that out, do all your comprised stuff there—your 'real estate' fight.'"

When the riggers begin, the sound staff begins to unload the trucks. "The exact times differ from tour to tour, but we begin anywhere from 9:00 until 10:00 [in the morning] to start unloading sound trucks. We try to get everything out on the floor by about 11:00." The sound equipment cannot be *flown*, attached to the overhead beams, until the riggers have done their job. "So if they are not [ready], you stand around and wait for the points to be available, but there are certain things you can do while you wait."

While waiting for your points, "you can put your amplifiers in position, you can plug in the AC distribution system, and start running cables from the AC distribution panel to the amplifiers, make other preparations like that. If there's not a lot of stuff out on the main floor, you could even, if the mix position is marked out, take some guys and go out there and set that up until the points are ready."

When the points are rigged, the P.A. system needs to go up. "Then you have to trim the P.A. system, which means you have to go out into the audience and make sure that one side's not six feet higher than the other side, and that the speakers are level and pointing in the right place." As the day progresses, the gear begins to look like a system. "After you get the P.A. trimmed, the guys start hooking up the amplifiers to the speakers, finish making all of those connections, and set the front-of-house (FOH) system up. Then you get the snakes out, turn the system on, and you cue the P.A. system. How you do it is all different, depending on the engineer."

When the stage is erected, the backline crew sets up the act's instruments and on-stage amp cabinets. Natale explains that the audio tech responsible for microphones on stage works quickly to "put all the mike stands together, get all the cabling out, and mike up the backline. And you do a *line check* [test of each microphone and direct input boxes] just to make sure that all your stuff is working from the stage out to the P.A. and to the monitor system."

After line check, the sound crew may have a sound check. However, some acts do not arrive at the venue in time for sound check, or they may not arrive at the prearranged time. "So if there is a sound check, you screw around and waste some time until the band shows up for sound check at 4:00 or 5:00. They play a couple of songs and [the sound engineers] make adjustments. And while I'm doing the sound check, I get one of the other guys to walk around the arena and just make sure everything's covered."

After sound check, the sound crew is able to have dinner. "Then you kill some more time. When the support act finishes their set, the crew must quickly do the *changeover*, removing the support act's gear and setting up the headline act's gear. Then, after the support band is off, you do another line check for the headline band. When the headline band comes on stage, they call you and say, 'Okay, we're ready to go.' They turn off the house lights, you fade out the walk-in music, and the headline act starts playing."

When the show is over, generally at 11:00, the sound crew dismantles the system, packs it safely into cases and crates, and loads the gear into the trucks. Natale says it may be 12:30, 1:00, or later before the sound crew is finished. "That's a pretty full day."

THE LIGHTING DIRECTOR

Ethan Weber is the lighting director, or LD, for the Rolling Stones. He says on show days he either goes "in" with the rigging call or the lighting call, which is usually first or second on the daily call sheets. "My show day start times vary, depending on the size and type of tour it is. On club or theater tours, the days usually start much later, any time between maybe 9 AM and noon. On arena tours I'll generally go in sometime between 6 AM and 9 AM, depending on the size of the show and whether or not the show needs to be ready for an early sound check. Stadium shows almost always load-in the day before the show and load-in times vary greatly—often dictated by the drive times."

According to Weber, "There are two different styles of LDs—the "white glove" designer, and the "hands-on" or working LD. "The 'white glove' usually starts his day once the system is either raised off the floor or once everything is tested and at full trim height. They may or may not set up their lighting consoles and test the lights, but they'll almost always touch-up focuses during the afternoon and possibly spend some time programming—either working on existing songs or building new ones that the band has added to their set. This depends on the type of designer and show.

"Some designers look at the show as being complete once they've left and don't want it touched, some hire directors they trust to 'grow' the show in a style that fits their own. In either case, their day usually begins [in the] late morning or early afternoon and finishes when the show is over."

For working designers/directors, the days are a bit different. "Personally, I like to come in with the riggers and lighting crew on the first call. Because I'm responsible for the show's lighting, I want to be at the venue to make any lighting decisions. I trust most of my crew chiefs and consult with them when needed, but ultimately I'm the one responsible and answerable to the band, so I'd rather be the one making the final call. Once decisions are made and trucks start dumping, I become part of the lighting crew."

Most of the lighting crew are given specific jobs by their crew chiefs. "I like to turn myself into kind of a rover, filling in wherever I see fit and doing the jobs I like to do, usually raising motors and trusses, hanging lights, et cetera. I enjoy all parts of the job and think that it's all part of the process: playing with the lights during programming and the show, and setting the system up and taking it down. Sounds stupid, but after spending the day hanging the system, you feel more at ease and comfortable when you finally sit down to focus/program. It feels a bit uncomfortable coming in cold to sit down at a console and start pressing buttons."

Being hands-on is also good for crew morale. "Loading in and out also helps keep you fit and I think it helps create a better work environment for you and your crew. It becomes more of a lighting team. I know that I can ask my crews to do almost anything within reason because they know that I wouldn't be asking them to do something I wouldn't/don't do myself."

Once the rig is off the ground Weber usually goes out front and sets up his lighting consoles and tests the lights. "Once that's done, it's a good time to grab lunch and let the carpenters and backline techs finish off the stage. After lunch I usually try to get a few lights turned out (never everything—makes you very unpopular) and spend an hour or two focusing. Once focused, I spend the rest of the afternoon programming, usually two or three hours."

Weber takes notes from every show and always finds room for tweaking. "Many of the bands I work for change their set lists regularly, so after taking care of my notes from the previous show I sometimes have new songs to work on. Most days I'll program until either the doors open or until I have to turn the console over to the opening act, anywhere between 5 and 7 PM. Some LDs like to use their afternoons for Internet or bus time to relax before the show after their focus session, but, again, I find that the console feels kind of alien if I don't spend a few hours a day on it."

When Weber is finally torn away from the console, he'll either go to catering and have some dinner, or find somewhere backstage to sit on a case and relax for a few minutes. "About a half hour before the opening act, I'll usually have a spot meeting. If we're using two to four spots, I usually wait until we're on headsets before the main act and go over everything then. Otherwise, I like to meet the spot operators face-to-face, get their names, show them a piece of paper with the stage layout, go over their assignments and tell them how I want them to run the show."

Fifteen minutes before the scheduled start time "I get on headset and do a roll call to make sure all the spots are there and ready, and go over everything we talked about in the spot meeting. After that, it's time to hand out the (intensely caffeinated) Black Black gum to anyone on the riser and wait for the houselights to go out."

After the show is over Weber packs up his front-of-house equipment and gets it on a truck, then chips in on load-out. "I usually leave to shower once everything is down, in boxes and ready to go onto a truck, anywhere between 1 and 2 AM on most tours. By then the whole lighting crew and most of the local crew is there helping out and I feel a bit unnecessary."

THE LOCAL STAGE CREW

A major tour requires an army of local stagehands to mount the show. The production rider lists the number of local crew required for the show. "A few weeks to a few days before the show, the tour manager or promoter rep will advance their *crew call*, the list of labor needed for the load in, show call and load out," says Melanie Hansel, vice president of Crew One Productions. "Like the tour techs, local stagehands are assigned to a department."

Hansel says most tours require a crew chief to break the stagehands and riggers into their departments of specialty, including loaders, audio, lighting, video, carpentry, and backline technicians. The local crew call can range "from twenty stagehands to more than 100."

The local crew can either be a non-union contractor specializing in live entertainment or *IATSE*, the stagehand union. The *crew chief* leads the local crew with the direction from the tour's stage manager. The production crew knows how many local stagehands load in and load out should take. Therefore, the crew contractor must provide stagehands who work hard alongside the touring techs. "The local crews are the first people in the venue, starting with rolling up the semi doors to unload them. They are the last to leave, ending with shutting the last truck door and sending it off to the next city. A typical day for the crew chief and show call hands can easily be a sixteen- to twenty-hour day."

The load-in generally averages six to eight hours and a load-out average is ninety minutes to three hours. "The tour will add extra hands to speed up the pace of the load-out, as they usually have hundreds of miles to travel before starting the process all over the next morning. The tour generally color codes the hands into departments with T-shirts or armbands during the load out, so the department heads can easily keep track of them."

Thank you, you've been a wonderful audience. Good night!

INDEX